The Political Philosophy
of Hobbes

The Political Philosophy of Hobbes

Its Basis and Its Genesis

By

Leo Strauss

Translated from the German Manuscript
By Elsa M. Sinclair

THE UNIVERSITY OF CHICAGO PRESS

CHICAGO & LONDON

The Political Philosophy of Hobbes was first published in 1936 by
The Clarendon Press, Oxford, England. Acknowledgment is grate-
fully extended for permission to issue this reprinting
in the United States.

THE UNIVERSITY OF CHICAGO PRESS, CHICAGO 60637
THE UNIVERSITY OF CHICAGO PRESS, LTD., LONDON

Published 1952. Sixth Impression 1973. First Phoenix Edition 1963
Printed in the United States of America
International Standard Book Number: 0–226–77695–6 (clothbound)
Library of Congress Catalog Card Number: 52–9720

TO
MY WIFE

PREFACE

THE intention of the present study is to prepare an analysis of the principles of Hobbes's political philosophy and of that of his successors. A new analysis of those principles has become necessary as a consequence of the deepened knowledge, which has been gained during the last decades, of the tradition of political thought. The time is now past when one could safely without any further qualifications characterize the seventeenth and eighteenth centuries as the hey-day of natural law theories. This characterization was tacitly based on a comparison of the political theories of the age of rationalism with those of the nineteenth century, and within the limits of such a comparison it still holds true; but it can no longer be maintained when the medieval and classical tradition is duly taken into account. The effect of this change of orientation on the interpretation of Hobbes's political philosophy is obvious. J. Laird in his recent book on Hobbes could try to establish the view that in ethical and political theory Hobbes's 'voice and hands are both mediaeval'. Though this statement is hardly justified, it clearly proves that the older opinion, according to which Hobbes's originality was beyond question, is somewhat shaken and now needs some qualifications which were not required at an earlier stage of research. Generally speaking, if theories of natural law, far from being a feature peculiar to the age of rationalism, are almost a matter of course in the medieval and classical tradition, we cannot avoid asking why the seventeenth and eighteenth centuries gained the reputation of being the period *par excellence* of natural law theories. And, to exclude from the outset the inadequate answer that for well-known political reasons the practical bearing of natural law theories was greater during that period than in any other age, we must raise the more precise question, whether there is not a difference of principle between the modern and the traditional view of natural law. Such a difference does in fact exist. Traditional natural law is primarily and mainly an objective 'rule and measure', a binding order prior to, and independent of, the human will, while modern natural law is, or tends to be, primarily and mainly a series of 'rights', of subjective claims, originating in the human will. I have tried to establish this view in the present study by comparing the political doctrine of Hobbes, as the founder of modern political philosophy, with that of Plato and Aristotle, as the founders of traditional political philosophy. Essentially the same result is reached if one compares the doctrines of Locke, Montesquieu, and Rousseau with those of, e.g., Hooker, Suarez, and Grotius. Even Leibniz's doctrine, which at first sight seems to be the most important exception to the afore-mentioned rule, confirms that rule, as is seen if one takes into account not only the content but also the form—the conditional character—which he attributes to the propositions of natural law.[1] However, although Hobbes attaches much less practical importance to the 'rights of men' than do most exponents of natural law, the essence of modern natural law and all its essential implications are nowhere more clearly seen than in his doctrine. For Hobbes obviously starts, not, as the great tradition did, from natural 'law', i.e. from an objective order, but from natural 'right', i.e. from an absolutely justified subjective claim which, far from being dependent on any previous law, order, or obligation, is itself the origin of all law, order, or obligation. It is by this conception of 'right' as the principle of morals and politics that the originality of Hobbes's political philosophy (which includes his moral philosophy) is least ambiguously evinced. For, by starting from 'right' and thus denying the primacy of 'law' (or, what amounts fundamentally to the same, of 'virtue'), Hobbes makes a stand against the idealistic tradition. On the other hand, by basing morals and politics on 'right', and not on purely natural inclinations or appetites, Hobbes makes a stand against the naturalistic tradition. That is to say, the principle of 'right' stands midway between strictly moral principles (such as those of the traditional natural law) on the one hand, and purely natural principles (such as pleasure, appetite, or even utility) on the other. 'Right', we may say, is a specifi-

[1] It is because of this view of Leibniz, which was held by Hobbes before Leibniz, that Kant's doctrine of the categorical imperative as distinguished from hypothetical imperatives became necessary. The rules of traditional natural law doubtless were, and were understood to be, categorical imperatives.

cally juridical conception. Some of the assumptions underlying
the philosophical application of that conception are indicated
in the last chapter of the present study. A full analysis of the
significance of that philosophical application had, however, to
be postponed; for before such an analysis could be made, it
was necessary to remove the obstacles which stand in the way
of even a mere recognition of the obvious fact that Hobbes's
political philosophy starts from natural 'right', as distinguished
from both natural 'law' and natural inclinations or appetites.

These obstacles are mainly due to the fact that Hobbes tried
to base his political philosophy on modern natural science.
The temptation to take this way could hardly be resisted. As
traditional moral and political philosophy was, to some extent,
based on traditional metaphysics, it seemed necessary, when
traditional metaphysics were replaced by modern natural
science, to base the new moral and political philosophy on the
new science. Attempts of this kind could never succeed: traditional metaphysics were, to use the language of Hobbes's
successors, 'anthropomorphistic' and, therefore, a proper basis
for a philosophy of things human; modern science, on the
other hand, which tried to interpret nature by renouncing all
'anthropomorphisms', all conceptions of purpose and perfec-
tion, could, therefore, to say the least, contribute nothing to
the understanding of things human, to the foundation of morals
and politics. In the case of Hobbes, the attempt to base political
philosophy on modern science led to the consequence that the
fundamental difference between natural 'right' and natural
appetite could not be consistently maintained. If the significance of Hobbes's principle of 'right' was to be duly recognized, it had, therefore, first to be shown that the real basis of
his political philosophy is not modern science. To show this,
is the particular object of the present study.

As G. C. Robertson observed in his *Hobbes*, fifty years ago,
'the whole of (Hobbes's) political doctrine . . . doubtless had
its main lines fixed when he was still a mere observer of men
and manners, and not yet a mechanical philosopher' (p. 57).
It is, therefore, only natural to attempt a coherent exposition
of Hobbes's 'pre-scientific' thought on 'men and manners', of
his original view, not yet distorted by scientific 'explanations',

of human life. I hope to have shown by the present study that such an exposition is possible, and even necessary, if we desire any coherent understanding of Hobbes's thought. Such an understanding is not so easy to gain as it seems at first sight. It is true that every reader of Hobbes is struck by the clarity, rigour, and decision of his thought. But every student of Hobbes is also amazed by the numerous contradictions which occur in his writings. There are but few of his most important and most characteristic assertions which are not contradicted, either directly or by the denial of their obvious consequences, somewhere in his works. In order to find out which of the contradictory statements express his real opinion, we have to hold fast to our first impression of the rigour and unity of his thought. For that impression is nothing other than the perception of Hobbes's fundamental view of human life, and that view is not contradictory, but one and indivisible. It is this view, and not modern science, which is the real basis of his political philosophy. That view has its origin not so much in any learned or scientific preoccupation, but in actual experience of how men behave in daily life and in 'public conversation'. The experience, underlying Hobbes's view of human life, must, in its turn, be traced back to a specific moral attitude which compels its holder to experience and see man in Hobbes's particular way. Thus that view might find an adequate expression, e.g. in maxims and reflections, in the style of Hobbes's contemporary La Rochefoucauld (whose opinions about the importance of *amour-propre* are, by the way, very much akin to Hobbes's opinions about the importance of 'glory' or 'pride'), rather than in a philosophic system. And in Hobbes's works there are important parts which are written in such a style. However, Hobbes's intention is not only to expound his view of human life as the expression of his own experience, but above all to justify this view as the only true and universally valid view. It is by starting from this intention that we can grasp the ultimate reason for the contradictions which are to be found in his writings. For, as he has at his disposal no method suitable to the demands of such a view of human life as he holds, he has no choice but to borrow the methods and conceptions supplied either by the philosophical tradition or by modern science. But neither corresponds to those demands. The traditional conceptions are not appropriate to a fundamentally untraditional view, and the conceptions provided by modern science are not congenial to a view of human life originating in a moral attitude. The basic difference between Hobbes's original view of human life on the one hand, and the conceptions provided by tradition or modern science on the other, explains all the contradictions of any consequence which occur in his works. The establishment of this fact is the necessary condition not only for any coherent interpretation of Hobbes's political philosophy, but even, as I have already indicated, for recognition of the principle of that philosophy.

In order to see that Hobbes's original view is independent both of tradition and modern science, we must study the genesis of his moral and political ideas. For by studying Hobbes's early thought, we are enabled to perceive that his original conception of human life was present in his mind before he was acquainted with modern science, and thus to establish the fact that that conception is independent of modern science; and by studying his later development we can arrive at a further corroboration of that finding, for there we witness the actual conflict between his original view and the demands of modern science. On the other hand, by studying Hobbes's development as a whole, which is a gradual emancipation from tradition, we are enabled to realize that at least the presuppositions and consequences of his original view became clearer to him, the more he freed himself from the shackles of tradition, and thus to show that his original conception, understood in its full meaning, is not only independent of tradition, but even contrary to it. Now, while it is one and the same reason—an interest in Hobbes's original view of human life—which leads us to study his development with regard both to the (in the main) increasing influence of modern science and to the (in the main) decreasing power of tradition, the method to be followed in the two cases is different. In the first case, we are particularly interested in Hobbes's early thought, in the views he held before he studied exact science. In the second case, we particularly want to see the working of the tendency, which is

revealed most clearly in Hobbes's later period, towards emancipation from tradition. It is, however, impossible to separate
those two lines of research completely. For as the early writings
of Hobbes are very sparse, we have in some cases to complete
the insufficient materials by construing Hobbes's early view as
the hypothetical starting-point of his later development, which
in itself is clearly evinced. This point must be stressed because
the interdependence of the two lines of investigation justifies
the otherwise hardly defensible composition of the present
study.

The term 'early writings' has in Hobbes's case a somewhat
unusual meaning. If we understand by early writings all those
which he composed before his first systematic treatment of
political philosophy (*The Elements of Law*, finished in 1640),
they comprise all he had written up to the time he was fifty.
In this sense, the 'early writings' are: (1) his introduction to
his translation of Thucydides (not later than 1628); (2) the
poem *De mirabilibus Pecci* (*c.* 1627); (3) the little treatise discovered and edited by Tönnies, called by its editor *A Short
Tract on First Principles* (perhaps 1630); (4) two English digests
of Aristotle's *Rhetoric* (*c.* 1635). The second and the third of
the writings mentioned are of no great interest for our purpose.
On the other hand, one must add the autobiographical and
biographical accounts of Hobbes's early period, as well as some
letters from and to Hobbes. This very sparse material does not
permit of a definite answer to the question of Hobbes's early
thought in all its aspects. The case would be different if a
Chatsworth MS., not indeed belonging to the Hobbes papers,
but, as far as I can judge, written in Hobbes's hand, could be
used as a source for Hobbes's early thought. There is reason
for assuming that if this manuscript is not the earliest writing
of Hobbes himself, his was the decisive influence in its
composition.[1]

---

[1] The manuscript in question is entitled 'Essayes' and was composed by
W. Cavendish, who dedicated it to his father as 'this dayes present'. As
Mr. S. C. Roberts has pointed out to me, the 'Essayes' are the earlier and
much shorter manuscript version of *Horae subsecivae*, anonymously published in 1620. As the 'Essayes' and the *Horae subsecivae* are based on some
essays of Bacon's which were not published before 1612, they must both
have been composed between 1612 and 1620. *Horae subsecivae* was tra-

With the exceptions immediately to be mentioned, I have
followed the edition of Hobbes's writings by Molesworth
(quoted as *English Works* or *Opera latina*). For the *Elements of
Law* and *Behemoth*, I have used Tönnies's editions, and for the
Leviathan the edition by A. D. Lindsay.

I wish to acknowledge my debt of gratitude to His Grace
the Duke of Devonshire for his generosity in permitting me
to examine the Hobbes papers at Chatsworth, and to quote
some passages from them. I am also very much indebted to
Mr. Francis Thompson, Librarian at Chatsworth, whose help
and advice were invaluable to me when I was studying the
Hobbes papers.

I have to thank Professor Ernest Barker, who read the manuscript of the present study and made very helpful suggestions, and
to whose kindness and interest it is primarily due that I was able
to continue my work.

I wish further to express my gratitude to Professor R. H.
Tawney, to the Master of Balliol, to Professor N. F. Hall, and
to Mr. E. J. Passant for the help and encouragement they have
given me.

ditionally attributed to 'Lord Chandos' or to 'Lord Candish, after Earle of
Devonshire'. The latter attribution is borne out by the discovery of the
manuscript version signed by W. Cavendish, and the former may well be
derived from a misreading of 'Candish' as 'Chandos'. W. Cavendish might
stand, of course, for any Earl of Devonshire, since they were all named
William; but the possibilities are limited by the date of composition of the
'Essayes' and the *Horae subsecivae* (between 1612 and 1620) in such a way
that only the 1st Earl of Devonshire or his son, afterwards 2nd Earl of
Devonshire, could claim the authorship of those writings. The authorship
of the 1st Earl is out of the question, for the 'Essayes' are dedicated by
W. Cavendish to his father, then living, and the 1st Earl's father died in
1557. Thus the (nominal or actual) author of the 'Essayes' and very probably
also of the *Horae subsecivae* can be nobody else but W. Cavendish, afterwards 2nd Earl of Devonshire. Now, this W. Cavendish was Hobbes's
pupil and friend. Hobbes lived with him as his tutor and secretary from
1608 until 1628, therefore also during the whole period within which the
'Essayes' and the *Horae subsecivae* can have been written. There were
personal connexions between Bacon and W. Cavendish, afterwards 2nd
Earl, and between Bacon and Hobbes; these connexions help to explain the
literary relation which exists between Bacon's *Essays* and the Cavendish
'Essayes'. In spite of the considerable borrowings from Bacon's *Essays* in the
'Essayes', there are, however, no less significant differences of view between
the model and the imitation—differences which correspond to the difference
between Bacon's thought and that of Hobbes.

I am very much indebted to the Rockefeller Foundation, the Academic Assistance Council, and the Master and Governing Body of Sidney Sussex College for financial help.

Finally, I wish to thank Mrs. E. M. Sinclair, who generously undertook the difficult task of translating the present study.

L. S.

PREFACE TO THE AMERICAN EDITION

For various reasons this study is here reissued in its original form. It is, no doubt, in need of considerable revision. But it still seems to me that the way in which I approached Hobbes is preferable to the available alternatives. Hobbes appeared to me as the originator of modern political philosophy. This was an error: not Hobbes, but Machiavelli, deserves this honor. But I still prefer that easily corrected error, or rather its characteristic premises, to the more generally accepted views which I was forced to oppose and which are less easily corrected.

I had seen that the modern mind had lost its self-confidence or its certainty of having made decisive progress beyond pre-modern thought; and I saw that it was turning into nihilism, or what is in practice the same thing, fanatical obscurantism. I concluded that the case of the moderns against the ancients must be reopened, without any regard to cherished opinions or convictions, *sine ira et studio*. I concluded in other words that we must learn to consider seriously, i.e. detachedly, the possibility that Swift was right when he compared the modern world to Lilliput and the ancient world to Brobdingnag. I assumed that political philosophy as quest for the final truth regarding the political fundamentals is possible and necessary: I regarded Hobbes as a political philosopher and not as an ideologist or mythologist. I assumed that political philosophy, as an essentially non-historical pursuit, is today in need of a critical study of its history; that such a critical history presupposes that one understand the great thinkers of the past as they understood themselves; that the history of political philosophy requires an adequate division into periods; and that only such a division can be considered adequate as corresponds to the self-consciousness of the actors, i.e. of the great political philosophers. I concluded that Hobbes was the founder of modern political philosophy because he had expressed the conviction that he had effected, in his capacity as a political philosopher, a radical break with all earlier political philosophy much more clearly than Zeno of Citium, Marsilius of

Padua, Machiavelli, Bodin, and even Bacon had done. I was confirmed in this view by the judgment of competent men, of Bayle and Rousseau.

The immediate and perhaps sufficient cause of my error was inadequate reflection on the opening of Machiavelli's *Discorsi*. I had learned from Spinoza to appreciate the clarion call of the Fifteenth Chapter of the *Principe*. But I had been told by all authorities that the *magnum opus* of Machiavelli is not the *Principe* but the *Discorsi;* and the *Discorsi* present themselves at first glance as an attempt to restore something lost or forgotten rather than as an attempt to open an entirely new vista. I did not consider the possibility that Machiavelli still exercised a kind of reserve which Hobbes disdained to exercise: that the difference in degree to which Machiavelli's and Hobbes' claims to originality are audible is due to a difference in degree not of clarity of thought but of outspokenness. The reason for this failure was that I was not sufficiently attentive to the question whether wisdom can be divorced from moderation or to the sacrifices which we must make so that our minds may be free.

L. S.

CONTENTS

I

INTRODUCTION

HOBBES'S political philosophy is the first peculiarly modern attempt to give a coherent and exhaustive answer to the question of man's right life, which is at the same time the question of the right order of society. There is perhaps no element of Hobbes's teaching which cannot be traced back to one or other of his predecessors; and it may be that one or other of them was in some respects less bound by tradition than was Hobbes. But such elements as had emerged separately before his time find their specifically modern unity only in Hobbes; and none of Hobbes's forerunners attempted that definite break with tradition in its entirety which the modern answer to the question of man's right life implies. Hobbes was the first who felt the necessity of seeking, and succeeded in finding, a *nuova scienza* of man and State. On this new doctrine all later moral and political thought is expressly or tacitly based. To indicate its political importance one might stress the fact that the ideal of civilization in its modern form, the ideal both of the bourgeois-capitalist development and of the socialist movement, was founded and expounded by Hobbes with a depth, clarity, and sincerity never rivalled before or since. To give an indication of its philosophical bearing one might point out that the moral philosophy, not merely of eighteenth-century rationalism, but also of Rousseau, Kant, and Hegel, would not have been possible without Hobbes's work. But above all, as a fundamental answer to the question of man's right life, Hobbes's political philosophy is of supreme importance not only for political philosophy as such, i.e. for one branch of knowledge among others, but for modern philosophy altogether, if the discussion and elucidation of the ideal of life is indeed the primary and decisive task of philosophy.

It is almost universally admitted that Hobbes marks an epoch in the history of natural law and of the theory of the State. That the importance of his achievement is far greater,

that it is truly universal, is usually not even considered. This
lack of recognition is partly due—paradoxical as it may sound
—to the influence of Hobbes himself. According to his own
statements, his achievement in political philosophy was made
possible by the application of a new method, the method by
which Galileo raised physics to the rank of a science.[1] In
conformity with this method, which is called the 'resolutive-
compositive', the given political facts (the disputable justice or
injustice of any particular action, or the current conception of
justice in general, or the State itself, which as the primary condition of justice is the political fact *par excellence*) are analysed,
reduced to their elements (the 'individual wills'), and then,
converso itinere, starting from those elements, the necessity and
possibility of a 'collective will' is developed *evidentissimâ con-
nexione*, by a completely lucid deduction, and what was at first
an 'irrational' whole is 'rationalised'.[2] It would thus seem that
the characteristic contents of Hobbes's political philosophy—
the absolute priority of the individual to the State, the conceptions of the individual as asocial, of the relation between
the state of nature and the State as an absolute antithesis, and
finally of the State itself as Leviathan—is determined by and,
as it were, implied in the method. As this method, however,
was applied only subsequently, only in imitation of Galileo's
founding of the new physics, Hobbes's achievement, from this
point of view, however great it may be, is nevertheless of the
second order—secondary in comparison with the founding of
modern science by Galileo and Descartes.

The universal importance of Hobbes's political philosophy
cannot but remain unrecognized so long as, in accordance with
Hobbes's own statements, the method is considered to be the
decisive feature of his politics. Now it is obvious that the
method is not its only and even not its most important characteristic. Precisely on the assumptions of the 'resolutive-compositive' method—and by no means on the assumptions of
Aristotle's 'genetic' method—the question of the aim and
quality of the individual will, of man's will in the state of

[1] Compare in this connexion particularly E. Cassirer, *Die Philosophie der
Aufklärung* (Tübingen, 1932), pp. 339 ff.
[2] *De cive*, Praefatio and Epistula dedicatoria; *De corpore*, cap. 6, art. 7.

nature, becomes decisive for the concrete development of the idea of the State. And the answer to this decisive question is not unequivocally traced out in advance by the method. As Rousseau's polemic against Hobbes sufficiently proves, there remains the antithesis between the assertions that man is by nature good (more accurately, innocent) and that he is by nature evil (rapacious). Hobbes's adoption of the latter view, without which his political philosophy would lose all its character, must therefore have an origin other than the method, and as a result his political philosophy must have a more immediate and concrete origin than the method. Where is this origin—the origin not of the method, of the form, but of the material of Hobbes's political philosophy—to be sought?

To this question research has up to the present given two different answers. The obvious answer, forced upon us by the structure of Hobbes's political philosophy itself, is that Hobbes draws the concrete definition of the aim and quality of the individual will from the mechanistic psychology which precedes political philosophy in his system. This psychology provides as data on the negative side the denial of freedom of will, on the positive the assertion that man is under all conditions determined by his sense-impressions and by his automatic reactions to those impressions (his desires and passions) rather than by reason. Now it is not difficult to see that this psychology is by no means the necessary assumption for Hobbes's political philosophy. Hobbes's characteristic theories—the denial that 'altruism' is natural, the theses of man's rapacious nature, of the war of every one against every one as the natural condition of mankind, of the essential impotence of reason—can also be maintained on the indeterminist assumptions. In addition, this 'pessimistic' view of human nature is marked in Hobbes before he had or could have the least conception of a mechanistic psychology. These and kindred considerations led W. Dilthey to seek the origin of the material of Hobbes's political philosophy, not in modern scientific psychology but in tradition. According to Dilthey, modern science decided only 'the form which anthropology now took on (sc. for Hobbes among others), while as far as material was concerned it had its basis in the descriptions, classifications, and explanations of the previous age'.[1] Dilthey then traced this material back to sources in classical antiquity. He attached particular importance to the proof that for the fundamental part of his political philosophy, the theory of the passions, Hobbes is greatly indebted to the Stoa.[2] We cannot here discuss in detail Dilthey's analysis of the sources. One point must, however, be raised. Dilthey takes his bearings from the theory of the passions in *De homine*, which is, indeed, influenced by the Stoa. He makes no mention of the theory of the passions as developed in the *Elements of Law*, a theory which betrays no Stoic influence at all, and which in addition is worked out in much greater detail than the corresponding passage in *De homine*. As a matter of principle, it must be remarked that Dilthey never investigated whether the traditional theories which recur in Hobbes's writings are really integral elements of his political philosophy or whether they are not rather mere residues of a tradition which Hobbes had in the main rejected, but from which he could not always free himself and never completely cast off. Dilthey never asked himself this question because he did not take Hobbes's express and systematic opposition to the whole tradition—including the Stoa and Epicureanism—seriously enough. Had he compared the material of Hobbes's political philosophy with the material of traditional political philosophy —the investigation of sources which he began is the basis, but only the basis of such a comparison—he would have seen that the traditional theses and concepts take on an entirely untraditional meaning in Hobbes's work.[3] To keep to the example already quoted—the Stoic conception of passion must be basically modified when it is taken over by a philosopher who

---

[1] *Gesammelte Schriften*, vol. ii, p. 452.

[2] Loc. cit., pp. 293 ff.

[3] Completely independent of Dilthey, in one sense in opposition to him, J. Laird (*Hobbes*, London, 1934) has recently investigated the relation of Hobbes's political philosophy to tradition. He asserts that Hobbes, who introduces the new mechanistic doctrine into metaphysics, even though by means of medieval 'technique', is completely medieval in his ethics and politics (p. 57). For Laird, the essential difference between Hobbes and his medieval forerunners accordingly lies in Hobbes's 'logical vigour and ruthlessness' (p. 58) or in the proof of the traditional theories by the methods and principles of modern science (cf. p. 90 and p. 181). The same objection must be raised to this attempt as above to Dilthey's.

systematically denies the possibility of *beatitudo*, and for whom the contrary of passion is no longer a state of repose.

If Hobbes's importance is to be duly recognized and understood, the necessary condition is thus that the fundamental difference between the 'material' of Hobbes's political philosophy, i.e. the characteristic moral attitude which determines Hobbes's way of thinking, on the one hand, and the classical as well as the Christian attitude on the other, should be grasped. The moral attitude which underlies Hobbes's political philosophy is independent of the foundation of modern science, and at least in that sense 'pre-scientific'. It is at the same time specifically modern. One is inclined to say that it is the deepest stratum of the modern mind. It found its fullest and sincerest expression in Hobbes's political philosophy. For, from the very beginning, it has been covered over by classical and Christian tradition, but, generally speaking, more completely before Hobbes than after him, and after him particularly by mechanistic psychology, to which Hobbes himself opened the door, and finally by sociology. Hobbes, however, philosophized in the fertile moment when the classical and theological tradition was already shaken, and a tradition of modern science not yet formed and established. At this time he and he only posed the fundamental question of man's right life and of the right ordering of society. This moment was decisive for the whole age to come; in it the foundation was laid, on which the modern development of political philosophy is wholly based, and it is the point from which every attempt at a thorough understanding of modern thought must start. This foundation has never again been visible as it was then. The structure which Hobbes, led by the inspiration of that moment, began to raise, hid the foundation as long as the structure stood, i.e. as long as its stability was believed in.

II

THE MORAL BASIS

POLITICAL philosophy, as that branch of knowledge which consists of moral philosophy on the one hand, and politics in the narrower sense on the other,[1] was treated systematically and exhaustively by Hobbes three times: in the *Elements of Law* (1640), in the second and third parts of the *Elementa philosophiae* (Section II, *De homine*, 1658; Section III, *De cive*, 1642), and in the *Leviathan* (1651). In all three presentations this political philosophy is based in method and material on natural science. The method is Galileo's 'resolutive-compositive' method. The material is borrowed from the mechanistic explanation of the passions and previously of sense-perception. It is therefore understandable that almost every one who has written about Hobbes has interpreted his political philosophy as dependent on natural science, for either material or method or for both. This interpretation, which at a first glance seems to be merely the recognition of an obvious fact, proves on closer examination to be extremely questionable.

The attempt to work out political philosophy as a part or annexe of natural science by means of scientific method is constantly questioned in Hobbes's work, because he was aware of the fundamental differences between the two disciplines in material and method. On this awareness is based his conviction that political philosophy is essentially independent of natural science. He was therefore able to write and publish *De cive*, the third part of his system, many years before the two systematically earlier parts. In justification of the premature publication of this book, he expressly says in the preface ' . . . factum est ut quae ordine ultima (pars) esset, tempore tamen prior prodierit; praesertim cum eam principiis propriis experientiâ cognitis innixam, praecedentibus indigere non viderem'.[2]

---

[1] *De corpore*, cap. 1, art. 9; *De homine*, Ep. ded.

[2] It follows from the dedication to *De homine* that what is said in the preface to *De cive* of politics in the narrower sense holds also for the other part of political philosophy, moral philosophy.

Political philosophy is independent of natural science because its principles are not borrowed from natural science, are not, indeed, borrowed from any science, but are provided by experience, by the experience which every one has of himself, or, to put it more accurately, are discovered by the efforts of self-knowledge and the self-examination of every one.[1] As a result, evidence in political philosophy is of quite a different kind from evidence in natural science. On the one hand, it is much easier to understand: its subject and its concepts are not so remote from the average man as are the subject and concepts of mathematics which form the basis of natural science.[2] On the other hand, 'the politiques are the harder study of the two'; by reason of their passions, men obscure the, in itself, clear and simple knowledge of the norms which political philosophy builds up. Moreover, man with his passions and his self-seeking is the particular subject of political philosophy, and man opposes by every kind of hypocrisy the self-knowledge on which the proof of these norms rests.[3]

According to Hobbes, political philosophy is not only independent of natural science, but it is a main component of human knowledge, of which the other main component is natural science. The whole body of knowledge is divided into natural science on the one hand, and political philosophy on the other.[4] Every classification of knowledge is based on a classification of the existent.[5] Hobbes's classification of the sciences is based on a classification of existing things into natural and artificial.[6] But this classification does not fully correspond to his intention, for most things which are produced by art, in particular all machines, are the subject of natural science.[7] It is not so much the artificially produced things that are basically

[1] *De corpore*, cap. 6, art. 7; *Leviathan*, Introduction.

[2] *De homine*, Ep. ded.; *Leviathan*, ch. 31 (p. 197) and Conclusion (p. 385).

[3] *Leviathan*, ch. 30 (pp. 180 and 187) and Introduction; *Elements of Law*, Ep. ded.; *English Works*, vol. vii, p. 399.

[4] The immediate source for this classification may well be Marius Nizolius, *De veris principiis et vera ratione philosophandi* (Parma, 1553), lib. 3, capp. 3–4.

[5] *De cive*, Ep. ded.

[6] *De corpore*, cap. 1, art. 9; *De homine*, Ep. ded.; *Leviathan*, Introduction.

[7] *De corpore*, cap. 1, art. 7; *De cive*, Ep. ded.; *Leviathan*, Introduction and ch. 9.

different from all natural things as the production, the human activity itself, i.e. man as an essentially productive being, especially as the being who by his art produces from his own nature the citizen or the State, who, by working on himself, makes himself into a citizen. In so far as man works on himself, influencing and changing his nature, so that he becomes a citizen, a part of that artificial being called the State, he is not a natural being: 'Homo . . . non modo corpus naturale est, sed etiam civitatis, id est (ut ita loquar) corporis politici pars.'[1] 'Manners of men' are something different from 'natural causes'.[2] The basic classification of existing things which in truth underlies Hobbes's classification of the sciences is classification under nature on the one side, and under man as productive and active being on the other.[3]

The question whether Hobbes understood political philosophy as a part or annexe of natural science or as a fully independent branch of knowledge, in other words, whether his political philosophy is intended to be naturalistic or anthropological, thus bears not only on the method but above all on the matter. The significance of the antithesis between naturalistic and anthropological political philosophy for the matter becomes fully apparent if one grasps that this antithesis is only the abstract form of a concrete antithesis in the interpretation of and judgement on human nature which extends throughout the whole of Hobbes's work. Hobbes eliminated the latter contradiction as little as the former.

Hobbes summed up his theory of human nature as it underlies his political philosophy in 'two most certain postulates of human nature'. The first postulate is that of 'natural appetite', 'qua quisque rerum communium usum postulat sibi proprium'.[4] As a result of the scientific explanation, this appetite is taken as having its roots in man's sensuousness, in his animal nature. Man is an animal like all other animals, as a percipient being constantly exposed to manifold impressions which automatically call forth desires and aversions, so that his life, like that of

[1] *De homine*, Ep. ded.
[2] *English Works*, vol. iv, p. 445; cf. *Leviathan*, ch. 37 (p. 238).
[3] *Elements of Law*, Ep. ded.; *Leviathan*, ch. 9; *De corpore*, cap. 1, art. 9; *De cive*, Ep. ded.
[4] *De cive*, Ep. ded.

all other animals, is constant movement. There is, however, one important difference: the specific difference between man and all other animals is reason. Thus man is much less at the mercy of momentary sense-impressions, he can envisage the future much better than can animals; for this very reason he is not like animals hungry only with the hunger of the moment, but also with future hunger, and thus he is the most predatory, the most cunning, the strongest, and most dangerous animal.[1] Human appetite is thus not in itself different from animal appetite, but only by the fact that in the case of man appetite has reason at its service. This view of human appetite, which at first sight seems to be the specifically Hobbian view, is, however, contradicted in Hobbes's writings by his repeated and emphatic statement that human appetite is infinite in itself and not as a result of the infinite number of external impressions.[2] But if this is the case, then human appetite is essentially distinguished from animal appetite in that the latter is nothing but reaction to external impressions, and, therefore, the animal desires only finite objects as such, while man spontaneously desires infinitely. There can be no doubt that only this latter view of human appetite corresponds to the intention of Hobbes's political philosophy.

The two conceptions of human appetite differ not only in substance as mechanistic and vitalistic conceptions. They differ also in method. The mechanistic conception is based on the mechanistic explanation of perception and therewith on the general theory of motion; on the other hand, the apparently vitalistic conception is based not on any general scientific theory, but on insight into human nature, deepened and substantiated by self-knowledge and self-examination. In spite of their opposed matter and methods, the two conceptions of human appetite have, however—below the surface—something

---

[1] *De homine*, cap. 10, art. 3.

[2] *Elements of Law*, Pt. I, ch. 7, § 7; *Leviathan*, ch. 11 (p. 49); *De homine*, cap. 11, art. 15. In all three passages Hobbes bases the proposition that life is limitless appetite mechanistically on the assumption that appetite is only an automatic consequence of perception, but also on the incompatible assumption that appetite is essentially spontaneous. On closer investigation it is seen that the mechanistic argument is not sufficient proof of the proposition, and that therefore the proposition itself cannot possibly owe the self-evidence, which it has for Hobbes, to the mechanistic argument.

in common, which allows us to characterize both of them as naturalistic.

The clearest and most perfect expression for the naturalistic conception of human appetite is the proposition that man desires power and ever greater power, spontaneously and continuously, in one jet of appetite, and not by reason of a summation of innumerable isolated desires caused by innumerable isolated perceptions: ' . . . in the first place, I put for a generall inclination of all mankind, a perpetuall and restlesse desire of power after power, that ceaseth only in Death.'[1] But this apparently perfectly clear proposition is fundamentally equivocal, for the boundless striving after power is itself equivocal. Hobbes continues: 'And the cause of this, is not alwayes that a man hopes for a more intensive delight, than he has already attained to; or that he cannot be content with a moderate power: but because he cannot assure the power and the means to live well, which he hath present, without the acquisition of more.' The striving after power may thus be rational as well as irrational. Only the irrational striving after power, which is found more frequently than the rational striving, is to be taken as natural human appetite. For the rational striving after power rests on already rational reflection and is for that very reason not natural, i.e. not innate, not in existence prior to all external motivations, to all experience and education.[2] The only natural striving after power, and thus man's natural appetite, is described by Hobbes as follows: 'men from their very birth, and naturally, scramble for everything they covet, and would have all the world, if they could, to fear and obey them.'[3] It depends on impressions from without and thus on perception that the child 'desires' that particular thing which he sees and not another thing, of whose existence he knows nothing; but that he 'would have all the world . . . to fear and obey (him)'—that, on the occasion of a particular desire which was awakened and caused by sense-perception, he 'desires' absolute rule over the whole world—cannot originate in the impression of things per-

---

[1] *Leviathan*, ch. 11 (p. 49).

[2] For Hobbes's concept of 'natural', see especially *De cive*, cap. 1, art. 2, annot. 1.

[3] *English Works*, vol. vii, p. 73.

ceived, for animals who also perceive and desire do not aspire
to absolute dominion. In the case of man, animal desire is
taken up and transformed by a spontaneous infinite and absolute desire which arises out of the depths of man himself.

We find a more detailed definition of the irrational striving
after power, the natural appetite of man as man, in the following
differentiation between irrational and therefore unpermissible
striving after power, and rational and therefore permissible
striving:

'because there be some, that taking pleasure in contemplating their
own power in the acts of conquest, which they pursue farther than
their security requires; if others, that otherwise would be glad to
be at ease within modest bounds, should not by invasion increase
their power, they would not be able, long time, by standing only on
their defence, to subsist. And by consequence, such augmentation
of dominion over men, being necessary to a man's conservation, it
ought to be allowed him.'[1]

We here clearly see that rational permissible striving after
power is in itself finite. The man guided by it would remain
'within modest bounds', would 'be content with a moderate
power'. Only the unpermissible, irrational, lustful striving
after power is infinite. Now irrational striving after power,
man's natural appetite, has its basis in the pleasure which man
takes in the consideration of his own power, i.e. in vanity. The
origin of man's natural appetite is, therefore, not perception but
vanity.

In four different arguments, Hobbes does not tire of desig-
nating the characteristic difference between man and animal
as the striving after honour and positions of honour, after
precedence over others and recognition of this precedence by
others, ambition, pride, and the passion for fame.[2] Because
man's natural appetite is nothing other than a striving after
precedence over others and recognition of this precedence by
others, the particularities of natural appetite, the passions, are
nothing other than particular ways of striving after precedence
and recognition: 'all joy and grief of mind (consists) in a

[1] *Leviathan*, ch. 13 (p. 64).
[2] *Elements of Law*, Pt. I, ch. 19, § 5; *De cive*, cap. 5, art. 5; *Leviathan*,
ch. 17 (pp. 88–9).

contention for precedence to them with whom they compare themselves.'[1] And as 'to have stronger, and more violent Passions for anything, than is ordinarily seen in others, is that which men call Madnesse', madness must show with particular clearness the nature of the passions. Speaking of the cause of madness, Hobbes says: 'The Passion, whose violence, or continuance maketh Madnesse, is either great vaine-glory; which is commonly called Pride, and selfe-conceipt; or great Dejection of mind.'[2] All passions and all forms of madness are modifications of conceit or of a sense of inferiority, or in principle, of the striving after precedence and recognition of that precedence. According to Hobbes's view, the motive of this striving is man's wish to take pleasure in himself by considering his own superiority, his own recognized superiority, i.e. vanity.[3]

The same conclusion is reached if one analyses and compares the arguments by which Hobbes in the three presentations of his political philosophy proves his assertion that the war of every one against every one arises of necessity from man's very nature. Every man is for that very reason the enemy of every other man, because each desires to surpass every other and thereby offends every other. The astonishing discrepancies between the three presentations, the still more astonishing obscurities, even the logical defects of the individual presentations show that Hobbes himself never completed the proofs of his fundamental assertion, and, as is seen on closer study, did not complete them simply because he could not make up his mind explicitly to take as his point of departure the reduction of man's natural appetite to vanity. We cannot here produce the proofs for this assertion.[4] Instead we would remind the reader of one fact, which, although it is so obvious, has, so far as we know, always been overlooked—the reason which caused Hobbes to call his most detailed exposition of political philosophy the

[1] *Elements of Law*, Pt. II, ch. 8, § 3; cf. *Elements*, Pt. I, ch. 8, § 8, and ch. 9; also *De cive*, cap. 1, art. 2.

[3] *Leviathan*, ch. 8 (p. 36); cf. *Elements*, Pt. I, ch. 10, §§ 9–11.

[3] 'Gloria . . . sive bene opinari de se ipso . . .' *De cive*, cap. 1, art. 2; cf. *Elements*, Pt. I, ch. 9, § 1; *De cive*, cap. 4, art. 9; *De homine*, cap. 12, art. 6. Cf. pp. 133 and 135, note 1, below.

[4] The author hopes to present these proofs in the near future within the framework of an exposition of Hobbes's political philosophy.

Leviathan. At the end of the most important part of this work, he says:

'Hitherto I have set forth the nature of Man, (whose *Pride* and other passions have compelled him to submit himselfe to Government;) together with the great Power of his Governour, whom I compared to Leviathan, taking that comparison out of the last two verses of the one and fortieth of Job; where God having set forth the great power of Leviathan, called him King of the *Proud*.'[1]

It is not mighty power as such which is the *tertium comparationis* between Leviathan and the State, but the mighty power which subdues the proud. The State is compared to Leviathan, because it and it especially is the 'King of all the children of pride'. Only the State is capable of keeping pride down in the long run, indeed it has no other *raison d'être* except that man's natural appetite is pride, ambition, and vanity. It is with this thought in mind that Hobbes says of his book *Leviathan* that it is 'Justitiae mensura, atque ambitionis elenchus'.[2]

Why could Hobbes not make up his mind to treat the view which is in reality conclusive for him, that man's natural appetite is vanity, unequivocally as the basis of his political philosophy? If this conception of natural appetite is right, if man by nature finds his pleasure in triumphing over all others, then man is by nature evil. But he did not dare to uphold this consequence or assumption of his theory. For this reason, in the enumeration of the causes which lead to the war of every man against every man, in the final presentation (in the *Leviathan*) he puts vanity at the end.[3] That it was the above-mentioned reason[4] which determined Hobbes may be seen from a passage in the preface to *De cive*. The objection had been raised that, according to Hobbes's theory, man is by nature evil. He replies:

'Quamquam . . . a natura, hoc est, ab ipsa nativitate, ex eo quod nascantur, *animalia* hoc habeant, ut statim omnia quae sibi placent, cupiant faciantque quantum possunt, ut quae impendent mala, aut metu fugiant, aut ira repellant, non tamen ob eam causam mala

---

[1] *Leviathan*, ch. 28, *in fine*.   [2] *Opera latina*, vol. i, p. xciv.
[3] Compare the different order of the argument in *Leviathan*, ch. 13 (pp. 63–4) on the one hand, in *Elements*, Pt. I, ch. 14, §§ 3–5 and *De cive*, cap. 1, art. 4–6 on the other. Cf. p. 169, note 2, below.
[4] Cf. p. 33, l. 23.

censeri solent: nam affectus animi qui a natura *animali* profisci-
cuntur, mali non sunt ipsi, sed actiones inde provenientes . . . con-
fitendum est, posse homines a natura cupiditatem, metum, iram,
caeterosque affectus habere *animales*, ut tamen mali facti a natura
non sint.'

Because man is by nature animal, therefore he is not by nature
evil, therefore he is as innocent as the animals; thus vanity
cannot characterize his natural appetite. It is indicative that
Hobbes in his defence against the reproach that according to
his theory man is by nature evil does not mention vanity at all.
Natural vanity disappears in the *caeteros affectus*.[1] It must
vanish into them, it must be hidden by them, if man's natural
innocence is to be asserted, if human wickedness is to be understood as the innocent 'wickedness' of the brutes. In laying the
foundations of his political philosophy, Hobbes puts vanity
more and more into the background in favour of innocent competition, innocent striving after power, innocent animal appetite, because the definition of man's natural appetite in terms
of vanity is intended as a moral judgement. But he is no better
able than any other to make us forget that man does not happen
to be an innocent animal. Not only is he finally obliged to
attribute to the judges the wickedness which he disallows in
the case of the guilty, the criminals;[2] he betrays particularly

---

[1] With consistent naturalism Hobbes tries to derive vanity from animal
nature (cf. *Elements*, Pt. I, ch. 8, §§ 3–5 and *Leviathan*, ch. 10). Thus he
can conclude the description of the social pleasures, which according to his
presentation, are nothing other than the pleasures of vanity, with the
following words: 'Atque hae verae sunt deliciae societatis, ad quas naturâ,
id est, ab affectibus omni animanti insitis ferimur . . .' (*De cive*, cap. 1, art. 2).
The precise comparison of animal and human nature, according to which
vanity is never present in animals, contradicts this indication of the animal
character of vanity; cf. *De cive*, cap. 5, art. 5, and the parallel passages in
the *Elements* and the *Leviathan*.

[2] '. . . it seems the Bishop takes blame, not for the dispraise of a thing,
but for a pretext and colour of malice and revenge against him he blameth
. . . we do as much blame (fire for burning cities and poison for destroying
men) as we do men. For we say fire hath done hurt, and the poison hath
killed a man, as well as we say that the man hath done unjustly; but we do
not seek to be revenged of the fire and of poison, because we cannot make
them to ask forgiveness, as we would make men to do when they hurt us.
So that the blaming of the one and the other, that is, the declaring of hurt
evil action done by them, is the same in both; but the malice of man is only
against man.' *English Works*, vol. v, pp. 53–4. That desire for revenge

in his description of the striving after power itself, that the innocence, neutrality, and moral indifference of that striving is only apparent. The striving after power, as human striving after power, is always either good and permissible or evil and unpermissible. The apparent moral indifference arises simply and solely through abstraction of the necessary moral difference, which Hobbes himself immediately stresses. Hobbes's political philosophy rests not on the illusion of an amoral morality, but on a new morality, or, to speak according to Hobbes's intention, on a new grounding of the one eternal morality.

The second of the 'two most certain postulates of human nature' which Hobbes takes as basis of his political philosophy, along with the 'postulate of natural appetite', is 'the postulate of natural reason', 'qua quisque mortem violentam tanquam summum naturae malum studet evitare'. In accordance with naturalistic reasoning this postulate is reduced to the principle of self-preservation: since the preservation of life is the condition *sine qua non* for the satisfaction of any appetite, it is 'the primary good'.[1] As a logical conclusion of this thought, Hobbes attempts to deduce natural right, natural law, and all the virtues—the four Platonic cardinal virtues—from the principle of self-preservation.[2]

It is striking that Hobbes prefers the negative expression 'avoiding death' to the positive expression 'preserving life'. It is not difficult to discover the reason. That preservation of life is the primary good is affirmed by reason and by reason only. On the other hand, that death is the primary evil is affirmed by passion, the passion of fear of death. And as reason itself is powerless, man would not be minded to think of the preservation of life as the primary and most urgent good, if the passion of fear of death did not compel him to do so.[3] A further reason, which is closely connected with the one already mentioned, recommends the negative expression. According to Hobbes, the preservation of life is the *primary* good, an

arises from vanity is said by Hobbes in *Elements*, Pt. I, ch. 16, § 10, and ch. 9, § 6.

[1] *De homine*, cap. 11, art. 6.
[2] See particularly *De cive*, cap. 3, art. 32.
[3] Cf. *Elements*, Pt. I, ch. 14, § 6 with the Ep. ded. to this work.

unhindered progress to ever further goals, a 'continuall prosper-ing'—in a word, happiness is the *greatest* good, but there is no *supreme* good, in the sense of a good in the enjoyment of which the spirit might find repose.[1] On the other hand, death is the *primary* as well as the *greatest* and *supreme* evil.[2] For death is not only the negation of the primary good, but is therewith the negation of all goods, including the greatest good; and at the same time, death—being the *summum malum*, while there is no *summum bonum*—is the only absolute standard by reference to which man may coherently order his life. While in the order of goods there is no real limit, and while, in addition, the primary and the greatest good are completely different, the primary and greatest and supreme evil are one and the same, and it is thus only in consideration of evil that a limit to desiring, a coherent orientation of human life, is possible. Only through death has man an aim, because only through death has he one compelling aim—the aim which is forced upon him by the sight of death—the aim of avoiding death. For this reason Hobbes prefers the negative expression 'avoiding death' to the positive expression 'preserving life': because we feel death and not life; because we fear death immediately and directly, while we desire life only because rational reflection tells us that it is the condition of our happiness; because we fear death infinitely more than we desire life.

But Hobbes cannot after all acquiesce in the assertion that death is the primary and greatest and supreme evil. For he knows that a miserable tortured life can be a greater evil than death. Thus it is not death in itself which is the greatest and supreme evil, but an agonizing death or, what seems at first to mean the same thing, a violent death.[3] But if Hobbes had really considered an agonizing death as the supreme and greatest evil, he would have attributed an even greater importance to medicine than did Descartes[4] or Spinoza.[5] This is so little the

---

[1] *De homine*, cap. 11, art. 15; *Elements*, Pt. I, ch. 7, § 7; *Leviathan*, ch. 6 (p. 30) and 11 *in princ.*

[2] *De homine*, cap. 11, art. 6; *De cive*, Ep. ded. and cap. 1, art. 7.

[3] *De homine*, cap. 11, art. 6; cf. *Elements*, Pt. I, ch. 14, § 6; *De cive*, Ep. ded.; ibid., cap. 3, art. 12 and cap. 6, art. 13.

[4] *Discours de la méthode, in fine.*

[5] *Tractatus de intellectus emendatione*, ed. Bruder, § 15.

case that he actually forgets medicine: 'Calamitates autem *omnes*, quae humana industria evitari possunt a *bello* oriuntur, praecipue vero a bello civili; hinc enim caedes, solitudo, inopiaque rerum omnium derivatur.'[1] Not an agonizing death in itself, but a violent death which threatens a man at the hand of other men, is the only one which Hobbes considers worthy of mention. When he says of an agonizing death that it is the greatest evil, he thinks exclusively of violent death at the hand of other men. The 'postulate of natural reason' expresses this thought in the formula '(unusquisque) mortem *violentam* tanquam summum naturae malum studet evitare'.

Not the rational and therefore always uncertain[2] knowledge that death is the greatest and supreme evil, but the fear of death, i.e. the emotional and inevitable, and therefore necessary and certain, aversion from death is the origin of law and the State.[3] This fear is a mutual fear, i.e. it is the fear each man has of every other man as his potential murderer.[4] This fear of a violent death, pre-rational in its origin, but rational in its effect, and not the rational principle of self-preservation, is, according

---

[1] *De corpore*, cap. 1, art. 7. It must further be pointed out that in almost all the passages in which Hobbes treats of the utility of natural science, he does not mention medicine at all. Compare the following passages: *Elements*, Pt. I, ch. 13, § 3; *De cive*, Ep. ded. and cap. 17, art. 12; *Leviathan*, ch. 13 (pp. 64–5) and ch. 46 *in princ.*; *De corpore*, cap. 1, art. 7.

[2] Speaking of the laws of nature, Hobbes says: '(the dictates of reason) are but theorems, tending to peace, and those *uncertain*, as being but conclusions of particular men, and therefore not properly laws.' *English Works*, vol. iv, p. 285. Cf. *De cive*, cap. 2, art. 1, annot., and *Leviathan*, ch. 26 (p. 141).

[3] 'Fertur enim unusquisque ad appetitum ejus quod sibi bonum, et ad fugam ejus quod sibi malum est, maxime autem maximi malorum naturalium, quae est mors; idque necessitate quadam naturae non minore, quam qua fertur lapis deorsum. Non igitur absurdum neque reprehendendum, neque contra rectam rationem est, si quis omnem operam det, ut a morte et doloribus proprium corpus et membra defendat conservetque. . . . Itaque Juris naturalis fundamentum primum est, ut quisque vitam et membra sua quantum potest tueatur.' *De cive*, cap. 1, art. 7. That *necessitas* is not here to be understood in the naturalistic-determinist sense is shown by parallel passages, such as the following: 'You that make it so heinous a crime for a man to save himself from violent death, by a *forced* submission to a usurper, should have considered what crime it was to submit *voluntarily* to the usurping Parliament . . . he (Hobbes) justified their submission by their former obedience, and present *necessity* . . .' *English Works*, vol. iv, pp. 423 ff.

[4] *De cive*, cap. 1, art. 2–3.

to Hobbes, the root of all right and therewith of all morality. He drew all his logical conclusions from this: he finally denied the moral value of all virtues which do not contribute to the making of the State, to consolidating peace, to protecting man against the danger of violent death, or, more exactly expressed, of all virtues which do not proceed from fear of violent death: 'Sunt enim tum fortitudo, tum prudentia, vis animi potius quam bonitas morum; et temperantia privatio potius vitiorum quae oriuntur ab ingeniis cupidis . . . quam virtus moralis.'[1]

The antithesis from which Hobbes's political philosophy starts is thus the antithesis between vanity as the root of natural appetite on the one hand, and on the other, fear of violent death as the passion which brings man to reason. More accurately expressed: because Hobbes reduces man's natural appetite to vanity, he cannot but recognize the fear of a violent death—not the fear of a painful death, and certainly not the striving after self-preservation—as the principle of morality. For if man's natural appetite is vanity, this means that man by nature strives to surpass all his fellows and to have his superiority recognized by all others, in order that he may take pleasure in himself; that he naturally wishes the whole world to fear and obey him. The ever-greater triumph over others— this, and not the ever-increasing, but rationally increasing, power—is the aim and happiness of natural man: 'Continually to out-go the next before, is felicity.' Man's life may be compared to a race: 'but this race we must suppose to have no other goal, nor other garland, but being foremost.'[2] Absorbed in the race after the happiness of triumph, man cannot be

[1] *De homine*, cap. 13, art. 9. In *De cive*, cap. 3, art. 32, Hobbes had still recognized the Platonic cardinal virtues; in the *Leviathan*, ch. 15 (p. 81), he mentions only temperance besides justice. It must further be pointed out that in the *Leviathan*, ch. 6 (p. 26), courage is characterized as a passion, and that as early as the *Elements* (Pt. I, ch. 17, § 14) a clear distinction is drawn between justice, equity, gratitude, temperance, prudence, which are always virtues, on the one hand, and on the other, courage, liberality, &c., which can be virtues, but also vices. See also pp. 50 and 113-15 below. Cf. Voltaire, *Dictionnaire philosophique*, art. 'Vertu' and 'Fausseté des vertus humaines,' and Kant, *Fundamental Principles of the Metaphysic of Morals*, first section (the paragraphs at the beginning).

[2] *Elements*, Pt. I, ch. 9, § 21.

aware of his dependence on the insignificant primary good, the preservation of life and limb; failing to recognize his bodily needs, man experiences only joys and sorrows of the mind, i.e. imaginary joys and sorrows. While it is in accordance with reason 'si quis omnem operam det, ut a morte et doloribus proprium *corpus* et membra defendat conservetque', it is of the essence of natural, irrational appetite that 'omnis *animi* voluptas omnisque alacritas in eo sita est . . . quod quis habeat, quibuscum conferens se possit magnifice sentire de se ipso'.[1] Living in the world of his imagination, he need do nothing, in order to convince himself of his superiority to others, but simply think out his deeds for himself; in this world, in which indeed 'the whole world obeys him', everything is accomplished according to his wishes.[2] He can awaken from this dream-world and come to himself only when he feels in his own person—by bodily hurt—the resistance of the real world. By *damnorum experientia*[3] man becomes reasonable. But if experience of injury is to show him not only the limit of his physical powers, about which he does not greatly care, but the limit of his insight and intelligence—and he is primarily concerned with the superiority of his intelligence[4]—the injury must be unforeseen. 'Men have *no other means* to acknowledge their own Darknesse, but onely by reasoning from the unforeseen mischances, that befall them in their ways.'[5] This self-knowledge is especially brought about by the unforeseen perception of the greatest and supreme evil, death. Because man by nature lives in the dream of the happiness of triumph, of a glittering, imposing, apparent good, he requires a no less imposing power to awaken him from his dream: this imposing power is the imperious majesty of death.

The ideal condition for self-knowledge is, therefore, unforeseen mortal danger. Why and how does the natural vain man

[1] *De cive*, cap. 1, art. 5 and 7. Cf. also ibid., cap. 1, art. 2, as well as the antithesis of 'corporeall hurt' and 'phantasticall hurt' (the latter=mortified vanity) in the *Leviathan*, ch. 27 (p. 159).

[2] Compare the description of vain-glory in *Elements*, Pt. I, ch. 9, § 1, and *Leviathan*, ch. 6 (p. 27).

[3] *De cive*, Praefatio.

[4] In ibid., cap. 1, art. 5, vanity is bluntly characterized as 'Comparatio ingeniorum'. Cf. also *Leviathan*, ch. 13 (p. 63).

[5] *Leviathan*, ch. 44 (p. 331).

gain this experience? Only by the answer to this question does one grasp the real reason which caused Hobbes to recognize the origin of morality not in the fear of death itself but in the fear of violent death. The vain man, who, in his imagination, believes himself superior to others, cannot convince himself of the rightness of his estimate of himself; he requires the recognition of his superiority by others. He therefore steps outside his imaginary world. He makes his claim to superiority and to recognition of his superiority: 'omnia licere sibi soli vult, et prae caeteris honorem sibi arrogat.' Now, either the others take his claim seriously and feel themselves slighted, or they do not take his claim seriously and he feels himself slighted. In either case, the making of the claim leads to contempt. But to be slighted is the greatest *animi molestia*, and from the feeling of being slighted arises the greatest will to injure.[1] The one slighted longs for revenge. In order to avenge himself he attacks the other, indifferent whether he loses his life in so doing.[2] Unconcerned as to the preservation of his own life, he desires, however, above all that the other should remain alive; for 'revenge aimeth not at the death, but at the captivity and subjection of an enemy . . . revenge aimeth at triumph, which over the dead is not'.[3] The struggle which thus breaks out, in which, according to the opinion of both opponents, the object is not the killing but the subjection of the other, of necessity becomes serious, because it is a struggle between bodies, a real struggle. From the beginning of the conflict the two opponents have, without realizing and foreseeing it, completely left the imaginary world. At some point in the conflict, actual injury, or, more accurately, physical pain, arouses a fear for life. Fear moderates anger, puts the sense of being slighted into the background,[4] and transforms the desire for revenge into hatred. The aim of the hater is no longer triumph over the enemy, but

---

[1] *De cive*, cap. 1, art. 4–5; *Leviathan*, ch. 13 (p. 64). Cf. also *Opera latina*, vol. iv, p. 195.

[2] ' . . . all signs which we shew to one another of hatred and contempt, provoke in the highest degree to quarrel and battle (inasmuch as life itself, with the condition of enduring scorn, is not esteemed worth the enjoying . . .)'. *Elements*, Pt. I, ch. 16, § 11. Cf. *De cive*, cap. 3, art. 12.

[3] *Elements*, Pt. I, ch. 9, § 6.

[4] 'Ira . . . oritur quidem saepissime ab opinione contemptus . . . Iram . . . metus temperat.' *De homine*, cap. 12, art. 4.

his death.[1] The struggle for pre-eminence, about 'trifles', has become a life-and-death struggle. In this way natural man happens unforeseen upon the danger of death; in this way he comes to know this primary and greatest and supreme evil for the first time, to recognize death as the greatest and supreme evil in the moment of being irresistibly driven to fall back before death in order to struggle for his life.

Only for a moment can he free himself from the danger of death by killing his enemy, for since every man is his enemy, after the killing of the first enemy he is 'again in the like danger of another',[2] indeed of all others. The killing of the enemy is thus the least far-sighted consequence of the withdrawal from death. In order to safeguard his life, not only for the moment, but in the long run, man needs companions, with whose help he can successfully defend his life against the others. Companions can be gained in two ways, by force or by agreement.[3] The first way is less far-sighted than the second; it stands as it were midway between the killing of the enemy and agreement with him; but for that very reason it is more 'natural', more congenial to natural man than the second.

Fear for his life, which came upon the man in his struggle for triumph, moderates, even kills, the will to triumph, and makes him ready to submit, to leave triumph to the enemy, in order that he may save his own life. But then his enemy, who has reached his goal, the safeguarding of the recognition of his superiority, of his honour, cannot, for honour's sake, take his life; for 'nothing but fear can justify the taking away of another's life. And because fear can hardly be made manifest, but by some action dishonourable, that betrayeth the conscience of one's own weakness; all men in whom the passion of courage or magnanimity have been predominated, have abstained from cruelty. . . . In one word, therefore, the only law of actions in war is honour.'[4] Thus arises the relationship of master and servant. The victor who has safeguarded his honour

[1] 'To kill is the aim of them that hate, to rid themselves of fear.' *Elements*, Pt. I, ch. 9, § 6.

[2] *Leviathan*, ch. 13 (p. 63).

[3] *De cive*, cap. 1, art. 13-14.

[4] *Elements*, Pt. I, ch. 19, § 2. Cf. *De cive*, cap. 5, art. 2, and *Leviathan*, ch. 17 (p. 87).

becomes the master. The vanquished, who 'submitteth . . . for fear of death', who admits his weakness and with that has forfeited his honour, becomes the servant.[1] The dominion of the master over the servant—despotic rule—is one form of the natural State;[2] and as the other form of the natural State, patriarchy, is construed by Hobbes entirely according to the pattern of despotic rule, we may even say: despotic rule is the natural State.

The artificial State, which is as such more perfect, arises when the two opponents are both seized with fear for their lives,[3] overcome their vanity and shame of confessing their fear, and recognize as their real enemy not the rival, but 'that terrible enemy of nature, death',[4] who, as their common enemy, forces them to mutual understanding, trust, and union, and thus procures them the possibility of completing the founding of the State for the purpose of providing safeguards for the longest possible term, against the common enemy. And while in the unforeseen life-and-death struggle, in which vanity comes to grief, the futility of vanity is shown, it is revealed in the concord of living, and of living in common, to which their pre-rational fear of death leads them, that the fear of death is appropriate to human conditions, and that it is 'rational'. It is even shown that it is only on the basis of fear of death that life comes to concord and that the fear of death is the only 'postulate of natural reason'.

A close connexion thus exists between the two 'postulates of human nature', on which Hobbes bases his political philosophy. Vanity left to itself of necessity leads to mortal combat, and since 'every man looketh that his companion should value him, at the same rate he sets upon himselfe',[5] the vanity of each of necessity leads to the 'warre of every one against every one'. And as man by nature lives first in the world of his imagination

---

[1] *Elements*, Pt. II, ch. 3, § 2; *De cive*, cap. 8, art. 1; *Leviathan*, ch. 20 (p. 106).

[2] *Elements*, Pt. I, ch. 19, § 11; *De cive*, cap. 5, art. 12; *Leviathan*, ch. 17, *in fine*.

[3] ' . . . men who choose their Soveraign, do it for fear of one another, and not of him whom they institute.' *Leviathan*, ch. 20, *in princ*.

[4] *Elements*, Pt. I, ch 14, § 6.

[5] *Leviathan*, ch. 13 (p. 64).

and then in the opinion of others, he can originally experience the real world only by feeling it, all unforeseen, in a conflict with others; he comes to know death, the primary and greatest and supreme evil, the only and absolute standard of human life, the beginning of all knowledge of the real world, originally only as *violent* death.

If, by his reduction of natural human appetite to vanity, Hobbes attributes guilt to man, then the affirmation of the fear of death (which is opposed to vanity) must also have moral significance. That is, Hobbes must have systematically differentiated between the fear of death, as the origin of all law and all morality, and all amoral or immoral motives. His contention that the State originates only in mutual fear and can only so originate has thus moral, not merely technical, significance.

Hobbes distinguishes no less precisely than any other moralist between legality and morality. Not the legality of the action, but the morality of the purpose, makes the just man. That man is just who fulfils the law because it is law and not for fear of punishment or for the sake of reputation.[1] Although Hobbes states that those are 'too severe, both to themselves, and others, that maintain, that the First motions of the mind, (though checked with the fear of God) be Sinnes', he yet 'confesses' that 'it is safer to erre on that hand, than on the other'.[2] In believing that the moral attitude, conscience, intention, is of more importance than the action, Hobbes is at one with Kant as with the Christian tradition.[3] He differs from this tradition at first sight only by his denial of the possibility that just and unjust actions may be distinguished independently of human legislation. In the state of nature the distinction between just and unjust actions depends wholly on the judgement of the individual conscience. In the state of nature every action is in principle permitted which the conscience of the individual recognizes as necessary for self-preservation, and every action is in principle forbidden which according to the judgement of the individual conscience does not serve the purpose of self-

---

[1] *Elements*, Pt. I, ch. 16, § 4; *De cive*, cap. 3, art. 5, and cap. 14, art. 18; *Leviathan*, ch. 15 (pp. 77 and 82).

[2] *Leviathan*, ch. 27, *in princ.*

[3] See particularly *De cive*, cap. 4, art. 21, and *Leviathan*, ch. 44 (p. 348).

preservation. Now, in the state of nature every action can be judged to be necessary for self-preservation. If, then, in the state of nature, any and every *action* is permitted, even in the state of nature not every *intention* is permitted, but only the intention of self-preservation. Thus the unequivocal distinction between just and unjust intentions holds even for the state of nature and is, therefore, absolute.[1]

Hobbes might have left it at that, if there were a natural law which obliged man unconditionally, and therefore obliged him even in the state of nature. But he expressly denies the existence of such a law: 'These dictates of Reason (*sc.* the laws of nature), men use to call by the name of Lawes; but *improperly*: for they are but Conclusions, or Theoremes concerning what conduceth to the conservation and defence of themselves; whereas Law, properly is the word of him, that by right hath command over others.'[2] Law is obligation.[3] But obligation comes only on the basis of a covenant between formerly free and unbound men. Thus 'where no Covenant hath preceded, there hath no Right been transferred, and every man has right to every thing. . . . But when a Covenant is made, then to break it is unjust: And the definition of Injustice, is no other than the not Performance of Covenant.'[4] Originally the just attitude cannot be anything but earnest striving to keep one's given word; the justice of this striving cannot, however, consist of respect for the law as such, of obedience to the law as such, because there is no law in the true sense of the word. The just attitude is therefore so far from being obedience that it is, on the contrary, nothing else but proud self-reliance: 'That which gives to human Actions the relish of Justice, is a certain Noblenesse or Gallantnesse of courage, (rarely found,) by which a man scorns to be beholding for the contentment of his life, to fraud, or breach of promise.' '. . . there are in mans nature, but two imaginable helps to strengthen (the force of words). And those are either a Feare of the consequence of breaking their word; or a Glory,

---

[1] It is true that in the *Leviathan*, ch. 14 (p. 65), Hobbes says in passing that in the state of nature '*nothing* can be unjust', but he means by this '*no action* can be unjust'. See *Leviathan*, ch. 15, *in princ.* Compare particularly the passages indicated in note 1, p. 23.

[2] Ibid., ch. 15, *in fine.* Cf. further note 2, p. 17, and note 1, p. 69.

[3] Ibid., ch. 14 (p. 67).   [4] Ibid., ch. 15, *in princ.*

or Pride in appearing not to need to breake it.'[1] That this cannot be Hobbes's final word is already proved by the use of the word 'pride'. As we have seen, the very title of the book *Leviathan*, in which the two passages just quoted occur, expresses the opinion that pride, far from being the origin of the just attitude, is rather the only origin of the unjust attitude.[2] The reduction of the just intention to pride is a deviation from Hobbes's key-thought. Not pride, and still less obedience, but fear of violent death, is according to him the origin of the just intention. What man does from fear of death, in the consciousness of his weakness at the hands of other men, when he *honestly* confesses to himself and to others his weakness and his fear of death, unconcerned about his *honour*, this alone is fundamentally just: 'Breviter, in statu naturae, Justum et Injustum non ex actionibus, sed ex consilio et *conscientia* agentium aestimandum est. Quod *necessario*, quod studio pacis, quod sui conservandi causâ fit, recte fit.'[3] Self-preservation and the striving after peace for the sake of self-preservation are 'necessary', because man fears death with inescapable necessity.[4] Hobbes's last word is the identification of conscience with the fear of death.

However one may judge this identification, at all events it permits a systematic differentiation between justice and injustice, between moral and immoral motives. This identification alone allows Hobbes to say: 'Ad *naturalem* hominum proclivitatem ad se mutuo lacessendum, quam ab affectibus, praesertim vero ab inani sui aestimatione derivant, si *addas* jam *jus* omnium in omnia, quo alter jure invadit, alter jure resistit . . .';[5] that is to say, to distinguish between man's natural appetite and his natural right. In particular it makes possible the distinction between the attitude of the unjust man who obeys the laws of the State for fear of punishment, i.e. without inner conviction, and the attitude of the just man, who for fear of death, and therefore from inner conviction, as it were once

---

[1] *Leviathan*, ch. 15 (p. 77) and ch. 14 (p. 73).

[2] That 'pride' is always used in the derogatory sense is indicated by Hobbes in *Elements*, Pt. I, ch. 9, § 1.

[3] *De cive*, cap. 3, art. 27, annot.

[4] Ibid., cap. 1, art. 7.

[5] Ibid., cap. 1, art. 12. Cf. *Elements*, Part I, ch. 14, § 11.

more accomplishing in himself the founding of the State, obeys the laws of the State. Fear of death and fear of punishment remain as different as far-sighted consistent fear, which determines life in its depth and its entirety, is from short-sighted momentary fear which sees only the next step.

Hobbes identifies conscience with the fear of death; only through knowledge of mortal danger, knowledge which is at the same time a retreat from death, can man be radically liberated from natural vanity, from the natural absorption in the world of his imagination. If this is the case, the fear of death, the fear of violent death, is the necessary condition not only of society but also of science. Just as life in common is hindered by passion, science is hindered by prejudice. And what holds with regard to the root of our passions is equally true of the basis of our prejudices; they too are based on 'a false opinion that (we) know already the truth of that which is called in question', that is to say, 'a false opinion of our own knowledge'.[1] The matter of the fundamental prejudices which bar the way to science are phantasmata of sight or hearing; but that man assents to these phantasmata, that man believes in them, is the result of vanity.

'To say (God) hath spoken to him in a Dream, is no more than to say he dreamed that God spake to him . . . such dreams as that (may proceed) from selfe conceit, and foolish arrogance, and false opinion of a mans own godlinesse, or other vertue, by which he thinks he hath merited the favour of extraordinary Revelation. . . . To say he speaks by supernaturall Inspiration, is to say that he finds an ardent desire to speak, or some strong opinion of himself, for which he can alledge no naturall and sufficient reason.'[2]

Vanity is therefore the final reason of incapacity to learn, of prejudice and superstition, as well as of injustice. Vanity is concerned above all other superiorities with mental superiority, with superiority of intelligence. Vanity is therefore the reason

---

[1] *Elements*, Pt. I, ch. 10, § 8. The section concludes with the proposition 'The immediate cause therefore of indocibility, is prejudice; and of prejudice, false opinion of our own knowledge.'

[2] *Leviathan*, ch. 32 (p. 200). ' . . . how shall a man know his own Private spirit to be other than a beleef, grounded upon the Authority, and Arguments of his Teachers; or upon a Presumption of his own Gifts (in the Latin version: vel a spiritu arrogantiae)?' Ibid., ch. 43 (p. 321).

why 'no man can conceive there is any greater degree of (Understanding), than that which he already attained unto. And from hence it comes to passe, that men have no other means to acknowledge their own Darknesse, but onely by reasoning from the unforeseen mischances, that befall them in their ways'.[1] The extreme case of unforeseen mischance is unforeseen mortal danger. Thus it is pre-eminently through unforeseen mortal danger and the irresistibly compelling fear of death which arises from it that we are enabled to free ourselves from the power of our fantasies and our prejudices. Science bears traces of this origin: its principles 'non modo speciosa non (sunt), sed etiam humilia, arida, et pene deformia (videntur)'.[2] Science proceeds 'from most low and humble principles, evident even to the meanest capacity; going on slowly, and with most scrupulous ratiocination'.[3] Science stands in complete contrast to all dogmatic, rhetorical, and allegedly inspired pseudo-knowledge, which catches the eye and may, indeed, be 'suddenly'[4] gained.

Since man is by nature fast in his imaginary world, it is only by unforeseen mischance that he can attain to a knowledge of his own darkness and at the same time a modest and circumspect knowledge of the real world. That is to say: the world is originally revealed to man not by detachedly and spontaneously seeing its form, but by involuntary experience of its resistance. The least discriminating and detached sense is the sense of touch. This explains the place of honour which is tacitly granted to the sense of touch in Hobbes's physiology and psychology of perception; all sense-perception, particularly that of the most discriminating and detached sense, the sense of sight, is interpreted by experience of the sense of touch.

Thus not the naturalistic antithesis of morally indifferent animal appetite (or of morally indifferent human striving after power) on the one hand, and morally indifferent striving after self-preservation on the other, but the moral and humanist antithesis of fundamentally unjust vanity and fundamentally just fear of violent death is the basis of Hobbes's political

---

[1] *Leviathan*, ch. 44 (p. 331).   [2] *De corpore*, cap. 1, art. 1.
[3] *Elements*, Pt. I, ch. 13, § 3.
[4] *De cive*, Ep. ded.; *Leviathan*, ch. 43 (p. 324).

philosophy. It will be objected that this moral antithesis is to be found in Hobbes's political philosophy only because Hobbes had not yet completely freed himself from the influence of the Christian Biblical tradition. For what is the antithesis between vanity and fear of violent death, if not the 'secularized' form of the traditional antithesis between spiritual pride and fear of God (or humility), a secularized form which results from the Almighty God having been replaced by the over-mighty enemies and then by the over-mighty State, 'the Mortall God'?[1] But even if this affiliation is right, it by no means follows that the moral antithesis in Hobbes's work which we are at present discussing is simply the superfluous residue of a tradition which has in principle been cast aside. On the contrary, this antithesis is an essential indispensable element, or, more accurately, the essential basis, of Hobbes's political philosophy. Had Hobbes waived it, had he developed a naturalistic political philosophy, he would have renounced the possibility of distinguishing between 'the offensiveness of a man's *nature*' and 'the *right* of every man to every thing'.[2] He would have had to recognize man's natural appetite, all his passions, and particularly vanity, as justified by nature in the same degree as is reason. In other words, political philosophy deprived of its moral foundation is, indeed, Spinoza's political philosophy, but it is not Hobbes's political philosophy. Spinoza, indeed, and not Hobbes, made might equivalent to right.[3] Naturalistic political philosophy necessarily leads to the annulment of the conception of justice as such. Thanks to the moral basis of his political philosophy and thanks to it alone, Hobbes kept the possibility of acknowledging justice as such and distinguishing between right and might.

The essential advantage which Hobbes's political philosophy has over Spinoza's is that by natural right Hobbes understands primarily right of man, whereas Spinoza's point of departure is the natural right of all existing things, and he thus misses

---

[1] *Leviathan*, ch. 17 (p. 89); cf. *De cive*, cap. 6, art. 13; and *Leviathan*, ch. 30 (pp. 180 ff.).

[2] *Elements*, Pt. I, ch. 14, § 11.

[3] For the fundamental difference between Hobbes's political philosophy and Spinoza's, cf. Strauss, *Die Religionskritik Spinozas*, Berlin, 1930, pp. 222–30.

the specifically human problem of right. Hobbes's political philosophy is really, as its originator claims, based on a knowledge of men which is deepened and corroborated by the self-knowledge and self-examination of the individual, and not on a general scientific or metaphysical theory. And because it is based on experience of human life, it can never, in spite of all the temptations of natural science, fall completely into the danger of abstraction from moral life and neglect of moral difference. Hobbes's political philosophy has thus for that very reason a moral basis, because it is not derived from natural science but is founded on first-hand experience of human life.

The contention that Hobbes's humanist moral motivation of his political philosophy is more original than the naturalistic motivation, from which one must first disentangle it, would receive indirect corroboration, if it could be shown that either all or the most important points of that moral motivation were already established before he had turned his attention to natural science. That this is the case is probable from the outset. Hobbes was over forty when he 'discovered' Euclid's *Elements*, and not until after that did he begin to take a serious interest in natural science. The 'discovery' of Euclid was beyond doubt an epoch in his life; everything he thought and wrote after that is modified by this happening. But if one has once seen that his most original thoughts are hidden rather than shown forth by a form of proof borrowed from mathematics and a psychology borrowed from natural science, and if one is not disposed to take for granted that he was asleep up to the age of forty, so that he needed the 'discovery' of Euclid to awaken him, one is inclined to suppose that what he wrote in his youth (before he was forty) and thus before he was influenced by mathematics and natural science, expresses his most original thoughts better than the work of his maturity. Whether this is the case, and to what extent, can be decided only after the sparse remnants of his youthful philosophy have been investigated. Only at the close of this investigation will it be possible definitely to answer the question whether and to what extent the 'discovery' of Euclid and the subsequent pursuit of natural science prejudiced his political philosophy or furthered it.

III

ARISTOTELIANISM

W E shall begin by surveying the forces which exercised a decisive influence on Hobbes before he turned to mathematics and natural science. The primary place is occupied by humanism. From eight to fourteen (1596–1603) Hobbes was taught Latin and Greek at home, so successfully that he was able to translate Euripides' *Medea* 'eleganter' into Latin verse.[1] From 1603 to 1608 he studied at Oxford. During this time, dissatisfied with academic teaching, he turned again to the classical texts which he had already read at home.[2] Afterwards, when he had given up all study for some years, he once more turned especially to the reading of classical writers, and read them with the interpretations of famous grammarians. His purpose in this study was also to develop a clear, nervous Latin style.[3] The continuation and conclusion of this study was the English translation of Thucydides, which gradually grew and was published in 1628.[4]

At Oxford Hobbes was introduced to scholastic philosophy. He himself recounts that he studied Aristotle's logic and physics.[5] He makes no mention of studying Aristotle's morals and politics. After about five years' study he graduated as Baccalaureus artium, i.e. he was admitted 'ad lectionem cujuslibet libri logices'.[6] According to the traditional curriculum, in the first part of University study, which led to the B.A. degree, the formal disciplines—grammar, rhetoric, and logic—were in the foreground. We may therefore assume that scholastic studies were for Hobbes in the main formal training, and that he acquired the more detailed knowledge of scholasticism, which he afterwards needed for polemic defence of his own

---

[1] *Opera latina*, vol. i, pp. xiii, xxii f., and lxxxvi.

[2] Loc. cit., p. lxxxvii.

[3] Loc. cit., pp. xiii, xxiv, and lxxxviii.

[4] Loc. cit., pp. xiv and lxxxviii. The translation is entered in the 'Register of the Company of Stationers of London' on the 18th March 1627 (i.e. 1628).

[5] *Opera latina*, vol. i, pp. xiii and lxxxvi f.

[6] Loc. cit., p. xliv.

theory, at a later date, as and when it was needed. At all events
it was with reluctance that he followed the scholastic instruction, and as he had almost forgotten his beloved Greek and
Latin in the years after taking his degree,[1] there is all the less
reason for believing that he retained much of scholastic philosophy, particularly as he did not take up that study again as
he did that of the humanities. It is perhaps permissible to
point out in this connexion that the most detailed reference to
scholastic theories are found in the *Leviathan* and not in the
earlier writings.

Hobbes's college was Magdalen Hall, where he was educated
in the Puritan spirit.[2] After taking his degree, he was for twenty
years without a break first tutor, and then secretary, to William
Cavendish, later the second Earl of Devonshire, and on a
friendly footing with the Cavendish family. Intercourse with
members of the aristocracy—the Cavendishes were not the
only aristocrats he met—certainly countered the influence of
his Puritan upbringing, and at this time, when his own point
of view was not yet formed, the aristocratic point of view must
have influenced him much more than it did later.

Of the four influences mentioned—humanism, scholasticism,
Puritanism, and aristocracy—humanism is in Hobbes's youth
certainly the most decisive. He says of himself: 'Natura sua,
et primis annis ferebatur ad lectionem historiarum et poetarum.'[3] Here, as the context shows, he means by *primis annis*
the whole time up to the awakening of his mathematical and
scientific interests, and, as similar statements of his show, by
lectionem historiarum et poetarum he means reading of classical
authors.[4] So one is completely justified in calling the first
period of his life (up to 1629) the 'humanist' period.

Ascertaining this is, however, of no value if it does not
lead to the question of the philosophical reasons of Hobbes's
humanism. This question cannot be evaded in the case of a

---

[1] Loc. cit., vol. i, p. xiii.

[2] Wood, *Athenae Oxonienses*, ed. Bliss, col. 1206.

[3] *Opera latina*, vol. i, p. xx.

[4] The following account by Aubrey probably refers to the reading of
contemporary writers: 'Before Thucydides, he spent two yeares in reading
romances and playes, which he haz often repeated and sayd that these two
yeares were lost of him.' *Brief Lives*, ed. Clark, i. 361.

philosopher of Hobbes's rank, even if it were unnecessary to ask it of any other humanist. With a philosopher of Hobbes's importance, we would assert that this is the central problem of his biography: How was it possible, and what does it signify, that he turned away from philosophy, became a humanist, and remained one for twenty years? This question would certainly not appear paradoxical to R. Blackbourne, who writes in his *Vitae Hobbianae auctarium* :

' . . . (Hobbes) magno litteraturae Academicae fastidio affici coepit. . . . Aliam itaque philosophandi rationem sibi ineundam ratus, lectioni veterum philosophorum, poetarum, historicorum, tum e Graecis tum Latinis, diligenter incubuit, et ex eorum thesauris, quid in suos usus faceret, accurate deprompsit.'[1]

And if the objection is raised that Blackbourne probably means *philosophari* in a wider sense than the technical, we would reply that this wider sense is the true philosophic sense.

As one may gather from the passage quoted from Blackbourne, Hobbes, after the end of his University studies, read not only classical poets and historians but also classical philosophers. Which philosophers? Or—what is even more important —which philosopher did Hobbes accept as authority in his humanist period? In the foreword to his translation of Thucydides he says:

'It hath been noted by divers, that Homer in poesy, Aristotle in philosophy, Demosthenes in eloquence, and others of the ancients in other knowledge, do still maintain their primacy: none of them exceeded, some not approached, by any in these later ages. And in the number of these is justly ranked also our Thucydides; a workman no less perfect in his work, than any of the former.'[2]

Hobbes has thus, even at the end of his humanist period, no objection to raise against the ruling opinion that Aristotle is *the* classical philosopher. In order not to under-estimate the importance of the observation quoted one must compare it with Hobbes's later judgements. Afterwards he held not Aristotle, but Plato, to be 'the best of the ancient philosophers'.[3]

---

[1] *Opera latina*, vol. i, p. xxiv.
[2] *English Works*, vol. viii, p. vii.
[3] Ibid., vol. vii, p. 346. Cf. also *Leviathan*, ch. 46 (p. 365) and *English Works*, vol. vi, p. 100.

We shall try later to analyse what is implied in this change of view. In the present connexion it is only of importance that Hobbes, who later considered Plato to be the best philosopher, not the best philosopher of all, but the best philosopher of antiquity, at the end of his humanist period repeats without raising any objection the ruling opinion according to which Aristotle is the highest authority in philosophy.

The break with Aristotle was completed only in connexion with Hobbes's mathematical and scientific studies and even then by no means immediately in all rigour. The polemic against Aristotle in the *Elements* is not nearly so violent as in *De cive* or in the *Leviathan*. One fact of particular significance must be emphasized at this point. As late as in the *Elements*, in his definition of the State, i.e. at a central point, Hobbes asserts the aim of the State to be, along with peace and defence, common benefit. With this he tacitly admits Aristotle's distinction between the reason of the genesis of the State and the reason of its being (between ζῆν and εὖ ζῆν). On the other hand, in parallel passages in the later presentations, more faithful to his own intention, according to which the necessity and the possibility of the State are understood only from fear of violent death, he leaves out common benefit and thus rejects the above-mentioned Aristotelian distinction.[1]

The break with scholasticism, which Hobbes made very early, if indeed he ever required to make it, does not, therefore, mean from the outset a break with Aristotle. But which Aristotle—which aspect of Aristotle—takes the place of the scholastic Aristotle? The linkage of Aristotle with Homer,

---

[1] 'This union so made, is that which men call now-a-days a Body Politic or civil society; and the Greeks call it πόλις, that is to say, a city; which may be defined to be a multitude of men, united as one person by a common power, for their common peace, defence, and benefit.' *Elements*, Pt. I, ch. 19, § 8. (Notice also the mention of the πόλις in the definition of the State.) 'Civitas ergo (ut eam definiamus) est persona una, cujus voluntas, ex pactis plurium hominum, pro voluntate habenda est ipsorum omnium; ut singulorum viribus et facultatibus uti possit, ad pacem et defensionem communem.' *De cive*, cap. 5, art. 9. '(Commonwealth) is one person, of whose acts a great multitude, by mutual covenants one with another, have made themselves every one the author, to the end he may use the strength and means of them all, as he shall think expedient, for their peace and common defence.' *Leviathan*, ch. 17 (p. 90). Cf. also below, p. 63.

Demosthenes, and Thucydides provides the answer—Aristotle seen from the humanist point of view. What does this ambiguous assertion mean in Hobbes's case?

Fundamentally it means a shifting of interest from Aristotle's physics and metaphysics to his morals and politics, to his philosophy περὶ τὰ ἀνθρώπινα. In other words, it means the replacement of theory by the primacy of practice. Only if one assumes a fundamental change of this kind does Hobbes's turning away from scholasticism to poetry and history cease to be a biographical or historical peculiarity. This assertion is all the more justified, as Hobbes, even after natural science had become his favourite subject of investigation, acknowledged the precedence of practice over theory and of political philosophy over natural science.[1] He certainly knew and valued the joys of knowledge no less than any other philosopher; but these joys are for him not the justification of philosophy; he finds its justification only in benefit to man, i.e. the safeguarding of man's life and the increase of human power.[2] It is not a matter of chance that the (traditional) praise of the contemplative life is to be found mainly in dedications and forewords.[3] Where Hobbes develops his own view connectedly, he manifestly subordinates theory to practice. So it is to be understood that he did not, like Aristotle,[4] attribute prudence to practice and wisdom to theory. As he asserts the practical aim of prudence as well as of wisdom, the distinction between prudence and wisdom loses all reference to the distinction between practice and theory. Prudence is to wisdom what experience is to knowledge; wisdom is the knowledge 'of what is right and wrong and what is good and hurtful to the being and well-being of mankind. . . . For generally, not he that hath skill in geometry, or any other science speculative, but only he that understandeth what conduceth to the good and government of the people, is called a

---

[1] 'Scio philosophiam seriam unicam esse, quae versatur circa pacem et fortunas civium, principalem; caeteras nihil esse praeter ludum. Ludimus enim otiosi . . . in syllogismis Logici, in sonis Musici, in numeris Arithmetici, in motu Physici . . ., dum otium nostrum negotia tuentur principum.' *Opera latina*, vol. iv, p. 487 f. Cf. also below, p. 44, note 4.

[2] *Leviathan*, ch. 5 (p. 22); *De corpore*, cap. i, art. 6–7.

[3] *De cive*, praefatio; *De corpore*, praefatio; *English Works*, vol. vii, p. 467.

[4] *Eth. Nicom.* 1141ᵃ19 ff.; cf. *Metaph.* A.1.

wise man.'[1] The contrast with Aristotle has its ultimate reason
in Hobbes's conception of the place of man in the universe,
which is diametrically opposed to Aristotle's conception. Aristotle justified his placing of the theoretical sciences above moral
and political philosophy by the argument that man is not the
highest being of the universe.[2] This ultimate assumption of
the primacy of theory is rejected by Hobbes; in his contention
man is 'the most excellent work of nature'.[3] In this strict sense
Hobbes always remained a humanist, and only with the essential limitation which this brings could he recognize Aristotle's
authority in his humanist period.

Even when Hobbes had come to the conclusion that Aristotle
was 'the worst teacher that ever was', he excepted two works
from this condemnation: ' but his rhetorique and discourse of
animals was rare.'[4] Hobbes's study of the 'discourse of animals'
has left no trace; his study of the *Rhetoric* all the more. Two
English digests made by Hobbes from this work have been
published.[5] There is a Latin digest among the Hobbes papers
at Chatsworth. But these digests are not the only and certainly
not the most important testimony to Hobbes's preoccupation
with the *Rhetoric*. It would be difficult to find another classical
work whose importance for Hobbes's political philosophy can
be compared with that of the *Rhetoric*. The central chapters
of Hobbes's anthropology, those chapters on which, more than
on anything else he wrote, his fame as a stylist and as one who
knows men rests for all time, betray in style and contents that
their author was a zealous reader, not to say a disciple of the
Rhetoric. What we have in mind is the 8th and 9th chapters
of the first part of the *Elements*, the 10th chapter of the *Leviathan*, and the 11th, 12th, and 13th chapters of *De homine*.
Naturally Hobbes did not simply transcribe the parallel passages
of the *Rhetoric*, but his debt to the *Rhetoric* in themes, mode
of presentation, and even in details is best seen by a collation.
In the *Elements*, Pt. I, ch. 8, § 5, in the *Leviathan*, ch. 10, and

---

[1] *Elements*, Pt. II, ch. 8, § 13; cf. ibid., Pt. I, ch. 6, § 4, and *Leviathan*,
ch. 5 (p. 22).

[2] *Eth. Nicom.*, loc. cit.

[3] *Leviathan*, Introduction.

[4] Aubrey, loc. cit., p. 357.

[5] *English Works*, vol. vi, pp. 419–510 and 511–36.

in *De homine*, ch. 11, art. 13, Hobbes treats under the heading 'Honourable' (or *Pulchra*) what Aristotle in *Rhetoric*, i. 9, discussed under καλά.

Rhetoric[1]	Elements	Leviathan
And honourable are . . . the works of virtue. And the signs of virtue. . . . And the reward whereof is rather honour than money. And those things are honourable which, good of themselves, are not so to the owner. . . . And bestowing of benefits. . . . And honourable are . . . victory. . . . And things that excel. And what none can do but we. And possessions we reap no profit by. And those things which are had in honour. . . . And the signs of praise.	And honourable are those signs for which one man acknowledgeth power or excess above his concurrent in another. . . . And . . . victory in battle or duel. . . . And gifts, costs, and magnificence of houses, apparel, and the like, are honourable.	. . . Victory is Honourable . . . Magnanimity, Liberality, Hope, Courage, Confidence, are Honourable. . . . Actions proceeding from Equity, joyned with losse, are Honourable.

In the *Elements*, Pt. I, ch. 8, § 8, Hobbes begins the enumeration of the 'signs of honour' with 'To praise; to magnify; to bless, or call happy' (cf. *Leviathan*, ch. 10); in this he follows Aristotle, who in the passage quoted treats of ἔπαινος, μακαρισμός, and εὐδαιμονισμός.[2]

In chapter 10 of the *Leviathan* Hobbes treats of the various forms of 'dishonour'. Aristotle discusses these in connexion with his analysis of anger as 'desire for revenge, joined with grief, for that he, or some of his, is, or seems to be, neglected'.[3]

Rhetoric	Leviathan
To neglect, is to esteem little or nothing; and of three kinds: (1) Contempt, (2) Crossing, (3) Contumely. Contempt, is when a man thinks another of little worth in comparison to himself. Crossing, is the hinderance of another man's will, without design to profit	. . . to disobey, is to Dishonour. . . . To neglect, is to Dishonour. . . . To contemne . . . is to Dishonour; for 'tis undervaluing. . . . To revile, mock, or pity, is

---

[1] Quoted from Hobbes's *Rhetoric*-digest, *English Works*, vol. vi, pp. 436 ff.

[2] The parallel in *De homine*, cap. 11, art. 13, shows only the following coincidence with the *Rhetoric*: '(Ignoscere veniam petenti pulchrum . . .). Inimicos placare beneficiis, turpe.' Cf. *Rhetoric*, i. 9, § 24: καὶ τὸ τοὺς ἐχθροὺς τιμωρεῖσθαι μᾶλλον (καλὸν) καὶ μὴ καταλλάττεσθαι.

[3] *English Works*, vol. vi, p. 452 (=*Rhet*. ii. 2).

Rhetoric

himself. Contumely, is the disgracing of another for his own pastime. . . . Those that men are angry with, are: such as mock, deride, or jest at them. And such as show any kind of contumely towards them. And such as despise those things which we spend most labour and study upon. . . . And such as requite not our courtesy. And such as follow contrary courses, if they be our inferiors. . . . And such as neglect us in the presence of our competitors, of those we admire, of those we would have admire us, of those we reverence, and of those that reverence us. . . .

Leviathan

to Dishonour. . . . To refuse to do (those things to another which he takes for signes of Honour), is to Dishonour. . . . To dissent, is Dishonour. . . .

We shall now show the dependence of Hobbes's theory of the passions on the *Rhetoric*.

Rhetoric[1]	*Elements*[2]	*Leviathan*[3]	*De homine*[4]
Anger is desire of revenge, joined with grief, for that he, or some of his, is, or seems to be, neglected. (452=*Rhet.*ii.2.)	Anger . . . hath been commonly defined to be grief proceeding from an opinion of contempt. (5)		(Ira) oritur quidem saepissime ab opinione contemptus. (4)
ὁ δ' ὀργιζόμενος ἐφίεται δυνατῶν αὐτῷ. (*Rhet.* ii. 2, 2.)			Objectum ergo irae est molestum, sed quatenus vi superabile. (4)
Those to whom men are easily reconciled, are . . . such as they fear (453=*Rhet.* ii. 3). Cf. also *Rhet.* ii. 12, 9: οὔτε γὰρ ὀργιζόμενος οὐδεὶς φοβεῖται.			Iram . . . metus temperat. (4)
. . . anger seeks the vexation, hatred the damage, of one's adversary . . . anger	To kill is the aim of them that hate, . . . revenge aimeth at triumph. (6)		

[1] Loc. cit., pp. 452 ff.
[3] Ch. 6.

[2] Pt. I, ch. 9, §§ 5 ff.
[4] Cap. 12, art. 4 ff.

Rhetoric	Elements	Leviathan	De homine
may at length be satiated; but hatred never. (456 = *Rhet*. ii. 4.)			

Rhetoric	Elements	Leviathan	De homine
Shame is a perturbation of the mind arising from the apprehension of evil . . . to the prejudice of a man's . . . reputation. The things therefore which men are ashamed of, are those actions which proceed from vice. . . . (458 = *Rhet*. ii. 6.)		Griefe, for the discovery of some defect of ability, is Shame . . . and consisteth in the apprehension of some thing dishonourable. . . .	

Rhetoric	Elements	Leviathan	De homine
Pity is a perturbation of the mind, arising from the apprehension of hurt or trouble to another that doth not deserve it, and which he thinks may happen to himself or his. And because it appertains to pity to think that he, or his, may fall into the misery he pities in others; it follows that they be most compassionate : who have passed through misery. . . . And such as think there be honest men. . . . Less compassionate (are) they that think no	Pity is imagination or fiction of future calamity to ourselves, proceeding from the sense of another man's present calamity; but when it lighteth on such as we think have not deserved the same, the compassion is the greater, because then there appeareth the more probability that the same may happen to us. . . . The contrary of pity is Hardness of heart, proceeding . . . from extreme great opinion of their own exemption of the like cal-	Griefe, for the Calamity of another, is Pity; and ariseth from the imagination that the like calamity may befall himselfe . . . for the same Calamity, those have least Pity, that think themselves least obnoxious to the same.	Dolere ob malum alienum, id est, condolere sive compati, id est, malum alienum sibi accidere posse imaginari, misericordia dicitur. Itaque qui similibus malis assueti sunt, sunt magis misericordes; et contra. Nam malum quod quis minus expertus est, minus metuit sibi. (10)

Rhetoric	Elements	Leviathan	De homine
man honest . . . (and) who are in great prosperity. (461f.=*Rhet*. ii. 8.)	amity, or from hatred of all, or most men. (10)		
. . . indignation . . . is grief for the prosperity of a man unworthy (462=*Rhet*. ii. 9.)	Indignation is the grief which consisteth in the conception of good success happening to them whom they think unworthy thereof. (11)		
Envy is grief for the prosperity of such as ourselves, arising not from any hurt that we, but from the good that they receive. (464=*Rhet*. ii. 10.) Emulation is grief arising from that our equals possess such goods as are had in honour, and whereof we are capable, but have them not; not because they have them, but because not we also. No man therefore emulates another in things whereof himself is not capable. (465= *Rhet*. ii. 11.)	Emulation is grief arising from seeing one's self exceeded or excelled by his concurrent, together with hope to equal or exceed him in time to come, by his own ability. But, Envy is the same grief joined with pleasure conceived in imagination of some ill-fortune that may befall him. (12)	Griefe, for the successe of a Competitor in wealth, honour, or other good, if it be joyned with Endeavour to enforce our own abilities to equal or exceed him, is called Emulation: But joyned with Endeavour to supplant, or hinder a competitor, Envie.	Dolor ob praelatum sibi alium, conjunctus cum conatu proprio, est aemulatio: sed conjunctus cum voluntate praelatum sibi retrahendi, invidia est. (11)[1]

We would further emphasize that the 11th chapter of *De homine* in construction and in detail is modelled on the

---

[1] Cf. *Rhetoric*, ii. 11, *in princ*.

corresponding sections of the *Rhetoric*. In this chapter Hobbes discusses the *Bona* (6–11), the *Jucunda* (12), the *Pulchra* (13), and the *Bona comparata* (14). In this he follows Aristotle, who in the *Rhetoric* discusses the ἀγαθά (i. 6), the ἡδέα (i. 11), the καλά (i. 9), and the μείζω ἀγαθά (i. 7).

Rhetoric	*De homine*
(Good are) . . . health. . . . And riches. And friends. . . . And whatsoever art or science. And life. . . . (431 = *Rhet.* i. 6.)	(Bona sunt) Vita. Sanitas. . . . Amicitia. Divitiae. . . . Scientiae sive artes. . . . (6–10)
(Pleasant are) those things we remember whether they pleased or displeased then when they were present. . . . And victory: therefore also contentious games: as tables, chess, dice, tennis, etc.; and hunting; and suits in law. And honour and reputation. . . . And to be beloved and respected. And to be admired. And to be flattered. . . . And change or variety. . . . And to learn. And to admire. . . . And imitation; and therefore the art of painting; and the art of carving images; and the art of poetry; and pictures and statues. . . . And everyone himself. . . . And to be thought wise. . . . (441 f. = *Rhet.* i. 11.)	Imitatio jucundum; revocat enim praeterita. Praeterita autem si bona fuerint, jucunda sunt repraesentata, quia bona; si mala, quia praeterita. Jucunda igitur musica, poesis, pictura. Nova, jucunda: appetuntur enim ut animi pabulum. Bene sentire de sua ipsius potentia, sive merito sive immerito, jucundum. . . . victoria, jucunda . . . et ludi certaminaque omnia, jucunda; quia qui certant, victoriam imaginantur.[1] Placent autem maxime certamina ingeniorum.[2] (12)[3]
Of the colours or common opinions concerning good and evil, comparatively. (432)	Bona comparata.
. . . And that which is lasting (is a greater good), than that which is not lasting. . . . And what many desire than what few. (434 = *Rhet.* i. 7.)	Bona et mala si comparentur, majus est, caeteris paribus, quod est diuturnius. . . . Et, caeteris paribus, quod pluribus bonum, quam quod paucioribus. (14)

Finally, we would recall the connexion between *De homine*, cap. 13, art. 5, and the corresponding sections of the *Rhetoric*.

Rhetoric	*De homine*
τὰ δὲ ἤθη ποῖοί τινες κατὰ τύχας, διέλθωμεν . . . τύχην δὲ λέγω εὐγένειαν καὶ πλοῦτον καὶ δυνάμεις (*Rhet.* ii. 12, *in princ.*).	A bonis fortunae, hoc est, a divitiis, a nobilitate generis, a potentia civili fit ut ingenia aliquatenus varientur; nam a divitiis et potentia

---

[1] Cf. *Rhet.* i. 11, § 15: ὅπου γὰρ ἅμιλλα, ἐνταῦθα καὶ νίκη ἐστίν.

[2] Cf. ibid.: ἡ δικανικὴ καὶ ἐριστικὴ ἡδεῖα.

[3] As regards the following paragraph, see above, p. 36.

Rhetoric	*De homine*
Rich men are contumelious, and proud. . . . And think themselves worthy to command. . . . They do injury, with intention not to hurt, but to disgrace; and partly also through incontinence. There is a difference between new and ancient riches. For they that are newly come to wealth, have the same faults in a greater degree; for new riches are a kind of rudeness and apprenticeship of riches. (470 f.=*Rhet*. ii. 16.) The manners of men in power, are the same, or better than those of the rich. When they do injuries, they do great ones. (471=*Rhet*. ii. 17.)	civili, ingenia plerumque fiunt superbiora; nam qui plus possunt, plus licere sibi postulant, id est, ad injurias inferendas magis propensi sunt, et ad societatem cum iis, qui minus possunt, aequis legibus ineundam ineptiores sunt. Nobilitas antiqua ingenium facit come. . . . Nobilitatis novae ingenium magis est suspicax, ut qui, nondum satis certi quantus honor sibi tribui debet, fiunt versus inferiores saepe nimis asperi, versus aequales nimis verecundi.

Since Hobbes in his later writings uses passages from the *Rhetoric*, of which he had made no use in earlier writings, it follows that when composing all his systematic expositions of anthropology (*Elements* 1640, *Leviathan* 1651, *De homine* 1658) he studied Aristotle's *Rhetoric* afresh each time. So much was implied in his remark to Aubrey, 'But (Aristotle's) rhetorique was rare.'

Hobbes's preoccupation with the *Rhetoric* can be traced back as far as about 1635. The more exhaustive English digest of the *Rhetoric* (*Works*, vol. vi, pp. 419–510) was first published in February 1637.[1] As early as 1635 Hobbes had considered the

---

[1] See *A Transcript of the Registers of the Company of Stationers of London*, vol. iv, London, 1877, p. 346. One copy of the 1637 edition is in the British Museum Library. The two excerpts in English from the *Rhetoric* were published together in 1681 from Hobbes's posthumous papers. According to their editor they were written about 1650. This assertion can be contradicted with reference to the more exhaustive digest, the first edition of which (in 1637) was obviously unknown to the editor. It is extremely improbable also in the case of the shorter digest (*English Works*, vol. vi, pp. 511–36). The shorter digest, which treats the original much more freely than does the more exhaustive one, and omits the theory of the passions and so forth, is concerned exclusively with rhetoric in the narrow sense. That Hobbes was still preoccupied with rhetoric at the time alleged by the editor, i.e. at the time when he was living in Paris and working on the *Leviathan*, cannot be borne out by evidence. It may be stated that Hobbes's interest in rhetoric grew less and less in course of time. One has only to compare the corresponding chapters in the *Elements* (Pt. I, ch. 13 and Pt. II, ch. 8, § 13) with those of *De cive* (cap. 12, art. 12) and of the *Leviathan* (ch. 25 and ch. 29). As the shorter digest also makes the impression of

writing of a personal exposition of the theory of the passions;[1] and we have seen how much his earliest treatment of the theory of the passions was influenced by Aristotle's *Rhetoric*. In addition, he himself recounts that he instructed the third Earl of Devonshire in rhetoric among other things, in the years 1631–8.[2] It may therefore be taken as certain that at least the more exhaustive digest of the *Rhetoric* came into being in connexion with this teaching on the one side, and with the preparation of the *Elements* on the other. We may assume that the shorter digest of the *Rhetoric* was made about the same period.

Hobbes's closer study of Aristotle's *Rhetoric* may be proved with certainty only for the 1630's, i.e. in the time in which he had overtly completed the break with Aristotelianism. All the same, we must recall that at Oxford he attended lectures on rhetoric among other subjects. Moreover, one gathers from his introduction to the translation of Thucydides that the phenomena of eloquence on the one hand, and of the passions on the other, occupied his mind even in his humanist period—as political themes,[3] and it is as such that Aristotle treats them in the *Rhetoric*. On the whole, it seems to us more correct to assume that the use and appreciation of Aristotle's *Rhetoric* which may be traced in Hobbes's mature period are the last remnants of the Aristotelianism of his youth, than to consider that Hobbes, after exclusive preoccupation with poets and historians, should suddenly have discovered the *Rhetoric* for himself, after turning to systematic philosophy, as he had previously discovered Euclid's *Elements*.

Among the Hobbes papers at Chatsworth there is a free digest from the *Nicomachean Ethics* which is based on the interpretation of Aristotle by the Paduan Aristotelian, Franc. Piccolomini. It is perhaps permissible to see in this digest a further trace of the Aristotelianism of Hobbes's youth.[4] It

having been dictated to a pupil, we may take it that it arose from the instruction in rhetoric which Hobbes gave to the third Earl of Devonshire between 1631 and 1638. See also below, p. 76, note 3.

[1] See his letter to the Earl of Newcastle, Historical MSS. Commission, 13*th Report*, Appendix, Pt. II, p. 126.

[2] *Opera latina*, vol. i, p. lxxxix.

[3] Cf. *English Works*, vol. viii, pp. xvii, xxvi, and xxix f.

[4] Cf. pp. 46 f. and 116, note 3, below.

is true that it is not in Hobbes's handwriting. But if it has not come by chance into the Hobbes papers, one may suppose that Hobbes, at the time when he still believed that he could acquiesce in a modified Aristotelianism, had the digest of the interpretation of Aristotle by a student of Piccolomini made for him, or borrowed the digest which another had made. It is certain that this digest did not serve as a basis for Hobbes's later criticism of Aristotle, and therefore, if it had anything at all to do with Hobbes, it was used by him during his humanist period.

IV

ARISTOCRATIC VIRTUE

HOBBES'S translation of Thucydides was the crown and end of his humanist period. It is true that he read other historians as well and that he did not read history exclusively, but no other author filled his mind as did Thucydides. It is true, he also translated Homer into English, but that was in the leisure hours of his old age, when he had completed his philosophic life-work, 'because (he) had nothing else to do'.[1] Thucydides' history on the other hand, is the centre of his interests in his youth, heralding his philosophic life-work. Thucydides achieved this eminence as 'the most politic historiographer that ever writ'.[2] If one characterizes Hobbes's humanist studies with reference to their favourite subject, one must therefore assert that the peculiar form of this humanism is the interest in history, which itself proceeds from an interest in politics.

To Hobbes 'History and civil knowledge' are much more closely allied in his humanist period than was later the case. Now 'History and civil knowledge' are 'that kind of learning which best deserveth the pains and hours of great persons'.[3] In this connexion Hobbes particularly recommends the writings of Thucydides 'as having in them profitable instruction for noblemen, and such as may come to have the managing of great and weighty actions'.[4] 'History and civil knowledge', therefore, have exceptional importance for the aristocracy. Hobbes's humanism would thus have a philosophical significance, if the aristocracy among whom he lived were a decisive influence not only on the circumstances of his life but also on his thought; in other words, if Hobbes, after he had turned from metaphysics to moral and political philosophy, considered aristocratic virtue as the highest virtue.

[1] *English Works*, vol. x, p. x.
[2] Loc. cit., vol. viii, p. viii.　　　　　　　　[3] Loc. cit., p. iv.
[4] Loc. cit., p. v. Compare also the later statement in the preface to *De cive*: 'dignissima certe scientiarum haec ipsa est, quae ad Principes pertinet, hominesque in regendo genere humano occupatos . . .'

That this is the case may be gathered even from the very assertion in which Hobbes seems to contest the possibility of a virtue peculiar to the aristocracy. He says: 'honour and honesty are but the same thing in the different degrees of persons.'[1] But while he thus denies that the essence of virtue is touched by class-difference, he at the same time admits that the same virtue has different names in different classes and presents itself differently, and he indicates the possibility that the same virtue or some of the same virtues, which in principle may be acquired by all men, are most to be expected in the highest ranks. If Hobbes had not been of the opinion that virtue understood as 'honour' deserves precedence over virtue understood as 'honesty', he would not have been able to praise the 'heroic virtue' of the Cavendish family one page farther on. He could not have recommended the study of history with the remark that 'in history, actions of honour and dishonour do appear plainly and distinctly, which are which'.[2] He could not have said 'that though (Thucydides) had never written an history, yet had not his name not been extant, in regard of his honour and nobility',[3] i.e. on account of his noble descent.

Hobbes always held fast to his esteem of the aristocracy, in particular of the old aristocracy. In the *Elements*, he says 'nobility is honourable';[4] in the *Leviathan*, 'To be descended from conspicuous Parents, is honourable';[5] and in *De homine*, 'Nobilitas antiqua ingenium facit come, propterea quod in tribuendo cuique honorem, tuto largi et benigni esse possunt, cum debiti sibimet ipsis honoris satis sint securi.'[6]

There is an historic connexion between this esteem of aristocratic virtue and the Aristotelianism which we have previously tried to show as the philosophic basis of Hobbes's humanism. It has been said with all justice of the classical exposition of aristocratic virtue, Castiglione's *Cortegiano*: 'it is from

---

[1] *English Works*, vol. viii, p. v. Cf. Sir Thomas Elyot, *A preservation againste deth* (London, 1545): ' . . . honoure is nothynge but honestee, although it hath been usurped for the estimacion, that is in authoritee.'

[2] *English Works*, vol. viii, p. vi.

[3] Ibid., p. xiii. Cf. Cicero, *Orator*, ix. 32: ' . . . nec vero, si (Thucydides) historiam non scripsisset, nomen eius exstaret, quum praesertim fuisset honoratus et nobilis.'

[4] Pt. I, ch. 8, § 5.   [5] Ch. 10 (p. 46).

[6] Cap. 13, art. 5. Cf. also art. 3.

Aristotle's *Ethics* that Castiglione borrows the framework of his ideal character.'[1] But in this Aristotelianism undergoes a fundamental change. It is true that Castiglione expressly keeps to the superiority of the contemplative life over the life of action, and when he characterizes Plato and Aristotle as the ideal courtiers, beyond doubt he means by that that the courtier in the ideal form is, as it were, only the earthly embodiment of the philosopher. It would, perhaps, not be much of an exaggeration to take Castiglione's guide to the courtier's life as an ironical guide to the philosopher's. The courtier, in the ideal case a philosopher like Plato or Aristotle, and not the prince (whose education and guidance is entrusted to the courtier), is exalted to a vision of perfect beauty. And as in Plato the vision of the ideas, the indispensable condition for right government, has an intrinsic value, wholly independent of its political significance, in the same way in Castiglione's work is the love of ideal beauty which fills the perfect courtier much more than a mere means for the right education and guidance of the prince. However, confronted with the question whether the perfect courtier, a philosopher like Plato or Aristotle, is not in principle superior to any prince, i.e. with the question as to the order of precedence of theory and practice, Castiglione decides in favour of the perfect prince, and therewith in favour of practice.[2] The virtue after which the prince must strive, the highest virtue, is heroic virtue, the virtue of Hercules or Alexander the Great.[3]

The tendency to thrust theoretic virtue into the background in favour of heroic virtue shows itself, though less distinctly and in more scholastic form, in the digest of the *Nicomachean Ethics* which is found among the Hobbes papers at Chatsworth. The unknown author of the digest demands that the discussion of dianoetic virtues be excluded from ethics;[4] in accordance

[1] Sir Walter Raleigh, *Some Authors* (Oxford, 1923), p. 99. It may also be recalled that one of the best-known Aristotelians of the sixteenth century, Augustinus Niphus, wrote *De viro aulico*. See his *Opuscula moralia et politica*, Paris, 1645, vol. ii, pp. 240 ff.

[2] *The Book of the Courtier*, done into English by Sir Thomas Hoby, Everyman's Library, pp. 295, 297, and 300.

[3] Loc. cit., pp. 276, 289 f., and 300.

[4] 'Intellectualis virtus cum ad Ethicam disciplinam essentiali methodi jure non pertineat, ideo in praesens differenda eius tractatio, ut ne dicam penitus rejicienda' (p. 1).

with this he treats exclusively moral virtues and leaves out the analysis of the dianoetic virtues in the 6th Book of the *Nicomachean Ethics* and the discussion in the 10th Book which proves the superiority of theory over practice. On the other hand, in express divergence from Aristotle, and following Franc. Piccolomini's precedent,[1] he discusses much more fully than Aristotle heroic virtue as the 'excellens Virtus moralis, ex quâ magnum aliquis et publicum bonum ardenter cupit, constanter tentat, et foeliciter'.[2] A special section is devoted to the treatment of heroic virtue, and it is with this section that the digest ends.

Doubtless heroic virtue is not identical with aristocratic virtue, and the increase of interest in heroic virtue which may be seen also elsewhere in Renaissance Aristotelianism[3] is certainly not to be explained only, and probably not primarily, by the interest in aristocratic virtue. But in whatever way and for whatever reasons the assimilation of heroic virtue and aristocratic virtue took place,[4] for Hobbes, in any case, the identification of heroic and aristocratic virtue is established from the outset. When he praises the virtues of the Cavendish family in the dedication to the translation of Thucydides, he characterizes these virtues in the same breath as 'honour' and 'heroic virtue'.[5]

Hobbes held to the assimilation of 'heroic virtue' and 'honour' also later. 'Heroes' is for him the classical designation of princes and nobles, 'heroic virtue' is identical with the virtue of the Court.[6] The essentials of heroic virtue are valour, noble

---

[1] 'Egit Philosophus de Virtute Heroica succincte, et breviter. Piccolomineus vero satis copiose . . .' (p. 12).

[2] p. 38 f. This definition of *heroica virtus* is influenced by Cicero's treatment of *magnanimitas*; cf. *De officiis*, i. 20, 66.

[3] I would refer the reader to Johannes de Stobnicza's Commentary on Lionardo Bruni, *In moralem disciplinam introductio*, as well as to A. Niphus, *De sanctitate*, lib. i (*Opuscula moralia*, vol. i, pp. 157 ff.).

[4] How much the meaning of the word 'hero' approximates especially in the second half of the sixteenth century to the meaning of 'perfect aristocrat' may be seen from the *Oxford English Dictionary* under 'hero', &c. B. Gracian's book *El Heroe* (1637), which is to be counted among aristocratic literature, should also be recalled here.

[5] *English Works*, vol. viii, p. v and p. vi.

[6] 'As philosophers have divided the universe, their subject, into three regions, celestial, aerial, and terrestrial; so the poets . . . have lodged themselves in the three regions of mankind, court, city, and country. . . . For there is in princes, and men of conspicuous power, anciently called heroes,

descent, beauty, love, authority, wisdom, the art of diversion, ambition,[1] i.e. those virtues which according to Castiglione are the essentials of the perfect aristocrat. In his ethics Hobbes treats of those very virtues under the heading 'Honour'. He says there: 'Honourable are . . . Beauty of person, consisting in a lively aspect of the countenance . . . as also, general reputation amongst those of the other sex. . . . And actions proceeding from strength of body and open force . . . such as are victory in battle or duel. . . . Also to adventure upon great exploits and danger. . . . And to teach or persuade. . . . And nobility. . . . And authority.'[2] Thus the meaning of 'heroic virtue' and 'honour' coincide completely and the virtues indicated by the two expressions are the specific virtues of the aristocrat.

The original function of the sections in Hobbes's ethics which treat of 'honour' is, then, the explanation of aristocratic virtue. For 'honour' is co-ordinated with the aristocracy in the same way as 'honesty' is co-ordinated with the lower classes.[3] Moreover, there is even a literary connexion between Hobbes's analysis of honour and contemporary aristocratic literature. Compare the following passage from W. Segar's *Honour Military and Civill*:[4]

'. . . divers demonstrations of honour are also due by externall countenance, words, and gesture; as by attentive hearing of him

a lustre and influence upon the rest of men, resembling that of heavens. . . .' *English Works*, vol. iv, p. 443 f. 'By profit (of an heroic poem) I intend . . . accession of prudence, justice and fortitude, by the example of such great and noble persons as he introduceth speaking, or describeth acting.' Loc. cit., vol. x, p. iii.

[1] '. . . the work of an heroic poem is to raise admiration, principally for three virtues, valour, beauty, and love . . . a hero('s) . . . glory lies . . . in courage, nobility, and other virtues of nature, or in the command he has over other men.' Loc. cit., vol. x, p. iv. In Gondibert and Oswald, personages in Sir William Davenant's epic *Gondibert*, Hobbes finds 'nothing but settled valour, clean honour, calm counsel, learned diversion, and pure love; save only a torrent or two of ambition, which, though a fault, has somewhat heroic in it, and therefore must have place in an heroic poem'. Loc. cit., vol. iv, p. 451. Heroic poetry has to do with 'great persons, that have their minds employed on great designs'. Loc. cit., p. 454 f.

[2] *Elements*, Pt. I, ch. 8, § 5. Compare also the somewhat different enumeration in *Leviathan*, ch. 10 (p. 46 f.).   [3] See above, p. 45.

[4] London, 1602, p. 211 f. Cf. *Elements*, Pt. I, ch. 8, § 6, and *Leviathan*, ch. 10 (pp. 45 ff.).

that speaketh, by rising to him that passeth, etc. He that sitteth doth receive honour from him that standeth. . . . A man that sitteth at the table is more honoured than hee that serveth. . . . He is most honoured that walketh next the wall (unlesse they be three in number) for then he that is in the mids, is in the worthiest place. . . . A man is also honoured, when his Prince or other superiour is pleased to salute him by word or writing, or to grace him with gift of any Office or dignitie. . . . Men are honoured by bearing Armes: For who so hath Armes from Ancesters, is more honourable than he who is the first Gentleman of his race. . . . '

Hobbes takes such remarks on honour as his point of departure; he deepens them systematically from the beginning by including them in the framework which Aristotle's analysis of καλά in the *Rhetoric* offered.[1]

In his characterizations of heroic virtue Hobbes always names courage first.[2] Aristocratic virtue is primarily the virtue of the warrior, the virtue which is especially revealed in war. Castiglione says:

'I judge the principall and true profession of a Courtier ought to be in feates of armes, the which above all I will have him to practise lively, and to bee knowne among others of his hardines, for his atchieving of enterprises, and for his fidelitie towards him whom he serveth'; 'shewing alwaies and counting in effect, armes to bee his principall profession, and all the other good qualities for an ornament thereof.'[3]

Hobbes adopts this view, by unequivocally co-ordinating honour (aristocratic virtue) and war:

'The sum of virtue is to be sociable with them that will be sociable, and formidable to them that will not. And the same is the sum of the law of nature; for in being sociable, the law of nature taketh place by the way of peace and society; and to be formidable, is the law of nature in war, where to be feared is a protection a man hath from his own power; and as the former consisteth in actions of equity and justice, the latter consisteth in actions of honour.'[4] 'The only law of actions in war is honour.'[5]

The *analysis* of honour is found in the *Elements* and in the *Leviathan* and (as analysis of the *Pulchrum*) as late as *De homine*.

---

[1] See above, p. 36.
[2] See p. 48, note 1, above.
[3] *The Courtier*, ed. cit., pp. 35 ff. and 72.
[4] *Elements*, Pt. I, ch. 17, § 15.
[5] Loc. cit., ch. 19, § 2.

It is therefore all the more striking that the express characterization of honour as *virtue* (i.e. in war) occurs only in the earliest exposition. It is true, in *De cive* courage is still called virtue, but no longer in connexion with honour; moreover, in the *Leviathan* and in *De homine* courage itself is completely omitted. In place of the triad 'honour, justice and equity', we have more and more the two concepts 'justice and charity'.[1] Thus the more Hobbes elaborated his political philosophy, the further he departed from his original recognition of honour as virtue, from the original recognition of aristocratic virtue. We see in this fact a further indication that for Hobbes at the time before he entertained the idea of composing an independent and coherent treatment of political philosophy, and particularly during his humanist period, honour and heroic virtue was the decisive ideal.

In the course of his development Hobbes departed farther and farther from the recognition of aristocratic virtue. At the end of this process there is, however, not only the establishment of a peculiarly bourgeois morality, but at the same time aristocratic virtue itself becomes sublimated and spiritualized.

In accordance with Hobbes's definition, a man's honour is the recognition by others of his superiority over those others. Thus 'those signs for which one man acknowledgeth power or excess above his concurrent in another'[2] are 'honourable'. In particular, all emotions or actions which arise from consciousness of superiority are 'honourable'. This consciousness is called glory or pride.[3] But this formal definition, according to which consciousness of superiority is only a particular 'sign'

---

[1] Cf. *Elements*, Pt. I, ch. 17, § 15, with the parallel passages in *De cive*, cap. 3, art. 32, *Leviathan*, ch. 15 (pp. 81 ff.), and *De homine*, cap. 13, art. 9 (see above, p. 18). Cf. further *Elements*, Pt. I, ch. 19, § 2, and the parallels in *De cive* and *Leviathan*. It is true, in the *Leviathan*, ch. 17 (p. 87), the expression 'laws of honour' does occur, and this has no corresponding expression in *De cive*, cap. 5, art. 2. But, instead, in a series of other passages in the *Leviathan*, which have no parallels in the other two presentations, 'honour' and 'justice' are expressly no longer treated as complementary, but as antitheses, in accordance with *De cive*, cap. 5, art. 2, but much more pronouncedly. Cf. *Leviathan*, ch. 10 (p. 47), ch. 12 (p. 58), and ch. 13 (p. 66). See below, p. 113 f. and 120.

[2] *Elements*, Pt. I, ch. 8, § 5.

[3] Ibid., Pt. I, ch. 9, § 1; *De cive*, cap. 1, art. 2 and cap. 4, art. 9; *Leviathan*, ch. 6 (p. 27) and ch. 10 (p. 46).

of (recognizable) superiority,[1] hides the peculiar relationship between 'glory' (or 'pride') and 'honour'. For those actions which arise out of consciousness of superiority on the part of the man who carries them out are primarily 'honourable'. Thus one may say: glory or pride is the source of honour.[2] Glory or pride, consciousness of one's own superiority, when this consciousness is well founded, is magnanimity.[3] It is magnanimity which Hobbes later considers to be the source not only of honour but of all virtue.

The connexion between magnanimity and honour, consciousness of superiority and aristocracy, received its classical explanation from Aristotle.[4] To Aristotle magnanimity is on the one hand, one virtue among others—it is right behaviour towards great honours—on the other hand, it is 'a kind of ornament to the (other) virtues'. It presupposes the other virtues and enhances them. Magnanimity as it were sums up the other virtues, as virtues of the free superior individual, in the same way as justice[5] sums up the other virtues as virtues of the citizen who obeys the law and behaves rightly by his fellow citizens. If now instead of the unstable balance between magnanimity and justice which prevailed at least apparently in the *Nicomachean Ethics*, we have more and more the preponderance of magnanimity over justice, that means that as a moral principle obedience to the law is considered less and less and consciousness of superiority ('glory') on the part of the superior individual and his interest in recognition of that superiority by others ('honour') is considered more and more.

A development of this kind seems to have taken place in the Renaissance.[6] It is documented within certain limits in Castiglione's ideal of the courtier. 'Magnanimity is the soul of the Courtier, for it preserves him, in a world of minute observances, from laying stress on trifles, from losing sight of the

---

[1] Cf. *Elements*, Pt. I, ch. 8, § 5.

[2] Ibid., Pt. I, ch. 19, § 2; *De cive*, cap. 1, art. 4–5; *Leviathan*, ch. 13 (p. 64).

[3] *Elements*, Pt. I, ch. 9, § 20.

[4] *Eth. Nicom.* iv. 7–9.   [5] Ibid., v. 2–3.

[6] Cf. Jakob Burckhardt, *Die Kultur der Renaissance in Italien*, 10. Auflage, vol. i, pp. 152 ff. and vol. ii, pp. 155 ff., and also L. Einstein, *Tudor Ideals*, London, 1921, pp. 259 ff.

end in a sedulous study of the means. It is only by virtue of magnanimity that the Courtier can attain to that negligence . . . which is of the essence of good manners.'[1] What is more, it is not only magnanimity as consciousness of superiority, but also and particularly magnanimity as interest in superiority and in recognition of that superiority by others, which distinguishes Castiglione's courtier. The courtier must be versed in the arts of pleasing and attracting attention: 'And to conclude, I say that (to doe well) the Courtier ought to have a perfect understanding in that wee have saide is meete for him, so that every possible thing may be easie to him, and all men wonder at him, and hee at no man.'[2] The heightening of the interest in the right behaviour towards small and great honours is particularly shown in those sections of Castiglione's book which are most original, in his descriptions of grace. To be perfect, all the courtier's arts and accomplishments require grace. They gain grace only by the artistic concealment of all art, i.e. the very concealment of art must remain hidden.[3] The direct opposite of grace is affectation, i.e. boastful self-presentation and self-praise. But this does not by any means imply that grace is essentially modesty. On the contrary, grace is at the service of the art of pleasing and attracting attention. Grace is even a subtle deception, by means of which the courtier gains a reputation for aptitudes which he does not possess:

'And in every thing that (the Courtier) hath to doe or to speake, if it be possible, let him come alwaies provided and thinke on it before hand, shewing notwithstanding the whole to be done ex tempore, and at the first sight. As for the things he hath but a meane skill in, let him touch them (as it were) by the way, . . . in

[1] Sir Walter Raleigh, loc. cit., p. 99.
[2] Castiglione, loc. cit., p. 129; cf. also pp. 41 ff. and pp. 95 ff. Sir Thomas Elyot says in his *Governour*: 'Magnanimitie . . . is, as it were, the garment of Vertue, wherewith she is set out . . . to the uttermoste. . . . Semblably doth Magnanimitie, joined with any vertue, sette it wounderfully furthe to be beholden, and . . . mervayled at . . .' Compare also the following chapter-headings from Gracian's *El heroe* (quoted from the English translation, London, 1726): 'That (the Hero) should excel in what is great and noble. That he should aim at a priority in merit. That he should choose bright and shining qualities before others. That he should often be renewing his reputation. That he should have emulation in him.'
[3] Castiglione, loc. cit., p. 43 and p. 46 f.

such wise that a man may believe he hath a great deale more cunning therein, than he uttereth. . . . This . . . is rather an ornament that accompanieth the thing he doth, than a deceite: and though it be a deceite, yet it is not to be disalowed.'[1]

In all this Castiglione keeps fundamentally to the ground-work of Aristotle's *Ethics*. Hobbes's final theory of magna-nimity, on the other hand, assumes a complete break with Aristotelianism. He occasionally uses 'magnanimity' and 'courage' as synonymous.[2] This usage directly recalls Sir Thomas Elyot's *The Boke named the Governour* (1531) in which 'Magnanimitie, whiche may be named valyaunt courage' is treated,[3] and then Cicero's treatment of magnanimity in the first book of *De officiis*, on which Elyot's presentation is based.[4] According to the teaching of the Stoa, to which Cicero's state-ments in their turn go back, and which were later brought into harmony with the Aristotelian statements by Thomas Aquinas, magnanimity is more accurately defined as one part of courage.[5] Hobbes thus followed the tradition founded by the Stoa, when he speaks of 'courage or magnanimity'. But he already goes beyond this tradition, by taking magnanimity not as one part of courage, but conversely, by taking courage, and in addition also liberality, as parts of magnanimity: 'Contempt of little helps, and hindrances, Magnanimity. Magnanimity, in Danger of Death, or Wounds, Valour, Fortitude. Magnanimity, in the use of riches, Liberality.'[6] It would seem as though Hobbes wished to understand all the virtues of the aristocracy, all the brilliant virtues, as brought about by the self-consciousness of

[1] Castiglione, loc. cit., pp. 130 ff. Cf. pp. 46, 48 f., and 100.

[2] *Elements*, Pt. I, ch. 19, § 2.

[3] Elyot says: ' . . . nowe I remembre me, this worde Magnanimitie beinge yet straunge, as late borrowed out of the latyne, shall nat content all men. . . . I will adventure to put for Magnanimitie a worde more familiar, callynge it good courage . . .' Sir Thomas Hoby in his translation of the *Cortegiano* renders 'magnanimità' by 'noblenesse of courage' and 'stoutnesse of courage'.

[4] For Cicero (*De officiis*, i. 20 ff.) *fortitudo animi* and *magnitudo animi* are an indissoluble unity.

[5] Cf. G. Krüger, 'Die Herkunft des philosophischen Selbstbewusstseins,' *Logos*, vol. xxii, pp. 261 ff. Krüger investigates the history of the concept magnanimity in connexion with an interpretation of Descartes's theory of *générosité*.

[6] *Leviathan*, ch. 6 (p. 26).

the superior man. He follows this path farther, to its conclusion, by construing justice itself as a result of magnanimity.[1]
Magnanimity as 'contempt of little helps' is, however, not merely
 contempt of unjust helps', but also and particularly 'contempt
of dishonest helps'.[2] In the same way, magnanimity is the
origin of honour, as it is the origin of justice. If, indeed, honour
and justice are the 'sum of virtue',[3] then one may summarize
Hobbes's theory of magnanimity thus: magnanimity is the
origin of all virtue.[4] Perhaps more thought should be given
than is usually done to this extreme accentuation of the concept
of aristocratic virtue which is found in the *Leviathan*, if one
wishes to understand the fact that 'Hobbism (after the Restoration) became an almost essential part of the fine gentleman'.[5]

But what is the significance of this theory of magnanimity?
What is its final assumption? At a first glance, Hobbes's theory
differs from Aristotle's in that to Hobbes magnanimity no longer
is what it was to Aristotle, an 'ornament' of all virtues, among
them of a justice which is already in existence, but is the origin
of justice among other virtues. This change means fundamentally that virtue is no longer conceived to be a state (ἕξις) but
solely an intention. That this is the case is shown particularly
by Hobbes's express criticism of Aristotle's *Ethics*: ' . . . the
Writers of Morall Philosophie, though they acknowledge the
same Vertues and Vices (*sc.* as Hobbes); yet not seeing wherein
consisteth their Goodnesse . . . place them in a mediocrity of
passions: as if not the Cause, but the Degree of daring, made
Fortitude; or not the Cause, but the Quantity of a gift, made
Liberality.'[6] That is to say: the reason, the motive of an action

---

[1] See p. 24 f. above.

[2] 'Magnanimity is contempt of unjust, or dishonest helps.' *Leviathan*,
ch. 8 (p. 35). For an understanding of this passage, cf. *English Works*,
vol. vi, p. 25: ' . . . the rule of honest and dishonest refers to honour, and
. . . it is justice only, that the law respecteth.'

[3] See p. 49 above.

[4] Wisdom also is characterized as a 'kind of gallantry'. See *Behemoth*,
p. 38.

[5] Macaulay, *The History of England from the Accession of James the Second*,
vol. i, p. 181. Compare also Sir Thomas Browne's characterization of the
magnanimus as 'Aristotle's true gentleman' (*Christian Morals*, i, § 16).

[6] *Leviathan*, ch. 15 (p. 83); cf. also *Elements*, Pt. I, ch. 17, § 14 and
De cive, cap. 3, art. 32. Cf. Kant, *Metaphysik der Sitten* (Schriften, Akade-
mie-Ausgabe, vol. vi, p. 404).

or of a form of behaviour is the only criterion of its moral value. Independent of legislation, 'every man (is) his own Judge, and accused only by his own Conscience, and cleared by the Uprightnesse of his own Intention. When therefore his Intention is right, his fact is no Sinne . . .'[1] The intention becomes for Hobbes the one and only moral principle, because he no longer believes in the existence of an 'objective' principle according to which man must order his actions—in the existence of a natural law which precedes all human volition. He, as we have seen, expressly denies that the natural moral law is really a law.[2] The denial of a natural law, of an obligation which precedes all human contracts, is the final reason why the intention, why particularly 'a certain Noblenesse or Gallantnesse of courage', i.e. magnanimity, is considered as sufficient reason for all virtue.

The theory that magnanimity is the origin of all virtue is found only in the *Leviathan*. In the *Elements*, magnanimity is discussed as an estimable passion but as nothing more. In *De homine* it is no longer even mentioned. In its place we have the more colourless *justa sui aestimatio*,[3] which differs fundamentally from magnanimity in that it is not essentially consciousness of superiority. The mere fact that the theory of magnanimity which is under discussion occurs only in the *Leviathan* raises the suspicion that it is not an indispensable element in Hobbes's moral philosophy. And, indeed, it may be seen from the *Leviathan* itself that even in this work it is not only not indispensable but even diametrically opposed to its fundamental purpose. We have pointed out that with the progressive elaboration of his political philosophy Hobbes drew farther and farther away from his original recognition of aristocratic virtue. The *Leviathan* belongs to a very advanced stage of this development. As its very title expresses, it is directed primarily against the passion of 'pride'.[4] 'Glory or Pride' are used by Hobbes synonymously with 'Noblenesse of courage', i.e. magnanimity, in passages in which he characterizes magnanimity as the origin of justice. Precisely because magnanimity is a form of pride, even though it be the most

[1] *Leviathan*, ch. 27 (p. 155).   [2] See p. 24 above.
[3] *De homine*, cap. 12, art. 9.   [4] See above, p. 12 f. and p. 25.

'honourable' form, it cannot be accepted by Hobbes as the origin of justice. For as it rests on a sense of superiority, it runs counter to the recognition of the natural equality of all men, and in the last analysis it is only the recognition of this equality which Hobbes allows to stand as just self-estimation.[1] The theory that magnanimity is the origin of all virtue is thus directly opposed to Hobbes's real intention. As this theory occurs only in the *Leviathan*, one may assume that Hobbes momentarily adopted it, under the strength of the impression made by Descartes's *Passions de l'âme*, which appeared in 1649, at the time when the *Leviathan* was being composed. It would certainly not be the first and only time that Hobbes allowed himself to be carried away by the authority of Descartes. Descartes says: ' . . . la vertu de générosité (est) comme la clef de toutes les autres vertus, et un remède général contre tous les dérèglements des passions.'[2]

But how is one to judge the fact that Hobbes in passing borrowed Descartes's theory of *générosité*? Is one to say that it was only under Descartes's influence that Hobbes achieved a deepening of his moral doctrine, of which he was incapable before and after? We should consider it better to judge that Hobbes, who had wrestled all his life in vain to find a clear formulation of his own much deeper answer to the moral problem, was momentarily satisfied to take over Descartes's lucid though superficial answer, which as a result of the whole previous development seemed obvious. This judgement is all the more justified since Hobbes's own system of morals corresponds better to Descartes's deepest intention than does the morality of *Les passions de l'âme*.[3] Radical doubt, whose moral correlate is distrust and fear, comes earlier than the self-confidence of the ego grown conscious of its independence and freedom, whose moral correlate is *générosité*. Descartes begins the groundwork of philosophy with distrust of his own prejudices, with distrust above all of the potential *deus deceptor*,

[1] *Elements*, Pt. I, ch. 14, §§ 2–3, and ch. 17, § 1; *De cive*, cap. 1, art. 3–4 and cap. 3, art. 13; *Leviathan*, ch. 13 (p. 63) and ch. 15 (p. 79 f.).

[2] *Les Passions de l'âme*, art. 161. Cf. also art. 154.

[3] It may be recalled that Descartes was originally considered by some people to be the author of *De cive* and that Descartes himself spoke rather favourably of this work.

just as Hobbes begins interpreting the State and therewith all morality by starting from men's natural distrust. It is, however, not Descartes's morals, but Hobbes's, which explains the concrete meaning and the concrete implications of fundamental distrust. For Hobbes, except when confused as to his own real intention by Descartes, sees the origin of virtue not in magnanimity, but in fear, in fear of violent death. He considers not magnanimity but fear of violent death as the only adequate self-consciousness.

In questions which bear on the philosophy of self-consciousness, one can wish for no more authoritative judge than Hegel. Hegel tacitly recognizes the superiority of Hobbes's philosophic basis to that of Descartes when he characterizes the experience from which self-consciousness originally arises as the life-and-death struggle which is born of interest in recognition from others. In the *Phenomenology of Mind* he says:

'Self-consciousness exists in itself and for itself, in that, and by the fact that it exists for another self-consciousness; that is to say, it *is* only by being acknowledged or "recognised" . . . each is indeed certain of its own self, but not of the other, and hence its own certainty is still without truth. . . . The relationship of both self-consciousnesses is in this way so constituted that they prove themselves and each other through a life-and-death struggle. They must enter into this struggle, for they must bring their certainty of themselves, the certainty of being for themselves, to the level of objective truth, and make this a fact both in the case of the other and in their own case as well.'[1]

From this struggle arises together with the master-servant relationship the original form of self-consciousness. The consciousness of the servant is essentially determined according to both Hegel and Hobbes by fear of death;[2] and in principle to Hegel just as much as to Hobbes the consciousness of the servant represents a higher stage than the consciousness of the master. Hegel by prefacing his analysis of the pre-modern

---

[1] Op. cit., J. B. Baillie's translation, vol. i, pp. 175 ff.

[2] As Hegel says: ' . . . bondage . . . is a self-consciousness . . . this self-consciousness was not in peril and fear for this element or that, nor for this or that moment of time, it was afraid for its entire being; it felt the fear of death, it was in mortal terror of its sovereign master . . .' Op. cit., p. 185.

forms of self-consciousness—Stoa, scepticism, and 'unhappy consciousness'—by the analysis, based on Hobbes's philosophy,[1] of mastery and servitude, recognized that Hobbes's philosophy was the first to deal with the most elementary form of self-consciousness.

[1] M. Alexandre Kojevnikoff and the writer intend to undertake a detailed investigation of the connexion between Hegel and Hobbes.

V

THE STATE AND RELIGION

HOBBES carried on his historical studies with a view to politics. His favourite author was Thucydides, 'the most politic historiographer that ever writ'.[1] In his autobiographies he says he published his translation of Thucydides because he wished to communicate to his fellow citizens the teaching that democracy is wrong and monarchy to be preferred, to which belief Thucydides had converted him.[2] These later accounts are fully borne out by the introduction to the translation of Thucydides. In it Hobbes summarizes Thucydides' 'opinion touching the government of the state' to the effect that Thucydides 'least of all liked the democracy' and 'best approved of the regal government'.[3] The tone of the whole introduction is a testimony to the fact that Hobbes whole-heartedly adopts the point of view of his author. Thus Hobbes was from the outset a decided upholder of the monarchy and a decided opponent of democracy, and he kept to this opinion throughout his whole life.

At all stages in his development Hobbes considered hereditary absolute monarchy as the best form of State. In the introduction to the translation of Thucydides he certainly considers the formally monarchic government of Peisistratos and the nominally democratic but *de facto* monarchic government of Pericles as equivalent.[4] But likewise in all three systematic expositions of his political philosophy he recognizes the possibility of elective monarchy, which he compares with the Roman institution of dictatorship, and under which the people is 'sovereign in property', but not 'in use'.[5] As he asserts the legal equivalence of democracy and monarchy in principle, one

---

[1] *English Works*, vol. viii, p. viii.
[2] *Opera latina*, vol. i, pp. xiv and lxxxviii.
[3] *English Works*, vol. viii, p. xvi f.
[4] Loc. cit., p. xvii. Cf. also *Elements*, Pt. II, ch. 2, § 5 and ch. 5, *in fine*; *De cive*, cap. 10, art. 15; *Leviathan*, ch. 25, *in fine*.
[5] *Elements*, Pt. II, ch. 2, § 9; *De cive*, cap. 7, art. 15–16; *Leviathan*, ch. 19 (p. 100 f.).

may say that he regarded absolute monarchy and dictatorship as the only practical forms of government.[1] Hobbes maintained this position from the time of the translation of Thucydides until the *Leviathan*. In that respect also his opinion never changed, that while esteeming dictatorship he recognizes absolute monarchy as the superior form.

Hobbes's position with regard to monarchy did not change throughout his whole life.[2] But his conception of the term 'monarchy' changed. This is shown by the way he explains the pre-eminence of monarchy in the various presentations. In the earlier presentations he makes mention of the traditional arguments, which all amount to saying that monarchy is the only natural, i.e. original form of authority, the only form which corresponds to nature's original order, whereas aristocracy and democracy are artificially produced by man, merely 'cemented by human wit'.[3] It is true that as early as the *Elements* and again more clearly in *De cive* he lays no weight on arguments of this kind. Nevertheless, the fact that they are mentioned in the earlier presentations justifies the assumption that Hobbes came only gradually to cast them aside and that he at first considered monarchy to be the only natural form of authority. Moreover, he maintained up to the end that paternal authority and consequently patrimonial monarchy is, if not the legal, nevertheless the historical, origin of all or the majority of States.[4]

Hobbes at all times maintained the distinction between the

[1] Cf. F. Tönnies, *Thomas Hobbes*, 3rd edition, Stuttgart, 1925, pp. 252–5.

[2] Thus Hobbes did not come gradually from recognition of absolute monarchy alone to recognition of dictatorship also. The most decided affirmation of absolute monarchy is found not in the *Elements*, but in *De cive* (cap. 10, art. 17). While the *Elements* (Pt. II, ch. 2, § 10) and *Leviathan*, (ch. 19, p. 101) assert the possibility of limited monarchy, which is indeed no true monarchy, but a commission given by the sovereign people, this possibility is denied in *De cive* (cap. 7, art. 17). In addition, in a section of *De cive* which has no parallel in the other presentations (cap. 10, art. 18), the advantages of hereditary monarchy are asserted. Because in *De cive* Hobbes had advocated monarchy too decidedly, he was obliged in the preface, which he composed later, formally to declare that the advantages of monarchy had not been proved, but were only probable.

[3] *Elements*, Pt. II, ch. 5, § 3, and *De cive*, cap. 10, art. 3. Cf. Tönnies, loc. cit., p. 250 f. Cf. also *De cive*, Praefatio, and *Opera latina*, vol. v, p. 352.

[4] *Leviathan*, ch. 10 (p. 47 f.), ch. 13 (p. 65), ch. 20 (p. 105), ch. 22 (p. 124), ch. 27 (p. 164), and ch. 30 (p. 182); *Behemoth*, p. 147.

natural and the artificial State. He always distinguished between 'the commonwealth by acquisition', which is based on natural force, whether of the father or of the conqueror, and 'the commonwealth by institution', which comes into being by voluntary subjection to an elected government, i.e. artificially. For him the monarchic character of the natural State is at all times taken for granted.[1]

In all three presentations of his political philosophy Hobbes treats first of the artificial and then of the natural State. And in all three presentations, in accordance with his final point of view, in discussing the artificial State he also treats particularly of institutional and therefore artificial monarchy. But there is one highly noteworthy difference: whereas in the *Leviathan* the right of succession is treated as a specific problem of monarchy in the discussion of the 'commonwealth by institution', in the earlier presentations it is mentioned only in connexion with the discussion of the natural State.[2] Originally this specific problem of monarchy (i.e. the right of succession) was included only in the discussion of the natural State because, according to Hobbes's original point of view, monarchy and the natural State were identical.

But which natural State? Hobbes distinguishes two kinds of natural State: the despotic State which is based on conquest, and the patrimonial monarchy which is based on paternal authority. As is already indicated by the fact that in the earlier presentations the right of succession in monarchies was treated only with regard to patrimonial monarchy, and that even in the *Leviathan* it is only in this connexion and not in the discussion of the despotic State that there is a reference back to the previous discussions on the right of succession, the monarchy which Hobbes originally identified with the natural State was patrimonial monarchy and not despotic monarchy. It must

---

[1] 'The attayning to this Soveraigne Power, is by two wayes. One, by Naturall force; as when *a man* maketh his children, to submit themselves . . . to his government . . . or by Warre subdueth his enemies to his will. . . . The other, is when men agree amongst themselves, to submit to some *man or Assembly* of men, voluntarily . . .' *Leviathan*, ch. 17, *in fine*. Cf. *Elements*, Pt. I, ch. 19, § 11, and *De cive*, cap. 5, art. 12.

[2] Cf. *Elements*, Pt. II, ch. 4, §§ 11–17; *De cive*, cap. 9, art. 11–19; and *Leviathan*, ch. 19 (pp. 101–4).

above all be emphasized that the traditional arguments in favour of monarchy, which are mentioned in the earlier presentations, are exclusively related to patrimonial monarchy and not to despotic monarchy. Thus for Hobbes, monarchy and patrimonial kingdom were originally identical.

Only later did he come to consider the monarchy which is based on paternal authority and the monarchy based on conquest, as equivalent. This change is the result of his conception of the idea of an artificial ('instituted') monarchy, compared with which all forms of authority, which are not of artificial production and are not based on voluntary delegation, seem natural. The idea of the artificial monarchy, as of the artificial State altogether, becomes clearer from one exposition to the next. In the *Elements* it is said in passing: '(the monarch's) subjects . . . are to him as his children and servants.' This observation has disappeared without leaving a trace in the later presentations.[1] In the *De cive*, in a completely fresh paragraph,[2] a distinction is made with special reference to monarchy between the *jus imperii* and the *exercitium imperii*. Monarchy is to cease to be personal government in any higher degree than democracy or aristocracy. In the *Leviathan*, in the chapters headed 'Of those things that weaken, or tend to the dissolution of a Common-wealth' and 'Of the Office of the Soveraign Representative', in sections which have no parallel in earlier presentations, there is an effort towards a modification of the traditional conception of monarchy in the light of ideal institutional monarchy. On the other hand, the treatment of the natural State is at least relatively shortened.[3] The more sharply Hobbes elaborates the idea of representation,[4] the more clarity he achieves as to the essence of institutional monarchy and the differences between the king as natural person and the king as politic person, the less important does the natural State, patrimonial monarchy, and the affinity between monarchy and the paternal authority become for him. In the end paternal (and despotic) government and monarchy are diametrically

---

[1] *Elements*, Pt. II, ch. 4, § 12; *De cive*, cap. 9, art. 14; *Leviathan*, ch. 19 (p. 103).
[2] Cap. 13, art. 1.   [3] Cf. Tönnies, loc. cit., p. 255.
[4] Ibid., pp. 238 ff. and also p. 210 and p. 242.

opposed: 'The king, though as a father of children, and a master of domestic servants command many things which bind those children and servants, yet he commands the people in general never but by a precedent law, and as a politic, not a natural person.'[1]

According to Hobbes's final opinion, we must distinguish between the natural State, which is monarchic as a matter of course, and the artificial State, which in principle may with equal justification be democratic, aristocratic, or monarchic. But originally he considered democracy as the primary form of the artificial State. It is expressly said in the *Elements*, in the discussion of the artificial State: 'Democracy precedeth all other institution of government.' Aristocracy and (institutional) monarchy are derived from the original democracy. This thesis occurs in *De cive* only in a much weakened form and in the *Leviathan* it has completely disappeared.[2] Thus, according to Hobbes's original opinion, the artificial State is primarily democratic, as the natural State is the patrimonial monarchy.

It would be a mistake to believe that Hobbes originally preferred monarchy, on account of its natural origin, to artificial democracy. It happens that the earliest systematic exposition of his views is the most democratic. That the precedence of democracy over the other artificial forms of State is asserted most decisively in the *Elements* has already been mentioned. The following facts are less equivocal. In the *Elements*, Aristotle's assertion that the object of democracy is freedom meets with more justice at Hobbes's hands, in spite of his rejection of that opinion, than it does later.[3] Moreover, in the *Elements* there is a remark about the artificial State which seems

[1] *Behemoth*, p. 51. Cf. also *English Works*, vol vi, p. 152.

[2] Cf. *Elements*, Pt. II, ch. 2, § 1 with *De cive*, cap. 7, art. 5 (see Tönnies loc. cit., p. 243). There is a reminiscence of this conception in *Behemoth*, p. 76.

[3] 'Aristotle saith well, The ground or intention of a democracy, is liberty; which he confirmeth in these words: For men ordinarily say this; that no man can partake of liberty, but only in a popular common-wealth.' *Elements*, Pt. II, ch. 8, § 3. ' . . . hoc est quod voluit Aristoteles, ipse quoque consuetudine temporis libertatem pro imperio nominans . . .' *De cive*, cap. 10, art. 8. 'And because the Athenians were taught (to keep them from desire of changing their government,) that they were Freemen, and all that lived under Monarchy were slaves; therefore Aristotle puts it down in his Politiques . . .' *Leviathan*, ch. 21 (p. 113).

to be a residue of an argument in favour of democracy and which recurs in the later presentations only in a much weakened form. In the *Elements* he says:

'The subjection of them who institute a commonwealth amongst themselves, is no less absolute, than the subjection of servants. And herein they are in equal estate; but the hope of those is greater than the hope of these. For he that subjecteth himself uncompelled, thinketh there is reason he should be better used, than he that doth it upon compulsion; and coming in freely, calleth himself, though in subjection, a Freeman; whereby it appeareth, that liberty is . . . a state of better hope than theirs that have been subjected by force and conquest.'[1]

The following opinion seems to be implied: the motive which leads to the natural State is fear; on the other hand, the motive that leads to the artificial State is hope or trust. The artificial State which rests on hope or trust (in the sovereign) is opposed to the natural State which is based on fear. But this antithesis, in so far as democracy is the primary form of artificial State, means the preference for democracy over patrimonial monarchy.

But apart from all individual illustrative quotations, it is probable from the outset that Hobbes was open to democratic ideas in his humanist period, much more than later. In latter years he always named the classical authors as the chief causes of democratic ideas in his age. It is not to be assumed that, at a time when he was occupied with these authors, before he could confront their authority with his own political philosophy which raised a claim to mathematical certitude, and when only or almost only the authority of Thucydides was on his side, he was as steady in his rejection of the democratic tradition as he later became, to say nothing of the fact that Thucydides after all was not an absolutely indisputable authority for Hobbes's view in favour of absolute monarchy. It is in Thucydides, in the speech in which the Corinthians compare the Athenians and the Lacedaemonian State, i.e. classical democracy and classical aristocracy, that Hobbes finds the model for his early characterization of the relationship between demo-

---

[1] *Elements*, Pt. II, ch. 4, § 9. Compare with this *De cive*, cap. 9, art. 9 and cap. 5, art. 12, also *Leviathan*, ch. 20 (p. 107) and ch. 17, *in fine*, and further *Behemoth*, p. 12. Cf. also Spinoza, *Tractatus politicus*, cap. 5, § 6.

cracy and patrimonial monarchy. Just as Thucydides, in the speech which he puts into the mouth of the Corinthians, characterizes the Athenian democracy by its daring and its hopefulness, and on the other hand, the more 'old-fashioned' Lacedaemonian aristocracy by its hesitation and distrust,[1] Hobbes originally characterizes the motive of democracy as hope, and the motive of the 'older' natural State, and therewith the patrimonial monarchy in particular, as fear.

We have at all events to take cognizance of the paradoxical fact that the earliest presentation of Hobbes's political philosophy is at one and the same time the one most in favour of patrimonial monarchy and of democracy. The paradox disappears if one reflects that the ideas of patrimonial monarchy and of democracy which are brought out most clearly in the *Elements* are traditional ideas, that the untraditional union of these ideas, after which Hobbes was striving, was not fully successful until the *Leviathan*, and that, therefore, these ideas are of necessity imperfectly united in the earlier presentations, and, as a result, stand side by side in self-contradiction. In the *Elements* and even more during his humanist period, Hobbes had not yet found the means of reconciling these opposed traditional ideas, that is to say he had not yet developed his final conception of institutional artificial monarchy with sufficient clarity. From this comes the original contradiction between patrimonial monarchy and democracy. In the conflict between these two political opinions, Hobbes was from the beginning on the side of patrimonial monarchy; but from the outset he had scruples of democratic origin against this view.

Thus Hobbes's theory of the State, if one traces it to its starting-point, represents the union of two opposed traditions. Hobbes follows the monarchist tradition, in so far as he contends that patrimonial monarchy is the only natural, and thus the only legitimate, form of State. In contrast to this, the democratic tradition contends that all legitimacy has its origin in the decree of the sovereign people. Hobbes unites these opposed traditions first by a distinction between natural and artificial States. With reference to natural States he follows to the end the monarchist tradition, at least as far as the historical

[1] i. 70, 3.

origin of already existing States is concerned. With reference to artificial States, he follows, at least to begin with, the democratic tradition, taking pains from the beginning to show that democracy can do nothing better than to transform itself into an absolute monarchy, in fact or even also in name.

In this effort the reason which originally induced Hobbes to unite the opposed traditions is betrayed. Hobbes wished to present the advantages of monarchy, of which he was from the outset convinced, for reasons we shall discuss later, in a way which would gain recognition from all parties. The superiority of monarchy was naturally conceded by the monarchist party. It was therefore only a matter of convincing the upholders of the democratic tradition. The most convenient way to achieve this was first of all to grant the democratic assumption, without criticizing it, in order then to prove on the basis of this assumption the advantage of monarchy. The argument in favour of monarchy is thus originally linked with an alternative. Reduced to an expression of principle, it is the alternative of the monarchist and the democratic motive, of fear and hope, which still shines through in the passage quoted from the *Elements*. But Hobbes could not in the long run acquiesce in the juxtaposition of the natural and artificial State, of the monarchist and democratic principle, of fear and hope. He sought a common motive for the founding of the artificial as well as of the natural State. He found this motive in the fear of violent death, which he had originally, as it seems, connected only with the natural State. In this sense the precedence of the natural over the artificial State is acknowledged by Hobbes to the end.

Hobbes thus reconciles two fundamentally different theories of sovereignty. In accordance with the one, sovereignty is the right which is finally based on the authority of the father, thus completely independent of the will of the individual. In accordance with the other, all sovereignty is to be traced back to the voluntary delegation of authority on the part of the majority of free citizens. In the beginning Hobbes would probably have reconciled the antithesis in some such way as this: paternal government is the natural order of the family; the father is by nature absolute master of his children and servants; on the other hand, political rule is based on the voluntary delegation of paternal power to the king by the fathers.[1] In Hobbes's final theory of sovereignty the involuntary as well as the voluntary nature of subjection is more systematically reconciled: men —the individuals, not the fathers—at the founding of the artificial State delegate the highest power to a man or an assembly from mutual fear, the fear of violent death, and fear, in itself compulsive, is consistent with freedom. In other words, they voluntarily replace compulsive mutual fear by the again compulsive fear of a neutral third power, the government, and thus they substitute for an immeasurable, endless, and inevitable danger—the danger threatened by an enemy—a measurable, limited, and avoidable danger—the danger which threatens only the law-breakers from the courts of law.

Up to the time when Hobbes successfully reconciled the two opposed theories of sovereignty, he was compelled to reject as illegitimate those governments whose foundation could be explained neither by the traditional monarchist nor the traditional democratic principle. He therefore says in the introduction to the translation of Thucydides: Thucydides 'commendeth (the government of Athens), both when Peisistratus reigned (saving that it was an usurped power), and when in the beginning of the war it was democratical in name, but in effect monarchical under Pericles.'[2] Thus Hobbes could originally distinguish

---

[1] ' . . . originally, the Father of every man was also his Soveraign Lord, with power over him of life or death; and . . . the Fathers of families . . . by instituting a Common-wealth . . . resigned that absolute Power . . .' *Leviathan*, ch. 30 (p. 182). ' . . . the Parent ought to have the honour of a Soveraign, (though he have surrendered his power to the Civill Law,) . . .' Ibid., ch. 27 (p. 164). It is to be borne in mind that in these and similar passages Hobbes is speaking only of the *de facto*, and not of the legal origin of the State. According to Hobbes's final theory, it is not the father, but the mother, who has legally, i.e. by the law of nature, absolute power of the children. We may take it from the reasons developed in the text that Hobbes originally found not only the *de facto* but also the legal source of sovereignty in the authority of the father. The original reconciliation of the monarchist and democratic principle which we here assume is found in Hooker: 'To fathers within their private families Nature hath given a supreme power. . . . Howbeit over a whole grand multitude having no such dependency upon any one, . . . impossible it is that any should have complete lawful power, but by consent of men, or immediate appointment of God. . . .' *Ecclesiastical Polity*, Book I, x. 4.

[2] *English Works*, vol. viii, p. xvii.

between legitimate and usurped power (either according to the monarchist or the democratic principle); so it is to be understood that he originally considered only the patrimonial (and therefore legitimate) monarchy as the natural State, and not the despotic rule of a conqueror. His final theory is that every effective rule is *eo ipso* legitimate. The words 'tyranny' and 'despotism', therefore, lose all significance for him. He does not hesitate to declare that any or almost any State authority is based on usurpation, without the least prejudice to its legitimacy.[1]

If Hobbes originally recognized legal and not simply factual conditions of sovereignty, we may take it that he also originally assumed legal limits to sovereign power. Later he rejected any limitation or division of sovereignty as absurd. But in the introduction to the translation of Thucydides he mentions, without criticism and apparently still affirmatively, Thucydides' opinion that a mixed constitution of democracy and aristocracy deserves primacy over democracy on the one hand, and aristocracy on the other.[2] And in the *Elements*, in which he systematically, as in the later expositions, opposes the idea of a mixed constitution, he nevertheless admits the possibility not of a division of sovereignty but of a division of the administration of sovereignty into monarchist control and an aristocratic or democratic council.[3] This passage is left out in later expositions. Hobbes, therefore, progressed only gradually to wholehearted rejection of the idea of a mixed constitution. His original opinion will have been that the absolute monarch is by no means obliged, but would do well, to set up an aristocratic or democratic council, and thus unite the advantages of monarchy with those of aristocracy or democracy.

Hobbes did not, however, originally advise only voluntary limitations of the exercise of sovereignty but recognized also

---

[1] ' . . . there is scarce a Common-wealth in the world, whose beginnings can in conscience be justified. . . .' *Leviathan*, Conclusion (p. 388).

[2] *English Works*, vol. viii, p. xvii.

[3] 'But though the sovereignty be not mixed, but be always either simple democracy, or simple aristocracy, or pure monarchy; nevertheless in the administration thereof, all these sorts of government may have place subordinate. . . . So also in a monarchy there may be a council aristocratical of men chosen by the monarch; or democratical of men chosen by the consent (the monarch permitting) of all the particular men of the common-wealth.' *Elements*, Pt. II, ch. 1, § 17.

obligatory limitations of sovereignty. It is true that in all three presentations he rejected with equal decision the view that the sovereign is bound by civil laws, and even the view that the sovereign may under given conditions be called to account by the subjects; but originally he did not envisage sovereignty as nearly so absolute as it is in the *Leviathan*. According to his final view, the sovereign has no obligations of any kind in the real sense of the word; for the law of nature, which is apparently binding on the sovereign, takes on full binding force only by command of the sovereign; and no one can 'be bound to himselfe; because he that can bind, can release; and therefore he that is bound to himselfe onely, is not bound'.[1] Thus the sovereign has no real obligations. Hobbes does, indeed, say that the law of nature is obligatory not only on the basis of sovereign command but also 'as delivered in the word of God'. But this limitation is of no significance, because, according to his own assertion, the word of God itself becomes binding only on the basis of sovereign command. The theory of the *Elements*,[2] according to which natural law is binding not only by reason of revelation but also on account of natural knowledge of God, and thus obliges all men as rational beings and in particular the sovereign, is in sharp contrast to this. As duties of the sovereign Hobbes originally mentions solicitude for the eternal salvation of the subjects and for marriage laws which correspond to natural law. In *De cive* the first of these demands is even more weakened than it is in the *Elements*, and the second is completely dropped. Instead of it we are told in another connexion that the regulation of marriage and adultery depends entirely on civil law, and the natural law of marriage is thus denied. In the *Leviathan* the two demands are no longer even mentioned.[3]

---

[1] *Leviathan*, ch. 26 (p. 141). Two sections farther on he says: ' . . . the Lawes of nature . . . in the condition of meer nature . . . are not properly Lawes, but qualities that dispose men to peace, and to obedience. When a Common-wealth is once settled, then are they actually Lawes, and not before; as being then the commands of the Common-wealth; and therefore also Civill Lawes: For it is the Soveraign Power that obliges men to obey them.'

[2] Cf. *Elements*, Pt. I, ch. 17, § 12 with *De cive*, cap. 3, art. 33 and *Leviathan*, ch. 15, *in fine*. Cf. further *Leviathan*, ch. 33, *in fine*, and *De cive*, cap. 17, art. 17–18.

[3] Cf. *Elements*, Pt. II, ch. 9, §§ 2–3 and *De cive*, cap. 13, art. 5; cap. 6,

After what has been said Hobbes's original political views
may now be summarized as follows: Hereditary absolute
monarchy is the best form of State; the factual and legitimate
origin of monarchy is paternal authority; the fathers voluntarily delegated to the monarch and his issue the absolute power
which nature granted them over their own families. The
monarchy thus legitimized is fundamentally different from all
usurped power; it is the duty of the monarch by natural law,
which has its foundation in the order of nature, in the intelligence of God, who is the First Cause of all existing things, to
care not only and not primarily for the physical well-being of
his subjects, but above all for their moral well-being. Prudence
advises him to surround himself with an aristocratic or a democratic council, in order to unite the advantages of a monarchy
with those of an aristocracy or democracy. If for any reason
hereditary absolute monarchy is impossible in a State, actual
monarchic direction of State affairs is indispensable. A democratic tendency which has not been systematically overcome is
in conflict with this fundamentally monarchist conviction.

These contradictory opinions are, however, nothing other
than the *disjecta membra* of Aristotle's *Politics*. From this work
Hobbes borrows the view that the original form of State is the
patrimonial monarchy which arises out of paternal authority[1]
as well as the conception of democracy which he still permits
to obtain in the *Elements*.[2] The unity which Aristotle had
given to the monarchist and the democratic idea is certainly

art. 16; cap. 14, art. 9–10; and cap. 17, art. 10. In the *Leviathan* the natural
law of marriage is treated as based only on current opinion. See ch. 27
(p. 164) and ch. 30 (p. 182). The recasting of the section on the law of
succession shows that Hobbes, as he elaborated his political philosophy,
caused the law of nature to disappear more and more into positive law or
at least brought positive law more and more into the foreground. If the
monarch dies intestate, the successor, according to the *Elements*, is to be
chosen according to the natural law of succession. *De cive* holds to this,
with the reservation that no custom, i.e. no positive law (cf. *De cive*, cap. 14,
art. 15) is opposed to the natural law of succession. Finally, the *Leviathan*
expressly sets custom above natural law. Cf. *Elements*, Pt. II, ch. 5, §§ 12–17;
De cive, cap. 9, art. 14–19; *Leviathan*, ch. 19 (p. 103).

[1] Aristotle, *Politics*, i. 2.

[2] *Elements*, Pt. II, ch. 8, § 3. It may also be recalled that the definition
of the State in the *Elements* still shows traces of its origin in Aristotle's
definition. See p. 33 above.

no longer recognized by Hobbes, but, on the other hand, the new unity which these ideas finally gained in the *Leviathan* is hardly to be descried in outline.

Hobbes's three presentations of political philosophy may with scarcely less justice than Spinoza's expressly so entitled work be called theological-political treatises. Exactly as Spinoza did later, Hobbes with double intention becomes an interpreter of the Bible, in the first place in order to make use of the authority of the Scriptures for his own theory, and next and particularly in order to shake the authority of the Scriptures themselves. Only gradually does the second intention become clearly predominant. In *De cive* Hobbes devotes two special chapters to Scriptural proof of his own theories of natural law and of the absolute power of kings; in the *Leviathan* there is nothing that corresponds to the first of these chapters, and the content of the second is disposed of in two paragraphs in the chapter which treats of the natural State.[1] When Hobbes thus grants the theological motivation of political philosophy a last refuge in the discussion which treats of the natural State, he indicates the connexion between theology and the natural State in particular. This connexion is shown in the theological arguments in favour of monarchy, which Hobbes mentions in the earlier presentations, and which refer in the main to patrimonial monarchy, i.e. to the natural State. As the natural State becomes less and less important to Hobbes, the theological arguments in political philosophy also become less and less important. Originally, when he had not yet conceived the idea of the artificial State, or had not yet elaborated it in full clarity, he was incomparably more under the spell of theological tradition. That this is the case will be shown by a comparison of those parts of his three presentations of political philosophy which are concerned with criticism of religion.

It must first be stated that the space devoted to criticism of religion increases considerably on the way from the *Elements* to the *Leviathan*. Three chapters in the *Elements* correspond to four in *De cive* and seventeen in the *Leviathan*. This quantitative extension is accompanied by a deepening of the criticism. Hobbes's deviation from tradition becomes clearer from one

[1] Cf. Tönnies, loc. cit., p. 252.

presentation to another. The fundamental question: On what authority does one believe that Scripture is the word of God? is differently answered in the different presentations. In the *Elements*: On the authority of the Church, the successors of the Apostles. In *De Cive*: Not on the authority of the Church, but on that of Jesus. In the *Leviathan*: On the authority of the teachers whose teaching is permitted and organized by the sovereign power, i.e. one confesses verbally—for thoughts are free— that Scripture is the word of God, because secular authority commands this confession.[1] In all three presentations Hobbes contends that all that is needed for salvation is the belief in Jesus as Christ; in this fundamental article of faith he always includes also its premises (the existence of God, Providence, the resurrection of Christ, &c.). According to the earlier presentations the belief in the immortality of the soul belongs to these premises, whereas in a note which is inserted in the second edition of *De cive*,[2] the resurrection of the body is tacitly substituted for the immortality of the soul. The *Leviathan* finally openly opposes the resurrection of the body to the immortality of the soul and admits only the first as grounded in the Scriptures.[3] In all three presentations Hobbes declares that unconditional obedience to the secular power is the bounden duty of every Christian, in so far as that power does not forbid belief in Jesus as Christ. But the crucial question: Is the Christian obliged to obey the secular power when that power forbids him the profession of his faith? is answered in the earlier presentations with the finding that the right and duty of the Christian in such a case is only passive resistance and martyrdom, while the *Leviathan* denies the obligation and even the right of martyrdom to the ordinary Christian who has not the special vocation of preaching the Gospel.[4] According to *De cive* it is a Christian dogma that Christ's kingdom is

[1] *Elements*, Pt. I, ch. 11, §§ 9–10; *De cive*, cap. 18, art. 9; *Leviathan*, ch. 43 (p. 321 f.), ch. 33 (pp. 203 and 208 f.), and ch. 42 (pp. 280–4).

[2] A further difference in the sections dealing with criticism of religion in the two editions of *De cive* may be pointed out in passing: the ironical *etsi falso* at the end of cap. 17, art. 1, is an addition to the second edition.

[3] *Elements*, Pt. II, ch. 6, § 6; *De cive*, cap. 17, art. 13 and cap. 18, art. 6, annot.; *Leviathan*, ch. 43 (p. 326) and ch. 38 (p. 243).

[4] *Elements*, Pt. II, ch. 6, § 14; *De cive*, cap. 18, art. 13; *Leviathan*, ch. 42 (pp. 270–2) and ch. 43 (p. 328).

not of earth but of heaven; in the *Leviathan*, on the other hand, the Kingdom of God under the Old and also under the New Covenant is to be understood as a purely earthly kingdom.[1] According to the *Elements*, the first duty of the sovereign is 'to establish the religion they hold for best'; in *De cive* the corresponding paragraph concludes with the words: 'Difficultatem autem hanc in medio relinquemus'; in the *Leviathan* the whole matter is no longer even mentioned.[2] In the *Elements* Hobbes defends the episcopal constitution of the Church, whose rightness is proved by the fact that Christ in virtue of his sovereignty enthroned his apostles, who then inducted the presbyters, &c. At the same time he denies that in the Christian hierarchy there was a 'high priest' to whom the individual bishops were subordinate. Since in the *Elements* he also names the apostolic succession as the reason for the authority of the Scriptures, one must say that in this work he, at least to some extent, follows the Anglican episcopal conception. On the other hand, in the later presentations he rejects the episcopal constitution, even the view that officials of the Church can be instituted by any ecclesiastical authority which is not in every respect dependent on secular authority.[3] Moreover, in the final chapter of the *Leviathan* he emphatically declares that the episcopal and even the Presbyterian constitution is contrary to Evangelical freedom, with which Independentism is alone compatible.[4] It is all the more remarkable that in the *Leviathan* and as early as *De cive* the conception, apparently very favourable to the clergy, is put forward that in the age between the receiving of the Mosaic law and the election of Saul which God did not approve (with the sole exception that during his lifetime Moses was set above the High Priest) all spiritual and temporal power was united in the hands of the High Priest, whereas the *Elements* take for granted that the spiritual power

[1] *De cive*, cap. 17, art. 13; *Leviathan*, ch. 35.

[2] *Elements*, Pt. II, ch. 9, § 2; *De cive*, cap. 13, art. 5.

[3] *Elements*, Pt. II, ch. 7, § 8; and Pt. I, ch. 11, § 9; *De cive*, cap. 17, art. 24; *Leviathan*, ch. 42 (pp. 286–90). Compare particularly the diametrically opposed interpretation of Acts xiv. 23 in the *Elements* and in the *Leviathan*. The interpretation given in *Elements*, Pt. II, ch. 7, § 8 is rejected in *Leviathan*, ch. 42 (p. 288 f.) as right only 'at first sight'.

[4] *Leviathan*, ch. 47 (p. 380 f.).

was subordinate to the secular for the whole period of the Old Covenant.[1] But this apparent contradiction of the general tendency of the *Elements* on the one hand and of the later presentations on the other, is explained by the fact that in the later writings Hobbes attaches much less value to conformity with the teachings of Scripture. That Scripture vouches for priestly rule is from now on not an argument for priestly rule, but an argument against Scripture. Thus the single apparent exception is in reality the strongest corroboration of the assertion that on the path from the *Elements* via *De cive* to the *Leviathan* Hobbes drew farther and farther away from the religious tradition. If one will, one may say that Hobbes kept pace in his way—which was not very edifying—with the development from Anglican Episcopalianism to Independentism (with a characteristic omission of Presbyterianism).[2]

In the earliest presentation of his political philosophy Hobbes is thus relatively close to Anglican Episcopalianism. But he was as little a believing Christian then as later. Only political considerations can have induced him to defend the episcopal constitution of the Church and for this very reason to speak more circumspectly on dogma than during the Civil War and under the Republic and the Protectorate. Hobbes's personal attitude to positive religion was at all times the same: religion must serve the State and is to be esteemed or despised according to the services or disservices rendered to the State. This view may be seen as early as the introduction to the translation of Thucydides. There Hobbes defends his author against the charge of atheism in the following words:

'In some places of his history he noteth the equivocation of the oracles; and yet he confirmeth an assertion of his own, touching the time this war lasted, by the oracle's prediction. He taxeth Nicias for being too punctual in the observation of the ceremonies of their religion, when he overthrew himself and his army, and indeed the whole dominion and liberty of his country, by it. Yet he commendeth him in another place for his worshipping of the gods. . . .

[1] *Elements*, Pt. II, ch. 6, § 2; *De cive*, cap. 16, art. 13–15; *Leviathan*, ch. 40 (pp. 254–8).
[2] Compare Hobbes's judgement of the Presbyterians in *Leviathan*, ch. 44 (p. 338) and ch. 47 (p. 377), and also *Behemoth*, pp. 21 ff. See also p. 116 f. below.

So that in his writings, our author appeareth to be, on the one side not superstitious, on the other side not an atheist.'[1]

The golden mean between atheism and superstition consists in subordination to the religion which is prescribed by the State and never comes into conflict with the State.

The fact that Hobbes accommodated not his unbelief but his utterances of that unbelief to what was permissible in a good, and, in addition, prudent subject[2] justifies the assumption that in the decades before the Civil War, and particularly in his humanist period, Hobbes for political reasons hid his true opinions and was mindful of the maintenance of theological convention, even more than in the *Elements*. This assumption is strengthened by a letter written in 1636 in which he says:

'I long infinitely to see those books of the Sabbaoth, and am of your mind they will put such thoughts into the heads of the vulgar people, as will confer little to their good life. For when they see one of the ten commandments to be jus humanum merely, (as it must be if the Church can alter it), they will hope also that the other nine may be so too. For every man hitherto did believe that the ten commandments were the moral, that is, the eternal law.'[3]

As early as the *Elements* there is no longer this assimilation of the Decalogue with the moral law.

In general one may say that Hobbes's original attitude to religion was identical with the one Clarendon attributes to the Marquis of Newcastle:

'He loved . . . the Church, as it was constituted for the splendour and security of the Crown; and religion, as it maintained and cherished the order and obedience that was necessary to both, without any other passion for the particular opinions which were grown

[1] *English Works*, vol. viii, p. xv. Because Hobbes says in the dedication to the translation of Thucydides: 'I end with this prayer: that it will please God to give you virtues suitable to the fair dwelling he hath prepared for them, and the happiness that such virtues lead unto both in and after this world', is naturally no ground for deducing what he believed at the time of writing these lines, for the dedication to *De cive* concludes with the same phrase.

[2] Cf. his frank observations in *Leviathan*, ch. 38 (p. 244) and Conclusion (p. 390), in *Opera latina*, vol. i, pp. xvi and xciv, vol. iii, p. 560; *English Works*, vol. iv, pp. 355 and 407.

[3] *English Works*, vol. vii, p. 454.

up in it and distinguished it into parties, than as he detested what-
soever was like to disturb the public peace.'[1]

Hobbes wrote the *Elements* at Newcastle's command, after he
had already communicated his political doctrine to Newcastle
in private conversation.[2] And we have seen that the *Elements*
defend a much more conservative ecclesiastical policy than do
the later writings.

What has been said is true only of Hobbes's attitude to
positive religion. As for natural religion, it is unlikely that he
was originally as sceptical of its possibility as he was later.
Later—to put it mildly—he considered any natural knowledge
of God which is more than the knowledge that a First Cause
exists, completely impossible. For that reason he systematically
excluded not only revealed theology but also natural theology
from philosophy. In order to hide the dangerous nature of
this scepticism, to keep up an appearance that he attacked only
scholastic theology and not the religion of the Scripture itself,
Hobbes fought his battle against natural theology in the name
of strict belief in the Scriptures[3] and at the same time under-
mines that belief by his historical and philosophical criticism
of the authority of the Scriptures. Thus an apparent progress
in his Biblicism would be an indication of the real progress in
his criticism of natural theology, and thus a proof that he
originally judged natural theology more favourably than later.
Such an apparent increase of his Biblicism may be established
with relation to several important doctrines. According to the
Elements, the binding force of natural law is based on natural
knowledge of God, according to the later presentations it is

---

[1] Quoted from S. R. Gardiner, *History of England*, vol. viii, p. 243 f.
[2] *Elements*, Ep. ded.
[3] Closer investigation shows that Hobbes's criticism of theological tradition, as far as it is alleged to be based on Scripture, was decisively influenced by the Socinians. Leibniz recognized this connexion (see his *Réflexions
sur le livre de Hobbes* . . . , § 2). It is open to doubt whether one may draw
conclusions as to the history of Hobbes's own development from the fact
that the most conservative part of Hobbes's criticism is of Socinian origin.
But it may be pointed out that his 'Art of Sophistry', i.e. the last part of
the shorter *Rhetoric*-digest (written about 1635, cf. p. 41, note 1, above)
is an imitation of Faustus Socinus's *Elenchi Sophistici* . . . *explicati, et
exemplis Theologicis illustrati* (Racoviae, 1625). About 1635 Hobbes was
friendly with Falkland, who was said to be a Socinian.

based on revelation.[1] The *Elements* and *De cive* still defend
the doctrine of the immortality of the soul, whereas the *Leviathan* replaces this philosophical doctrine by the resurrection
of the body in the name of the Scriptures.[2] The *Elements* bring
forward the proofs of the existence of God more emphatically
and in more detail than does the *Leviathan*; if one compares
the formulation of these two works, one positively begins to
suspect that in the *Leviathan* the argument is not seriously
meant. The connecting link in this case as so often is in *De
cive*, where Hobbes says that without revelation atheism is
almost inevitable.[3] Thus in this case also there are signs of
Hobbes's tendency, as his criticism of religion progresses, to
replace natural theology by a pretended revealed theology.
We may further recall that the traditional arguments for the
supremacy of monarchy, which are at least mentioned in the
earlier presentations, rest on assumptions of natural theology.
Finally: in the *Elements* there is a remark countering the 'supernaturalists'' hostility to reason, to which there is practically no
parallel in the later works.[4] Later Hobbes fought his battle
against supernaturalism expressly, if only apparently, in the
name and with the weapons of supernaturalism, while his real
basis was materialism. In the beginning he could fight supernaturalism openly as supernaturalism because his arguments
were based on natural theology and thus on a point of view
which even in the least favourable case is incomparably closer
to revealed religion than is materialism. But Hobbes must have
broken relatively early with natural theology. At all events, as
early as 1641 in his correspondence with Descartes he defends
the conclusions of his materialism with reference to God and
the soul exactly as he did later. What we assume is only that

---

[1] *Elements*, Pt. I, ch. 17, § 12; *De cive*, cap. 3, art. 33; *Leviathan*, ch. 15, *in fine*.

[2] See p. 72 above.

[3] 'Habet hoc humanum genus, ab imbecillitatis propriae conscientia, et admiratione eventuum naturalium, ut plerique credant esse omnium rerum visibilium Opificem invisibilem Deum. . . Caeterum, ut eum recte colerent imperfectus usus rationis, et affectuum vehementia obstitere. . . . Hominibus itaque sine speciali Dei auxilio, utrumque scopulum effugere Atheismum et superstitionem, pene erat impossibile.' *De cive*, cap. 16, art. 1. Cf. *Elements*, Pt. I, ch. 11, § 2, and *Leviathan*, ch. 11 (p. 53) and ch. 12 (p. 55).

[4] *Elements*, Pt. I, ch. 18, § 12. Cf. *De cive*, cap. 12, art. 6.

before the complete elaboration of his materialism[1] and particularly during his humanist period, when he had not yet freed himself from the authority of Aristotle, he in principle recognized natural theology.

[1] In a letter to the Earl of Newcastle, written in 1636, he characterized Herbert of Cherbury's *De veritate* as 'a high point'. See Historical MSS. Commission, 13*th Report*, Appendix, Pt. II, p. 128.

VI

HISTORY

THE result of our investigation so far is that Hobbes's early moral and political views may, in the main, be traced back to the Aristotelian tradition, as it had been modified in the course of the sixteenth century. In so far as this is the case, those views are, at the most, materials of his political philosophy and by no means its germ. For his later theory is in systematic and express contrast to Aristotelianism however understood. Even if one may say that the fairly considerable modifications of Aristotelianism which Hobbes from the outset considered necessary, or took over as a matter of course, prepare the way for the later break with Aristotelianism, nevertheless a sense of a fundamental defect in Aristotelian philosophy, and in traditional philosophy generally, was necessary for this break. This sense made it impossible to leave the matter at a modification of Aristotelianism and forced Hobbes to understand and elaborate these modifications as systematic objections. Now, this deep dissatisfaction with traditional philosophy is latent in the turning away from philosophy to history which characterizes Hobbes's humanist period. In contrast to the traditional elements in his original position, which have so far engaged us, the function which history has in his early thought is revolutionary.

Our point of departure was that Hobbes turned to history with philosophic intentions. But precisely this fact is for the time being incomprehensible. If Hobbes held the moral and political views which we have tried to analyse in the preceding sections, it would have been natural for a philosopher such as he was first of all to give a coherent account and presentation of these views. Why then does he turn from the study of philosophy to the study of history? In which sense was this course decided by *alia ratio philosophandi*?

One may gather the following answer from the introduction to the translation of Thucydides. Philosophy and history are fundamentally different. Philosophy lays down precepts for

the right behaviour of men. But precepts are not nearly so
effective as examples. To widen man's experience by the
narration of examples which show how precept was followed
or disregarded and the success or failure which resulted and
thus more effectively than by the communication of precepts,
to make man capable of applying the precepts in the individual case—is the task of history. History, not philosophy,
gives man prudence.[1]

The authority of philosophy, of Aristotelian philosophy, remains unchallenged by this answer. Hobbes unquestioningly
takes it for granted that this philosophy rightly states the norms
for human actions; or at least he does not contest it. Even the
completion of philosophy by history which he demands may
perfectly well be ranged under Aristotelian philosophy. Practical wisdom is, if not the sufficient reason, at least the indispensable condition, for moral virtue; such wisdom is gained by
experience.[2] And nothing prevents the study of history, which
widens the experience of the individual beyond his own horizon
and age, from service to the acquisition of wisdom and thus
from service to moral education. What is irreconcilable with
Aristotle's *Ethics* is simply and solely the doubt cast on the
effectiveness of precept as such. Aristotle does not deny, he
even explicitly states, that rational precepts have no influence
on most men. But according to his view, what is true of most
men is not by any means true of free and noble-minded characters who love honour; they obey precepts.[3] As Hobbes doubts

[1] ' . . . the principal and proper work of history (is) to instruct and enable
men, by the knowledge of actions past, to bear themselves prudently in
the present and providently towards the future . . . ' *English Works*, vol.
viii, p. vii. ' . . . the nature (of history) is merely narrative . . . look how
much a man of understanding might have added to his experience, if he
had then lived a beholder of their proceedings, and familiar with the men
and business of the time: so much almost may he profit now, by attentive
reading of the same here [*sc*. in Thucydides] written. He may from the
narrations draw out lessons to himself . . .' Loc. cit., p. viii. 'Digressions
for instruction's cause, and other such open conveyances of precepts, (which
is the philosopher's part), he [*sc*. Thucydides] never useth; as having so
clearly set before men's eyes the ways and events of good and evil counsels,
that the narration itself doth secretly instruct the reader, and more effectually
than can possibly be done by precept.' Loc. cit., p. xxii.

[2] *Eth. Nicom.* vi. 13 (1144^{b}17 ff.) and vi. 8 (1142^{a}14 ff.).

[3] Loc. cit., x. 10 (1179^{b}3 ff.)

the effectiveness of precept altogether—does he not assert the impotence of reason with reference to all men, that is, as a principle?—must we not conclude that the impotence of reason was established for him even before he engaged in natural science?

This much may be said now: the question, by which history originally breaks into philosophy, is the question of the effectiveness of rational precept. It is to be noted that only the effectiveness, and not the rightness, of these precepts is called into question; it is purely a matter of the application of precept. This casts light at least on the *conditio sine qua non* of Hobbes's turning to history. The precepts, on whose rightness no doubt is cast, are in fact the precepts that were handed down by Aristotelian ethics. Because the formulation and the explanation of these precepts had been fully and adequately completed by Aristotle, because the primary philosophic problem had been solved, because its solution had become a matter of course, because of all this a philosopher like Hobbes had the leisure and the opportunity to give thought to the secondary problem of the application of the precepts.

Thus the problem is only the application of precepts duly handed down by the philosophic tradition. And in reference to the application the assertion is made that the precepts are not effective in themselves, that they are not followed for their own sake, but that under all circumstances—even in the case of noble natures—other measures must be taken to ensure their being followed. Aristotle characterizes the laws as such a measure—with particular reference to the general run of men. The necessity and effectiveness of laws is, of course, not questioned by Hobbes. But now the teachings to be drawn from history slip in as it were midway between the precepts of philosophy and the laws.[1] If the efficacy of those precepts is denied altogether, and if, on the other hand, it is still recognized that the laws have in view particularly 'the greater part of men', it follows that the teaching to be drawn from history

---

[1] ' . . . (history) doth things with more grace and modestie then the civill lawes and ordinances do: because it is more grace for a man to teach and instruct, then to chastise or punish.' Amiot's preface to Plutarch's *Lives* (quoted from Sir Thomas North's translation).

has from now on to fulfil the function for noble natures which, according to Aristotle, was the task of philosophic precepts. The teachings of history replace the precepts of philosophy in the education of the aristocracy.[1]

In order to understand Hobbes's intention aright, we must glance back at his predecessors. In the introduction to his translation of Thucydides he names as his authorities for his views on history Cicero (*De oratore*), Lucian (*Quomodo historia scribenda sit*), and Justus Lipsius (*Politica sive civilis doctrina*). Through Cicero and Lucian he is in touch with the rhetorical tradition, which, in contrast to the philosophical tradition and not without a certain amount of criticism of the philosophic tradition, had always urged the necessity of a study of the historians. Not to mention Cicero's praise of history, 'Historia vero testis temporum, lux veritatis, vita memoriae, magistra vitae, nuntia vetustatis',[2] which was always being quoted in the sixteenth and seventeenth centuries, we read in Quintilian:

'Neque ea solum, quae talibus disciplinis [*sc.* in philosophy] continentur, sed magis etiam, quae sunt tradita antiquitus dicta ac facta praeclare, et nosse et animo semper agitare conveniet. Quae profecto nusquam plura maioraque quam in nostrae civitatis monumentis reperientur. An fortitudinem, iustitiam, fidem, continentiam, frugalitatem, contemptum doloris ac mortis melius alii docebunt quam Fabricii, Curii, Reguli, Decii, Mucii aliique innumerabiles? Quantum enim Graeci praeceptis valent, tantum Romani, quod est maius, exemplis.'[3]

The opposition of philosophic precept and historical example, based on the doubt of the efficacy of precept, recurs again and again in the literature on the subject in the sixteenth century.[4]

---

[1] See p. 44 above.

[2] *De oratore*, ii. 9. 36. Cf. *De legibus*, i. 1. 4–2. 5.

[3] *Instit. orat.* xii. 2. 29–30.

[4] Thus Thomas Blundeville in his *True order and Methode of wryting and reading Hystories* (London, 1574) says: 'The way to come to (the inward peace of the heart), is partly taught by the Philosophers in generall precepts and rules, but the historiographers doe teach it much more plainlye by particular examples and experiences, and specially if they be written with that order, diligence, and judgement, that they ought to be.' Amiot says in the preface to *Plutarch*: ' . . . These things (History) doth with much greater grace, efficacie, and speed, then the books of morall Philosophie do: forasmuch as examples are of more force to move and instruct, then

But the same thought can be variously interpreted. It need only mean: we must attribute to a regrettable shortcoming on the part of the majority of men that they do not obey the precepts of philosophy, that they do not love virtue for itself, but for its reward, which is praise.[1] Doubt of the efficacy of precept can also mean that the true motive of virtue is honour and glory and that virtue is essentially aristocratic virtue. In this case the connexion with history becomes still closer. In his actions the aristocrat is swayed by the thought of his honour and glory, i.e. particularly by the thought of the survival of his deeds in history, and this thought is constantly strengthened by memories of the great deeds of Caesar, Alexander, Scipio, Hannibal, &c., which are handed down by the historians.[2] As a result of the close connexion between history and honour or glory, the more virtue is envisaged as aristocratic virtue, the keener will be the interest in history, an interest already favoured by the renascence of the rhetorical tradition.

Besides Cicero and Lucian, in the introduction to his translation of Thucydides, Hobbes quotes Justus Lipsius as authority for his views on history. Through Lipsius's political philosophy Hobbes is in touch with the systematic turning of political philosophy, and of philosophy altogether, to history, which took place in the sixteenth century. This turning is shown by the fact that now for the first time the methodic study of history is demanded. It is now discovered that classical authors who wrote on the writing of history so treat their theme *ut nec historiae quidem definitionem ex iis possis contexere.*[3] What is felt as a lack is not so much the scientific writing of history—it is recognized that from all time histories have been written which are adequate for every possible demand

are the arguments and proofes of reason, or their precise precepts, because examples be the verie formes of our deedes, and accompanied with all circumstances. Whereas reasons and demonstrations are generall, and tend to the proofe of things, and to the beating of them into understanding: and examples tend to the shewing of them in practise and execution, because they do not onely declare what is to be done, but also worke a desire to do it . . .' Cf. also Sir Thomas Elyot's *Governour*, Book III, ch. 25.

[1] See p. 84 below, note 1.

[2] Castiglione, loc. cit., p. 70.

[3] J. N. Stupanus in his preface to Franc. Patricius's *De legendae scribendaeque historiae ratione*, Basel, 1570.

—not even directions for the writing of history, but above all methodical reading, methodical utilization of the histories already in existence. History is to serve as material for a new study. The material offered by the historians is to be methodically read and methodically sifted with a view to the teaching which may be gained for the right ordering of human actions.[1]

[1] '. . . certe philosophia, quae ipsa vitae dux appellatur, propositis bonorum ac malorum finibus intermortua iaceret, nisi ad rerum praeteritarum historias omnia dicta, facta, consilia revocarentur: ex quibus non solum praesentia commode explicantur, sed etiam futura colliguntur, certissimaque rerum expetendarum ac fugiendarum praecepta conflantur. Itaque mirum mihi visum est in tanta scriptorum multitudine, tamque eruditis temporibus adhuc fuisse neminem, qui maiorum nostrorum claras historias inter se, et cum rebus gestis antiquorum compararet. id autem fieri commode poterat, si collectis omnibus humanarum actionum generibus, ad haec exemplorum varietas apte et suo quicque loco accomodaretur: ut ii qui se flagitiis penitus dedidissent, justissimis maledictis proscinderentur: qui autem ulla virtute claruissent, suo merito laudarentur. hic enim historiarum fructus est vel maximus, ut alii quidem ad virtutem inflammari, alii a vitiis deterreri possint. tametsi enim boni per se laudabiles sunt etiam si a nemine laudentur, nihilominus tamen praeter ea quae virtuti praemia proponuntur, hunc etiam laudis fructum, quem plerique solum ducunt, vivos ac mortuos consequi par est . . .' I. Bodin, *Methodus ad facilem historiarum cognitionem* (Paris, 1566), pp. 1–2. '. . . Quare cum ab historia penitus erudiamur, non solum artes ad vitam degendam necessarias, verumetiam quae omnino sunt expetenda, quae fugienda, quid turpe, quid honestum, quae optimae leges, quae optima Respublica, quae beata vita: postremo cum sublata historia Dei cultus, religiones, oracula temporum decursu tollantur: huius ego *scientiae* utilitate incredibili ad hanc scriptionem adductus sum, cum magnam historicorum ubertatem et copiam animadverterem non deesse, *qui tamen historiae artem ac methodum tradidisset, fuisse neminem*: ac plerosque temere, et sine ordine miscere historias, nullosque ex iis percipere fructus. antea quidem fuere nonnulli qui de instituenda historia libros scripserunt: quam sapienter non disputo. habent illi fortasse sui consilii causam probabilem. mihi tamen si judicium ferre liceat, consimiliter facere videntur, ut medici nonnulli, qui omni genere medicamentorum aegrotanti proposito, rursus de medicina facienda disputant, nec earum quae tot ac tam multae proponuntur, vim aut naturam docere morbisque praesentibus accomodare conantur: sic illi quoque de scribenda historia libros instituunt, cum pleni sint omnes omnium antiquitatum libri, plenae bibliothecae historicorum, quos utilius ad intuendum et ad imitandum proponere potuissent, quam de exordiis, narrationibus, verborum ac sententiarum luminibus oratorie disputare. Ut igitur aliquam doctrinae viam habeat hoc quicquid est quod de historica methodo scribere aggredimur, principio historiam partiemur ac definiemus . . .' Loc. cit., p. 8. 'Et quoniam triplex illud historiarum genus (*sc.* historia humana, naturalis et divina) viri graves et eruditi accurate scriptis mandarunt, illud tantum mihi proposui, ut in iis legendis, ac studiose diiudicandis ordinem et modum servarem; praesertim in historia rerum humanarum.' Loc. cit., p. 11.

The new study is concerned with the historicity of its material
only for this reason—that the only clear knowledge of the
application of the norms which obtain for human action is the
knowledge of actions which have taken place in the past.[1] It
is truth that is sought in this study, as in the writing of history.
In that it is at one with philosophy. Its distinction from philosophy lies in the fact that philosophy seeks general precepts,
while the study of history seeks the application and realization
of precepts, the conditions and results of that realization. And
for the reason by which philosophy and history are coupled,
they are both fundamentally different from poetry. For while
the main object of poetry is to give pleasure, philosophy and
history are both serious.[2] As late as the *Leviathan*, Hobbes
recognizes this pre-eminence of history over poetry. Charac-
teristically deviating from Aristotle's preference for the 'more
philosophical' poetry to history, as well as from Bacon's classification of knowledge into history, poetry, and philosophy,
Hobbes names history and philosophy as the two fundamental
branches of human knowledge.[3]

If the object of history is 'to instruct and enable men, to
bear themselves prudently in the present and providently
towards the future',[4] undertaking a methodic utilization of

[1] ' . . . in history, actions of honour and dishonour do appear plainly
and distinctly, which are which; but in the present age they are so disguised
that few there be, and those very careful, that be not grossly mistaken in
them.' *English Works*, vol. viii, p. vi.

[2] '(Historia) eosdem casus et humanas miserias serio explicatas continet,
quae in tragoediis ficta proponuntur.' Patricius, loc. cit., p. 165. Philosophers and historians both have as their task 'to tell things as they were done
without either augmenting or diminishing them, or swarving one iote from
the truth.' Blundeville, loc. cit. History 'doth things with greater weight
and gravitie, then the inventions and devises of the Poets: because it helpeth
not it selfe with anie other thing then with the plaine truth, whereas Poetry
doth commonly enrich things by commending them above the starres and
their deserving, because the chiefe intent thereof is to delight.' Amiot,
loc. cit. ' . . . molliores illas artes Musicen et Poesin sperno aut certe non
exigo.' Lipsius, *Politic*, i. 10, notae. ' . . . in truth consisteth the soul . . .
of history'. Hobbes, *English Works*, vol. viii, p. xx. '(Dionysius Halicar-
nassius) is contrary to the opinion of all men that ever spake of this subject
besides himself, and to common sense. For he makes the scope of history,
not profit by writing truth, but delight of the hearer, as if it were a song.'
Loc. cit., p. xxvi. See also Grotius, *De jure belli ac pacis*, Prolegg., §§ 46–7.

[3] *Leviathan*, ch. 9. Cf. also ch. 8 (p. 33 f.).

[4] *English Works*, vol. viii, p. vii.

history implies that a methodic education for prudence is aimed at. Education for prudence is not to be left to the experience of the individual, with all its chances, but, by placing the whole available experience of mankind at our disposal, chance is as far as possible to be excluded. That is to say, prudence is not so much to be furthered by methodical training, as it is actually to be replaced by the new study. To the question 'How is one to behave in this individual case?', one is no longer to receive the Aristotelian answer of how a sensible man would behave, but one receives for the particular case at least approximately adequate instructions, 'Receipts', by concrete maxims, gained from the study of history.

Because the study of history aims at training in prudence, words and deeds are less important to that study than aims, or, to put it more accurately, words and actions are important only in reference to aims. Through history the reader is to be taught which kinds of aims are salutary or destructive. It is the lack of a study of the aims that Bodin particularly deplores in historical investigation up to his time.[1] And it is precisely on the aims that Hobbes lays all emphasis in the introduction to his translation of Thucydides.[2]

The systematic transformation of philosophic interest, which brought about the turning to history, finds its most complete expression in Bacon's philosophy.[3] Bacon starts from the pre-

---

[1] '. . . nonnulli dicta factaque illustrium virorum, sed tenuiter admodum et sine ordine scripserunt . . . consilia vero ne attigerunt quidem, cum tamen in unius consilio saepe salus Reipublicae posita sit.' Loc. cit., p. 24 f. Cf. Cicero, *De oratore*, ii. 15. 63.

[2] '. . . conjectures at the secret aims and inward cogitations of such as fall under (the historiographer's) pen . . . is also none of the least virtues in a history, where conjecture is thoroughly grounded . . .' '(The attentive reader of Thucydides) may from the narrations draw out lessons to himself, and of himself be able to trace the drifts and counsels of the actors to their seat.' 'I saw that, for the greatest part, men came to the reading of history with an affection much like that of the people in Rome: who came to the spectacle of the gladiators with more delight to behold their blood, than their skill in fencing. For they be far more in number, that love to read of great armies, bloody battles, and many thousands slain at once, than that mind the art by which the affairs both of armies and cities be conducted to their ends.' *English Works*, vol. viii, p. viii f. Cf. also loc. cit., p. xxii (see above, p. 80, note 1). Hobbes is guided by the same view in his history of the Civil War; see *Behemoth*, p. 45.

[3] In the following remarks we are considering only Bacon's programme

miss that moral philosophy as the theory of virtue and duty has been perfectly worked out by classical philosophy. In his opinion, the fundamental shortcoming of ancient philosophy is that it limits itself to a description of 'the nature of good', to the 'heroical descriptions of virtue, duty, and felicity', and that it has neglected the other and no less important part of morals, 'concerning the husbandry and tillage (of the mind)', 'prescribing rules how to subdue, apply, and accommodate the will of man (unto the good)'.[1] Just because Bacon has in mind methodical and scientific guidance for the realization and application of precept, a number of themes, which classical philosophy treated cursorily or not at all, become central. Such themes are: 'the several characters and tempers of men's natures and dispositions';[2] the 'impressions of nature, which are imposed upon the mind by the sex, by the age, by the region . . . and again those which are caused by extern fortune', which 'are touched a little by Aristotle, . . . but they were never incorporated into moral philosophy, to which they do essentially appertain';[3] the passions: 'And here again I find it strange, as before, that Aristotle should have written divers volumes of ethics, and never handled the affections, which is the principal subject thereof; and yet in his Rhetorics . . . he findeth place for them, and handleth them well for the quantity; but where their true place is, he pretermitteth them. . . . Better travails, I suppose, had the Stoics taken in this argument. . . .

of moral philosophy. But it may be mentioned in passing that his criticism of traditional physics has the same motive, i.e. interest in application, as his criticism of traditional moral philosophy.

[1] 'In the handling of this science (sc. moral science), those which have written seem to me to have done as if a man, that professed to teach to write, did only exhibit fair copies of alphabets and letters joined, without giving any precepts or directions for the carriage of the hand and framing of the letters. So have they made good and fair examples and copies, carrying the draughts and portraitures of good, virtue, duty, felicity, propounding them well described as the true objects and scopes of man's will and desires. But how to attain these excellent marks, and how to frame and subdue the will of man to become true and comfortable to these pursuits, they pass it over altogether, or slightly and unprofitably.' *Works*, ed. Spedding and Ellis, vol. iii, p. 418. 'But allowing (Aristotle's) conclusion, that virtues and vices consist in habit, he ought so much the more to have taught the manner of superinducing that habit.' Loc. cit., p. 439. Cf. also p. 419 f.

[2] Loc. cit., p. 434 f.   [3] Ibid., p. 436 f.

But yet, it is like, it was after their manner, rather in subtility of definitions . . . than in active and ample descriptions and observations';[1] further, 'the wisdom touching negotiation and business', 'wisdom of counsel and advice';[2] further, 'fortune, as an organ of virtue and merit, deserveth the consideration';[3] and finally there has as yet been no branch of legal knowledge, taking as its field not so much the 'platform of justice' as 'the application thereof'.[4] All these disciplines, which, according to Bacon's contention, have as yet been insufficiently treated or even wholly ignored, take as their subject the application of moral precepts. As Bacon expressly says of a particular desideratum—a doctrine of the vices peculiar to the individual vocations—but as he thinks in all cases, they will seek not what men ought to do, but what men really do. They will not consider the good, but 'all forms and natures of evil', or, more generally, the matter of virtue, in order to find wise maxims for the creation and protection of virtue.[5] Traditional philosophy does not offer even the material of these disciplines. One finds this material rather in 'history, poesy, and daily experience',[6] and history can claim pre-eminence over poetry and individual experience.[7] It is thus primarily history which offers the material from which 'receipts might be made . . . for use of life'.[8] The neglect of history is therefore one of the

---

[1] *Works*, ed. Spedding and Ellis, vol. iii, p. 437. Compare also Descartes's judgement: 'Il n'y a *rien* en quoi paraisse mieux combien les sciences que nous avons des anciens sont défectueuses, qu'en ce qu'ils ont écrit des passions.' *Les passions de l'âme*, art. 1. Cf. also Spinoza, *Ethica*, III, praef.

[2] Loc. cit., p. 447 f.   [3] Ibid., p. 456.   [4] Ibid., p. 475 f.

[5] ' . . . there belongeth further to the handling of this part, touching the duties of professions and vocations, a relative or opposite, touching the frauds, cautels, impostures, and vices of every profession . . . the managing of this argument with integrity and truth, which I note as deficient, seemeth to me to be one of the best fortifications for honesty and virtue that can be planted. . . . So that we are much beholden to Machiavel and others, that write what men do, and not what they ought to do. For it is not possible to join serpentine wisdom with columbine innocency, except men know exactly all the conditions of the serpent . . . that is, all forms and natures of evil: for without this, virtue lieth open and unfenced.' Loc. cit., p. 430 f. The reference to Macchiavelli's programme (15th chapter of *Il Principe*) shows the direction and the lines which further investigation of the origins of the modern interest in history should take.

[6] Loc. cit., pp. 435 and 438.

[7] Ibid., pp. 453 and 271.   [8] Ibid., p. 435.

most weighty reasons for the inadequacy and uselessness of scholasticism.[1] Just as did Bodin, Bacon considers not so much the writing of history, as the philosophical utilization of history, as the need. Certainly as a result of the systematic turning to the problems of application, and therefore to history, the tasks set to history are widened; Bacon makes a plea for history of literature, which part of history had as yet been neglected. This branch of history should also serve the purpose of making men wise.[2] Bacon particularly desires a collection of the theories of the various philosophers, but not in the style of the classical doxography 'by titles packed and fagotted up together, as hath been done by Plutarch', but 'the philosophies of everyone throughout by themselves': 'For it is the harmony of a philosophy in itself which giveth it light and credence; whereas if it be singled and broken, it will seem more foreign and dissonant.'[3] The reason for this enhanced interest in all branches of history—most clearly seen in Bacon's case—is the enhanced interest in the problems of application. This interest is the motive of the study of history, as it is of the direct study of characters, passions, temperaments, humours, &c.,[4] in a word, the study of man as he really is, which study, according to Bacon's contention, was neglected by traditional philosophy in favour of the study—which he admits to be primary—of man as he ought to be.

The fact that a philosopher such as Bacon should make himself the advocate of philosophy's turning to history lightens

[1] Ibid., p. 285.

[2] 'History is natural, civil, ecclesiastical, and literary; whereof the first three I allow as extant, the fourth I note as deficient. For no man hath propounded to himself the general state of learning to be described and represented from age to age . . . without which the history of the world seemeth to me to be as the statua of Polyphemus with his eye out; that part being wanting which doth most shew the spirit and life of the person. . . . The use and end of which work I do not so much design for curiosity and satisfaction of those that are the lovers of learning, but chiefly for a more serious and grave purpose; which is this in few words, that it will make learned men wise in the *use and administration* of learning. For it is not St. Augustine's nor St. Ambrose's works that will make so wise a divine, as ecclesiastical history, thoroughly read and observed; and the same reason is of learning.' Loc. cit., p. 329 f.

[3] Loc. cit., p. 365 f.

[4] Compare the mention of these themes in Hobbes's introduction to his translation of Thucydides. *English Works*, vol. viii, p. xxix f.

the difficulty of answering the question 'What assumptions are involved in such turning?' The first reason why history becomes, if not the theme of philosophy, at least most important material for philosophy, seems to be that philosophic interest is shifting from physics and metaphysics to morals and politics; for 'eam praecipue philosophiae partem, quae vitam et mores informat, iuvari historiâ posse arbitramur'.[1] According to Aristotle's assertion, this change of interest takes place as soon as man is considered the highest being in the world.[2] If, however, one looks back to Plato, to whom moral and political problems are of incomparably greater importance than to Aristotle, and who yet no less than Aristotle raised his gaze away from man to the eternal order, one must hold that it is not the conviction of man's superiority to all existing creatures but the conviction of the transcendence of good over all being which is the reason why philosophic investigation begins with the ethical and political problem, with the question of the right life and the right society.[3] This retrospect to Plato at the same time makes clear that the shift of interest from natural philosophy to political philosophy, taken in itself, cannot possibly be the reason why philosophy turns to history. This turn is caused not by the enhanced interest in the question of the good and of the best form of State; but by the enhanced interest in man. This enhanced interest in man is shown in the case of Bacon by his compressing the traditional disciplines, Logic, Ethics, Politics, and Medicine, into one science of man; this science of man, as 'knowledge of ourselves, which deserveth the more accurate handling, by how much it toucheth us more nearly', is from now on to be distinguished as 'reflected' knowledge from 'direct' knowledge of nature.[4] The division of philosophy into natural philosophy and human philosophy is based

[1] A. Riccoboni, *De historia* (Basel, 1579), p. 74.

[2] See above, p. 35.

[3] Cf. W. Jaeger, *Ueber Ursprung und Kreislauf des philosophischen Lebensideals*, Sitzungsberichte der Preussischen Akademie der Wissenschaften, 1928, p. 409.

[4] ' . . . the . . . beams of man's knowledge; that is, radius directus, which is referred to nature . . . radius reflexus, whereby man beholdeth and contemplateth himself.' Bacon, loc. cit., p. 366. 'I do take the consideration in general and at large of human nature to be fit to be emancipate and made a knowledge by itself . . .' Loc. cit., p. 367.

on the systematic distinction between man and the world,
which Bacon makes in express controversy against ancient
philosophy.[1] The more man is considered 'the most excellent
work of nature',[2] the more does man, instead of the eternal
order which transcends man, become the central theme of
philosophy. Consequently, there is an increasing tendency to
take the 'superhuman' character (recognized by the founders of
the philosophic tradition) of the contemplative life[3]—the life
which is devoted to contemplating and understanding the
eternal order which transcends man—as a reason against the
contemplative life. An ideal is sought, with the realization of
which man does not transcend his humanity, but remains man,
a sensual-rational being.[4] That is—compared with the ideal of
the contemplative life—a more popular ideal. An ideal of this
kind seems to be moral virtue, which Aristotle designated as
that virtue which is becoming to man in his sensual-rational
nature. But the substitution of the ideal of contemplation by

[1] ' . . . the works of God . . . show the omnipotency and wisdom of the
Maker, but not his image: and therefore therein the heathen opinion
differeth from the sacred truth; for they supposed the world to. be the
image of God, and man to be an exact or compendious image of the world,
but the Scriptures never vouchsafe to attribute to the world that honour,
as to be the image of God, but only the work of His hands; neither do
they speak of any other image of God, but man . . .' Loc. cit., p. 349 f.
' . . . the forms of substances, man only except . . . are so perplexed, as
they are not to be inquired . . .' Loc. cit., p. 355.
[2] *Leviathan*, Introduction.
[3] See particularly *Eth. Nicom.* x. 7 (1177^b33 ff.).
[4] ' . . . sed quoniam vita civilis eget actione perpetua, nec potest in contemplatione tota civitas occupari: ut neque corpus ipsum aut animae
vires omnes intelligere: non erit hominis et totius civitatis eadem
felicitas, si sola contemplatione bonum definiamus: id quod Aristotelem
valde conturbavit, nec seipsum ex ea difficultate explicare potuit . . . neque
enim mens pura illa contemplatione prius frui potest, quam a corpore
penitus avulsa fuerit.' Bodin, loc. cit., p. 32. ' . . . those infinite disputations
. . . touching . . . felicity, beatitude, or the highest good . . . are by the
Christian faith discharged. And as Aristotle saith, That young men may
be happy, but not otherwise but by hope; so we must all acknowledge our
minority, and embrace the felicity which is by hope of the future world.'
Bacon, loc. cit., p. 419. 'It decideth the question touching the preferment
of the contemplative or active life; and decideth it against Aristotle . . .
men must know, that in this theatre of man's life it is reserved only for
God and angels to be lookers on . . .' Loc. cit., p. 421. In one of those
chapters in his *Politics* (i. 10), which treat of the benefits of history, Lipsius
demands that men shall keep the *modus sapientiae*.

moral virtue still fails to explain the turn of philosophy to
history. One sign is that the contemplative life has frequently
been challenged in the name of the norm of life set forth in
the Bible, without any enhanced interest in history as such
developing immediately from the challenge. Not the substitution of the contemplative ideal by moral virtue, in particular by the Biblical demands for justice and charity, but the
systematic doubt of the efficacy of precept, which is added to
this substitution, is the reason why philosophy turns to history.
We cannot here investigate whether the conviction of the in-
efficacy of precept, of the impotence of reason, is immediately
connected with the shifting of interest from the transcendent
order to man. It must suffice to emphasize that Bacon, no less
than his predecessors, doubts the efficacy of rational precepts.
The ancient philosophers, he says, 'fortified and entrenched
(virtue and duty), as much as discourse can do, against corrupt
and popular opinions'.[1] But this is not enough; for

'to show (virtue) to reason only in subtility of argument, was a
thing ever derided in Chrysippus and many of the Stoics; who
thought to trust virtue upon men by sharp disputations and conclusions, which have no sympathy with the will of man . . . if the
affections in themselves were pliant and obedient to reason, it were
true there should be no great use of persuasions and insinuations
to the will, more than of naked propositions and proofs; but in
regard of the continual mutinies and seditions of the affections . . .
reason would become captive and servile, if eloquence of persuasions
did not practise and win the imagination from the affections' part,
and contract a confederacy between the reason and imagination
against the affections.'[2]

But in order to hold the passions in check, one must not only
deprive them of the support of the imagination, but it is also
necessary to exploit the conflict of the passions among themselves for the purpose of conquering them. We must observe
how the passions 'do fight and encounter one with another . . .
this . . is of special use in moral and civil matters; how, I
say, to set affection against affection, and to master one by
another; even as we use to hunt beast with beast, and fly bird
with bird, which otherwise percase we could not so easily

---

[1] Loc. cit., p. 420.   [2] Loc. cit., p. 410.

recover . . .' Of this science 'the poets and writers of histories
are the best doctors'.[1]

The reason for the turning of philosophy to history is thus
the conviction of the impotence of reason, added to the enhanced interest in man. What is to be understood by the
impotence of reason is not the incapacity to establish or justify
norms. That reason is capable of this, is universally taken for
granted, particularly by Bacon; and even when this capacity
is contested, when the establishment of norms is expected not
of reason, but of revelation, the difficulty which leads to the
study of history would still remain. For it is not the way in
which precepts are given to man, whether by reason or by
revelation, but the fact that man does not obey the transcendent
norm, whether it be rational or revealed, which is the reason of
the study of history. History is taken up to remedy man's dis-
obedience. Historical examples are to make obedience easier.[2]
Bacon goes farther. He demands a technique based on induction from experience of life and particularly from history,
which would enable men to fulfil the precepts. Thus obedience
is evaded. In this case, in principle, the precedence of obedience
over every other, every selfish motive remains acknowledged.
If, however, aristocratic virtue takes the place of truly moral
virtue, obedience is replaced by honour.[3] But it was in the long
run impossible—for reasons which must be touched upon in
the next chapter—to leave the matter at aristocratic virtue. In
its turn aristocratic virtue is replaced by the identification of
virtue with prudence. We cannot here give more than this indication of the further development of modern moral philosophy
and the interest in history which is an integral part of it.[4] It

[1] Loc. cit., p. 438. See also p. 346. With the thesis here quoted Bacon
anticipates Spinoza's well-known theory; cf. *Ethica*, iv, propp. 7 and 14.

[2] ' . . . non facile assentiremur philosophis, qui praecipiunt patriae
utilitatem spectandam, et fidem, ac religionem sanctissime servandam,
proque iis dolores, et cruciatus omnes corporis perpetiendos, nisi accepisse-
mus quendam fuisse quondam hominem, incredibili animi robore praeditum,
qui captus a Poenis . . .' Riccoboni, loc. cit., p. 76.

[3] That honour is to replace obedience, of which man is not capable, is
indicated by Hobbes in *Leviathan*, ch. 14 (p. 73), quoted on p. 24 f. above.

[4] It may be in point to refer here to the connexion between Hegel's
philosophy of history and his criticism of the morality of obedience, and to
recall the connexion in Max Weber's theory between the 'responsibility-
ethic' and the study of history (see Max Weber, *Gesammelte Aufsätze zur*

must suffice to state that the development, at least in the sixteenth century, justifies the assertion that the reason why philosophy turned to history is the repression of the morality of obedience.[1]

Bacon clearly distinguishes between philosophic knowledge of the precepts, the norms, on the one hand, and, on the other, the knowledge of the technique of application, which is based on induction, especially from history. As long as this distinction, and with it, the primacy of the norms over application, is recognized, there is at least implicitly and in principle a recognition of the pre-eminence of obedience over every other motive for action. The situation is quite different if history is to lead not merely to the application of norms already established, but in the first place to the discovery of the norms themselves. For a consideration of history, induction from history, can lead to discovery of the norms only in one way— that it teaches one to distinguish between aims which justify themselves and lead to success, and aims which come to grief. The 'receipts' to be gained from history bear only on success or failure, not on moral goodness or baseness. If discovery of the norms is in any way expected from history, then—explicitly or implicitly—moral goodness must have been identified with success, and virtue with prudence. The anticipation that the study of history would lead to discovery of the norms is expressed with particular energy by Bodin; he says: 'ab historia penitus (erudimur), non solum artes ad vitam degendam necessarias, verumetiam quae omnino sunt expetenda, quae fugienda, quid turpe, quid honestum, quae optimae leges, quae optima Respublica, quae beata vita'.[2] For this reason history is 'incredibly useful'. Its significance is all the greater, as it is the easiest of all the arts and sciences; it requires no particular training and education to understand history. This extremely popular

Wissenschaftslehre, Tübingen, 1922, pp. 467 and 549, and also W. Brock, *An Introduction to Contemporary German Philosophy*, Cambridge, 1935, p. 39 f.).

[1] Hobbes's own development shows in another way that this is the case: the more virtue in general coincides with obedience to the law of the State, the more does history fall into the background; for the history of kings implies in principle that subjects criticize their sovereign, and thus threatens unconditional obedience.   [2] Loc. cit., p. 8.

character, far from impairing the dignity of history, is a token
of the superiority of history to every other branch of knowledge.[1] History, which is the easiest of all the sciences, is at
the same time, since its subject is human affairs in which
'maior est . . . quam in reliquis obscuritas et confusio', more
'incerta et confusa' than any other branch of knowledge.[2]

The conception of history, to which sixteenth-century development leads, particularly in the case of Bodin, may be thus
formulated. History is the easiest and the most obscure of
sciences. It is independent of every other science. Its special
subject is the study of aims and projects. By the distinction
between good (i.e. successful) and bad (i.e. unsuccessful) aims,
it makes possible a knowledge of the norms for human action.
History thus understood is in main issues at one with philosophy. One may therefore say: sixteenth-century development
tends to replace philosophy by history.

In his humanist period Hobbes had reservations against this
tendency. It predominated—however paradoxical this may
seem—only after his return to philosophy, i.e. in connexion
with his break with Aristotle. For his political philosophy,
which from this time on was gradually maturing, has precisely
the function of replacing history, as history was understood in
Bodin's extreme utterances. Hobbes's political philosophy is
also the easiest and the most obscure of sciences,[3] which, independent of every other science,[4] superior in dignity to every
other science,[5] deals particularly, or, to put it more exactly,
in its fundamental part, with aims, intentions, 'inward cogitations', 'secret aims', 'consilium et conscientia', the 'designe' of
men,[6] and by distinguishing between the good (i.e. successful)

[1] 'Sed praeter utilitatem incredibilem, quae duo res in omni disciplina
quaeri solent, facilitas et oblectatio, ambae in historiarum cognitione ita
conspirant, ut nec facilitas in ulla scientia maior, nec par voluptas inesse
videatur. facilitas quidem tanta est, ut sine ullius artis adiumento ipsa per
sese ab omnibus intelligatur. nam in aliis artibus, quod omnes inter se
aptae et iisdem vinculis colligatae sunt, altera sine alterius cognitione
percipi nequit. historia vero quasi supra scientias omnes in altissimo digni-
tatis gradu locata, nullius eget ope, ac ne literis quidem ipsis . . .' Loc. cit.,
p. 4.

[2] Loc. cit., pp. 14 and 25.   [3] See above, p. 7.

[4] See above, pp. 6–7.   [5] See above, p. 34, note 1.

[6] *English Works*, vol. viii, p. viii; *De cive*, cap. 3, art. 27, annot.; *Leviathan*
Introduction. See above, pp. 23–5.

intention and the bad (i.e. unsuccessful) leads to discovery of the norms. The need for history, which had arisen thanks to an alleged or real defect in traditional philosophy, is fulfilled by the new political philosophy. Thus from the time of the formation of the new political philosophy, history sinks back into its old philosophic insignificance—with the important difference, that in the new political philosophy, in contrast to the traditional, history is 'taken up' and conserved.

Only from this point of view can one appreciate the fact that Hobbes, who was particularly preoccupied with history up to the time of his return to philosophy, gives less and less thought to history as his political philosophy develops. As late as the *Elements* it is emphasized in a special paragraph that

'belief . . . in many cases is no less free from doubt, than perfect and manifest knowledge . . . there be many things which we receive from report of others, of which it is impossible to imagine any cause of doubt: for what can be opposed against the consent of all men, in things they can know, and have no cause to report otherwise than they are (such as is a great part of our histories), unless a man would say that all the world had conspired to deceive him.'

This justification of the authenticity of history is left out in the corresponding section of the *Leviathan*.[1] In the *Elements*, the estimation of frequently repeated legal verdicts as just verdicts figures as example of fallacies based on experience; in the *Leviathan*, in the same connexion, the problematic nature of all political knowledge based on history is emphasized, and thus the assumption on which the introduction to the translation of Thucydides rests is denied:

' . . . he that hath seen by what courses and degrees, a flourishing State hath first come into civil warre, and then to ruine; upon the sight of the ruines of any other state, will guesse, the like warre, and the like courses have been there also. But this conjecture, has the same incertainty almost with the conjecture of the Future; both being grounded onely upon Experience.'[2]

At variance with the *Elements*, there is in *De cive* and the *Leviathan* a reference to the harm done by the reading of history.[3] In

---

[1] *Elements*, Pt. I, ch. 6, § 9; *Leviathan*, ch. 7.
[2] *Leviathan*, ch. 3 (p. 11); cf. *Elements*, Pt. I, ch. 4, § 11.
[3] Cf. *De cive*, cap. 12, art. 10 and 12, and also *Leviathan*, ch. 5, *in fine*, and ch. 29 (p. 174) with *Elements*, Part II, ch. 8, §§ 3 and 13.

the Latin version of the *Leviathan*, not yet in the earlier English version of the work, it is said: 'historia dividitur autem in naturalem et civilem, quarum neutra pertinet ad institutum nostrum.'[1] In a section of the *Leviathan*, which has no parallel in the earlier presentations, Hobbes systematically rejects all criticism of political ideals, which is based on practice, i.e. on historical experience: 'For though in all places of the world, men should lay the foundation of their houses on the sand, it could not thence be inferred, that so it ought to be.' In full accordance with this, the observation in the earlier presentations, that in every State there is actually a sovereign power which corresponds to all the demands of political philosophy, is left out.[2] The more Hobbes learns to distinguish sharply between what is and what should be, the more the ideal character of the 'Leviathan' becomes clear in his mind, the less significance has history for him. As a result, the distinction between history, which is serious and seeks truth, and poetry, and the superiority of history over poetry, lose their former justification. As late as in the *Leviathan*, and in the more or less contemporary *Answer to the Preface of Gondibert* (1650), Hobbes still insists in the old way on the distinction between history and poetry.[3] In the introduction to the translation of Homer, which was composed much later, there is no longer any mention of it.[4] The turning away from history finds its most precise expression in the following sentences from *De homine*: 'Literae . . . utiles, praesertim historiae; suppeditant enim experimenta, quibus scientiae innituntur causarum; historia quidem naturalis physicae, historiae autem civiles scientiae civili et morali; idque *sive verae sint sive falsae*, modo non sint

---

[1] Cap. 9.

[2] Cf. *Leviathan*, ch. 20, *in fine*, with *Elements*, Pt. II, ch. 1, § 19, and *De cive*, cap. 6, art. 18. Compare with reference to these passages Tönnies, loc. cit., pp. 210 and 244.

[3] ' . . . the subject of a poem is the manners of men . . . manners feigned, as the name of poesy imports, not found in men.' *English Works*, vol. iv, p. 445. 'For as truth is the bound of historical, so the resemblance of truth is the utmost limit of poetical liberty.' Loc. cit., p. 451. Cf. *Leviathan*, ch. 8 (p. 34).

[4] The heroic poet tells 'an honest and delightful story, whether true or feigned'. *English Works*, vol. x, p. 111. Homer's, Virgil's, and Lucan's 'poems, except the introduction of their gods, are but so many histories in verse . . .' Loc. cit., p. vii.

impossibiles.'[1] History is thrust into the background in the measure that the new political philosophy gains clarity. For the new political philosophy fulfils the function which had to be fulfilled by history, as long as traditional political philosophy was acknowledged as valid.

That this is the case one recognizes fully when one scans Hobbes's political philosophy more closely. With the same argument which Hobbes himself, in the introduction to the translation of Thucydides, used to prove the need for studying history along with philosophy, he later argues the necessity for his political philosophy. Political philosophy is necessary, because 'most men' do not obey precepts. And the same presupposition which caused the turn to history is the basis of Hobbes's political philosophy: the replacement of the morality of obedience by the morality of prudence.[2] As a result, the difference between Hobbes's political philosophy and traditional political philosophy is identical with the difference, which in the opinion of Hobbes's predecessors and in accordance with Hobbes's own original view, exists between history and (traditional) philosophy. Bacon's criticism of Aristotelian morals (that it does not teach the realization of virtue) therefore becomes an element also in Hobbes's criticism of Aristotle.[3] For the turn to history had taken place precisely because (traditional) philosophy showed no way to the application of the norms. This failure is remedied by the new political

[1] *De homine*, cap. xi, art. 10.

[2] 'All that is required, both in faith and manners, for man's salvation, is, I confess, set down in Scripture as plainly as can be. "Children, obey your parents in all things. . . . Let all men be subject to the higher powers . . ." are words of the Scripture, which are well enough understood; but neither children, nor the greatest part of men, do understand why it is their duty to do so. They see not that the safety of the commonwealth, and consequently their own, depends upon their doing it. Every man by nature, without discipline, does in all his actions look upon, as far as he can see, the *benefit that shall redound to himself from his obedience* . . . the Scripture says one thing, and they think another, weighing the commodities or incommodities of this present life only, which are in their sight, never putting into the scales the good and evil of the life to come, which they see not.' *English Works*, vol. vi, p. 230 f.

[3] ' . . . the morals of Aristotle . . . have caused a great deal of dispute concerning virtue and vice, but no knowledge of what they are, nor any *method of obtaining virtue nor of avoiding vice.*' Loc. cit., p. 218. Compare Bacon's similar statement, quoted p. 87, note 1, above.

philosophy, whose boast it is, that it, in contrast to traditional
philosophy, teaches an applicable morality. Just as Bacon
acknowledged the traditional morals (with certain modifications)
and only wished to complete it by a theory (based mainly on
induction from history) of application, Hobbes allows the
validity of aristocratic virtue (although with more extensive
modifications and reservations), completing it by a morality
which is systematically applicable and which appeals to 'the
greatest part of men'.[1] It has the same meaning, when Hobbes
(in an argument *ad hominem*) acknowledges the binding force
of the Ten Commandments and 'only' denies that they are
applicable without more detailed interpretation by the secular
power.[2] In the same way Hobbes admits the natural inequality, the natural gradation of men, and 'only' contests that
this inequality is of any practical importance.[3] Finally, Hobbes
concedes 'that the Civill Government be ordained as a means
to bring us to a Spirituall felicity', and thus that all earthly
things are means, subordinate to the end, of eternal bliss. But
he denies that from this hierarchy of things earthly and things
eternal anything can be deduced as to the relative position of
the holder of secular power and the holder of spiritual power. In
the arguments for this denial Hobbes's premisses come clearly
to light. From the relation of ends and means nothing can be
deduced as to the relation of persons, for the objective relation
between means and ends is completely independent of human
will and is thus fundamentally different from the use of means
by men, a use which is essentially dependent on human will.[4]

---

[1] 'The force of Words, being . . . too weak to hold men to the performance
of their Covenants; there are in man's nature, but two imaginable helps to
strengthen it. And those are either a Feare of the consequence of breaking
their word; or a Glory, or Pride in appearing not to need to breake it. This
later is a Generosity too rarely found to be presumed on, especially in the
pursuers of Wealth, Command, or sensuall Pleasure; which are *the greatest
part of Mankind*. The Passion to be reckoned upon, is Fear.' *Leviathan*,
ch. 14 (p. 73). Compare the following judgement by Sir Walter Raleigh:
'When (Castiglione) failed, his good faith and lofty standards were to blame;
in his allegiance to the high canons of behaviour which he had laid down for
his Courtier, he omitted to take account of human duplicity and human
baseness.' Loc. cit., p. 47.

[2] *De cive*, cap. 6, art. 16; cap. 14, art. 17; cap. 17, art. 10.

[3] Ibid., cap. 3, art. 13; *Leviathan*, ch. 15 (p. 80).

[4] ' . . . let us consider in what sense it may be said intelligibly, that the

With this Hobbes lets us see that even if there were an eternal order, he would take into consideration only the actual behaviour of men, and that his whole interest is centred on man, on application, on the 'use of means'.

The shifting of interest from the eternal order to man, and thus to application, had, as we have seen, found expression earlier in the turning of philosophy to history. Carried to its logical conclusion, it leads to Hobbes's political philosophy. Hobbes is not content to ask 'How can the norms of traditional morality be realized?' He has not only the intention of justifying the traditional norms in a way more practicable for application than was the way of traditional philosophy; he altogether denies the applicability of traditional morals, whether of ancient philosophy or of Biblical Christianity, or even of aristocratic virtue. He even goes farther still. He does not merely assert that Aristotle did not show the way to a realization of the norms, but also that he did not even rightly define the norms. He does not merely contest that the natural inequality of men, as Aristotle assumes it in his *Politics*, or the preeminence of eternal bliss over all earthly good, is of practical importance, but he also denies that inequality and that preeminence. But though Hobbes's political philosophy finally denies not only the applicability but also the validity of the norms proclaimed by traditional political philosophy, the prin-

---

Temporall, or Civill Power is subject to the Spirituall. There be but two ways that those words can be made sense. For when wee say, one Power is subject to another Power, the meaning either is, that he which hath the one, is subject to him that hath the other; or that the one Power is to the other, as the means to the end. For wee cannot understand, that one Power hath Power over another Power; or that one Power can have Right or Command over another: For Subjection, Command, Right, and Power are accidents, not of Powers, but of Persons: One Power may be subordinate to another, as the art of a Sadler, to the art of a Rider. . . . Therefore as from subordination of an Art, cannot be inferred the Subjection of the Professor; so from the Subordination of a Government, cannot be inferred the Subjection of the Governor . . . And thus you see the laboured fallacy of the first Argument, to deceive such men as distinguish not between the Subordination of Actions in the way to the End; and the Subordination of Persons one to another in the administration of the Means. For to every End, the Means are determined by Nature, or by God himselfe supernaturally: but the Power to make men use the Means, is in every nation resigned (by the Law of Nature, which forbiddeth men to violate their Faith given) to the Civill Soveraign.' *Leviathan*, ch. 42 (pp. 313–15).

ciple of applicability remains the decisive factor even in the
final form of Hobbes's political philosophy.[1] In contrast to
tradition, Hobbes wishes to 'put such principles down for a
foundation, as passion not mistrusting, may not seek to dis-
place'.[2] He wishes then, not only, as Bacon did, to play the
passions one against the other, in order thus to show the way
to a realization of already established norms; he wishes to
draw up a political philosophy which will from the outset be
in harmony with the passions. The study of the passions,
which had found an entrance into morals first only in connexion
with the question as to the application of already established
norms, is from now on to become the foundation for a knowledge of the norms themselves. And after Hobbes found in the
fear of violent death (which conquers and convinces the passions
at the same time), a truly applicable principle of political
philosophy, it is again in accordance with the interest in
application that he progresses from this foundation (called
by him 'Right of Nature') to the establishment of the 'Law of
Nature'. The right to defend life and limb, which man has
from nature by reason of the inescapable fear of death, becomes
a right to all things and all actions, since a right to the end is
invalid without a right to the necessary means. For Hobbes
does not leave it to the judgement of the wise man to decide
which means are necessary; he does not say: 'those means are
necessary which a wise man would at the time judge necessary.'
He attempts instead to give a universally valid maxim, by
which the specific problem of application is overcome. In
order to avoid the 'arbitrariness', the uncertainty of what a wise
man would decide under unforeseen circumstances, he rules
that each man has a right to all things and all actions, since any
one under some circumstances may consider that any thing or
action is a necessary means for the defence of his life. The
express premiss of this finding is the equality of all men.[3]
Because all men are equal, i.e. because there is no natural order
in general, and therefore no natural gradation of mankind,

---

[1] Another way of putting this would be to say that Hobbes's political
philosophy calls into question the distinction between 'law' and 'polity'.
Cf. *English Works*, vol. vi, pp. 12–13.

[2] *Elements*, Ep. ded.   [3] *De cive*, cap. i, art. 7–10.

the difference between the wise minority and the unwise majority loses the fundamental importance it had for traditional political philosophy. And whereas, as long as the fundamental importance of this difference was recognized, it was necessary to study, along with philosophy which appeals only to the few, history also, in order to show 'the greater part of men' the way to realization, when the equality of all men is exalted to a principle, a new philosophy becomes possible which shows or aims at showing all men a way 'to obtain virtue and to avoid vice'.[1]

As Hobbes's political philosophy satisfies the need which had caused philosophy to turn to history, it at first pushes history back into its old insignificance for philosophy. For the time being philosophy and history are again completely separated. To this extent it is true to say that Hobbes's political philosophy is 'unhistorical'. What is usually meant by this judgement is, however, not so much that Hobbes took no interest in history as that he made incorrect assertions as to history being the basis of his political philosophy. Hobbes's fundamental historical error is supposed to be his assumption that man's primitive condition was the war of every one against every one. Against that assumption Maine in particular has maintained that the primitive condition of at least the European peoples 'may be fairly described as consisting of a number of little despotic governments, each perfectly distinct from the rest, each absolutely controlled by the prerogative of a single monarch'. ' . . . society in primitive times was not what it is assumed to be at present, a collection of individuals. In fact, and in the view of the men who composed it, it was an aggregation of families'.[2] These findings are especially directed against Hobbes.

' . . . nothing can be more worthless than Hobbes' conjectural account of the origin of society and government. . . . The theory is open to every sort of objection. . . . The universal disorder of the race in its infancy may be true of the contests of tribe with tribe and of family with family; but it is not true of the relations of individual man with individual man. . . . And, in addition, the theory is open to precisely the same objection as the counter-

---

[1] Cf. p. 98, note 3.
[2] *Ancient Law*, ed. C. K. Allen, pp. 104 and 152.

hypothesis of Locke, that it antedates the modern juridical conception of Contract.'

One understands from this Maine's comprehensive verdict: 'No geniuses of an equally high order so completely divorced themselves from history as Hobbes and Bentham, or appear, to me at all events, so completely under the impression that the world had always been more or less as they saw it.'[1] In answer to this criticism it must be recalled that the 'patriarchal theory' is not only no refutation of Hobbes's theory, but is itself defended by Hobbes.

'It may peradventure be thought, that there was never such a time, nor condition of warre as this (*sc.* of everyone against everyone); and I believe it was never generally so, over all the world: but there are many places, where they live so now. For the savage people in many places of America, *except the government of small Families*, the concord whereof dependeth on naturall lust, have no government at all; and live at this day in that brutish manner, as I said before. Howsoever, it may be perceived what manner of life there would be, where there were no common Power to feare; by the manner of life, which men that have formerly lived under a peacefull government, use to degenerate into, in a civill Warre.'[2]

' . . . originally the Father of every man was also his Soveraign Lord, with power over him of life and death; and . . . the Fathers of families . . . by instituting a Common-wealth . . . resigned that absolute Power.'[3]

'Germany, being antiently, as all other countries, in their beginnings, divided amongst an infinite number of little Lords, or Masters of families, that continually had wars one with another . . .'[4]

Hobbes, however, cannot rest content with such findings as to the historical origin of States, for they give no answer to the only important question, which concerns the right order of society. That he devoted no particular attention to the historical origin of States is to be understood from this point of view. Criticism of the patriarchal community, such as Maine —be it said, in complete harmony with Hobbes's views—continually offers,[5] could not satisfy him either. For his concern

---

[1] *Early History of Institutions*, London, 1875, pp. 356 and 396.
[2] *Leviathan*, ch. 13 (p. 65).   [3] Ibid., ch. 30 (p. 182).
[4] Ibid., ch. 10 (p. 47).
[5] *Ancient Law*, pp. 18, 109, 130 f., 133, 140 f., 195 f., and 259 f.

is the justification of this criticism, of the standards which first
make historical investigations *inter alia* possible. Thus he seeks
the most precise expression for the imperfection of the patriarchal communities in particular, and in general for the imperfection of all commonwealths up to his time, showing itself in
the constant danger of civil war; and he does this by pointing
out at the same time the possibility of the radical remedying
of this defect, the possibility of the 'movement from Status to
Contract', which he approves of as does Maine. Therefore,
going beyond the findings of history, that the original condition
of society was the patriarchal, he constructs a completely defective state of mankind. As such a state he conceives the lack
of any, even the most defective order, the war of every one
against every one. Finally, he derives this war from its origin
in human nature. So in the criticism that Hobbes's political
philosophy is 'unhistorical', the only statement that is justified
is that Hobbes considered the philosophic grounding of the
principles of all judgement on political subjects more fundamental, incomparably more important than the most thoroughly
founded historical knowledge.

The state of nature is thus for Hobbes not an historical fact,
but a necessary construction. Nevertheless, the appearance
that his theory of the state of nature has an historical meaning
is not entirely without foundation. It is essential to his political
philosophy that it should begin with the description of the state
of nature, and that it should let the State emerge from the state
of nature. Proceeding thus, Hobbes does not narrate a true
history, but he grasps a typical history. But, nevertheless, by
this very fact he acknowledges that the subject of at least the
fundamental part, and precisely of that fundamental part, of
his political philosophy, is an history, a genesis, and not an
order which is static and perfect. To see this more clearly one
does well to compare Hobbes's 'compositive' method with
Aristotle's 'genetic' method. Both philosophers are interested
in the typical element of history, but each in a different way.
When Aristotle depicts the genesis of the city as the perfect
community out of primitive communities, the understanding
of perfect organism is the main thread and the presupposition
for the understanding of its constituent parts, the more primi-

tive communities. The understanding of the standard, which is set up from the outset and which does not change at all during the analysis of the genesis, dominates the testing of the individual stages of the development.[1] Hobbes proceeds quite differently. For him, the imperfection of the primitive condition, or the state of nature, is perceived not by looking to the already, even if only cursorily clarified, idea of the State as the perfect community, but by fully understanding the experience of the state of nature. The standard for the test is not set up and proved beforehand, but is to produce itself and to prove itself. Hobbes, therefore, does not follow Aristotle, but opens up the way to Hegel. As for Hobbes the primitive condition is irrational, so for Hegel 'knowing, as it is found at the start, mind in its immediate and primitive stage, is without the essential nature of mind, is sense-consciousness'.[2] Just as Hobbes systematically makes the State or the need for the State emerge from the *natural* state, Hegel makes absolute knowledge emerge from *natural* consciousness. For both philosophers have no intention of measuring the imperfect by a standard which transcends it, but as they simply 'look on', while the imperfect by its own movement annuls itself, 'tests itself', they themselves are 'relieved of the task of testing'.[3] This is the meaning of Hobbes's argument that the man who wishes to remain in the state of nature contradicts himself,[4] that the mutual fear which characterizes the state of nature is the motive for abolishing the state of nature; or, to express it in Hegel's words, 'the passions work themselves and their aims out according to their constitution and produce the edifice of human society, in which *they* have provided law and order with power against themselves'.[5] The premiss for an 'immanent' testing of this kind which necessarily finds its expression within the framework of a typical history is for Hobbes, as for

---

[1] What has been said of Aristotle holds still more of Plato's statements about the genesis and decline of States; cf. particularly *Republic*, 545 D-E with *Meno*, 76 E.

[2] Hegel, *Phenomenology of Mind*, translated by J. B. Baillie, vol. i, p. 25.

[3] Loc. cit., p. 85.

[4] *Elements*, Pt. I, ch. 14, § 12; *De cive*, cap. 1, art. 13. Cf. also p. 151 below (on the 'materialistic' character of this procedure).

[5] *Vorlesungen über die Philosophie der Geschichte*, 3. Auflage, Berlin 1848, p. 34.

Hegel, the rejection of the morality of obedience. This premiss, which had at first caused philosophy to turn to history, finally brings it about that philosophy itself takes on the character of typical history. For Hobbes, at all events, history finally becomes superfluous, because for him political philosophy itself becomes a history, a typical history. His political philosophy becomes historical because for him order is not immutable, eternal, in existence from the beginning, but is produced only at the end of a process; because for him order is not independent of human volition, but is borne up by human volition alone. For this reason political philosophy now becomes an *a priori* science: not because the principles of political philosophy are eternal, but because 'principia, quibus justum et aequum, et contra, iniustum et iniquum, quid sint, cognoscitur; id est, justitiae causas, nimirum leges et pacta, ipsi fecimus'.[1] And for this reason political philosophy no longer has the function, as it had in classical antiquity, of reminding political life of the eternally immutable prototype of the perfect State, but the peculiarly modern task of delineating for the first time the programme of the essentially future perfect State. The repression of history in favour of philosophy from now on means in reality the repression of the past—of the ancient, which is an image of the eternal—in favour of the future. 'In scientiis ... quaeruntur causae non tam eorum quae fuere, quam eorum quae esse possunt.'[2] ' ... praestat enim scire quomodo possimus praesentibus causis optime uti, quam irrevocabile praeteritum, quale fuit, cognoscere.'[3]

If the order of man's world does not rest on a superhuman order, but springs from man's will alone, there is no philosophical or theological security for that order. Man then can convince himself of his capacity to order his world only by the fact of his ordering activity. That is to say, precisely on Hobbes's assumption, one cannot rest content with typical history: one must return to real history. Thus the state of nature, which at first was intended as merely typical, again

---

[1] *De homine*, cap. 10, art. 5.   [2] Ibid., cap. 11, art. 10.

[3] Ibid., cap. 10, art. 4. 'Finis autem seu scopus philosophiae est, ut *praevisis* effectibus uti possimus ad commoda nostra, vel ut effectibus animo conceptis ... effectus similes ... ad vitae humanae usus industria hominum producantur.' *De corpore*, cap. 1, art. 6.

takes on an historical significance—not, indeed, as a condition of absolute lack of order, but as a condition of extremely defective order. And the progress which may be traced in real history from the *prisca barbaries* to *hodiernum tempus* with reference to the conquest of nature, bears witness to the possibility of the progress still to be achieved in regard to the ordering of the world of man.[1] Thus real history has as its function to vouch for the possibility of further progress by perception of progress already made. After that—historically perhaps even earlier—its function is to free man from the might of the past, from the authority of antiquity, from 'prejudices'. Authority loses its prestige when its historical origin and evolution are traced; as a result of historical criticism man's limitations show themselves as limits set by himself, and therefore to be overpassed. Since there is no superhuman order which binds man from the beginning, since man has no set place in the universe, but has to make one for himself, he can extend the limits of his power at will. That he can, indeed, extend those limits is shown by history as the history of progress;[2] that present limits can be overstepped is proved by history as historical criticism. It is by the doubt of the transcendent eternal order by which man's reason was assumed to be guided and hence by the conviction of the impotence of reason, that first of all the turning of philosophy to history is caused, and then the process of 'historicising' philosophy itself.

[1] *De cive*, Ep. ded.

[2] Condorcet says in the introduction to his *Esquisse d'un tableau historique des progrès de l'esprit humain* (ed. Prior, pp. 2–3): 'Ces observations, sur ce que l'homme a été, sur ce qu'il est aujourd'hui, conduiront ensuite aux moyens d'assurer et d'accélérer les nouveaux progrès que sa nature lui permet d'espérer encore. Tel est le but de l'ouvrage que j'ai entrepris, et dont le résultat sera de montrer, par le raisonnement et par les faits, que la nature n'a marqué aucun terme au perfectionnement des facultés humaines; que la perfectibilité de l'homme est réellement indéfinie; que les progrès de cette perfectibilité, désormais indépendants de toute puissance qui voudrait les arrêter, n'ont d'autre terme que la durée du globe où la nature nous a jetés.' The last words betray Condorcet's (and his predecessors') ultimate presupposition: if nature had not *cast* us on this globe, infinite progress would be impossible. Compare below, p. 134 f.

VII

THE NEW MORALITY

HOBBES turns from philosophy to history because he finds that philosophy shows no way to the application of the norms which it establishes or proves; he turns back to philosophy as soon as he sees a possibility of developing a theory of application of the (traditional) norms, a theory based on the direct study of human nature, or of replacing the allegedly inapplicable traditional norms by applicable ones. In the end, however, he contests not only the applicability, but also the validity of the traditional norms. He was enabled to take this decisive step by the new moral attitude, which never found more sincere and eloquent expression than in his political philosophy. Only when vitalized by this moral attitude did the utilitarian morality which underlay philosophy's turn to history gain the fire and passion which gave it victory in afterdays. Whereas the principle of application conditioned only the form and method of Hobbes's political philosophy, this moral attitude gives it its peculiar substance.

The new moral attitude first appears within the horizon of the traditional ideals. Because the traditional norms are taken as a matter of course by Hobbes, he has the possibility of devoting himself exclusively to the problem of the application of those norms. Therefore, phenomena such as the passions, characters, temperaments, intentions, and motives, become central interests. Knowledge of these phenomena is provided not by (traditional) philosophy, but by history,[1] and among all historians according to Hobbes's view by none more than by Thucydides. Thucydides is 'the most politic historiographer that ever writ'. Not because he teaches the *arcana imperii* better than any other, but in the first place because, instead of dogmatically setting out precepts, he helps the reader to gain thorough and independent insight into the precepts as into teachings which are gained from experience, and in the second place, because he is aware of the peculiar difficulties of this

[1] See above, pp. 86-9.

kind of knowledge. His history contains no 'wise discourses
. . . of manners and policy', no 'open conveyances of precepts',
but is pure narrative. Not only does Thucydides keep strictly
to the sequence of events, but particularly 'the grounds and
motives of every action he setteth down before the action itself.
. . . After the action, when there is just occasion, he giveth his
judgment of them; shewing by what means the success came
either to be furthered or hindered.' By thus revealing 'the
ways and events of good and evil counsels' by his account, and
allowing the judgement on the connexion between motive, plan,
and result to arise from concrete experience, he teaches the
reader much more thoroughly than any philosopher could.[1]
Thucydides is concerned primarily with motives. The most
powerful motives are the passions.[2] Thucydides stands out
above other historians particularly because he reveals those
usually unavowed passions which primarily determine social
life. The depth of his insight finds adequate expression in the
obscurity of his sentences: 'the obscurity . . . proceedeth from
the profoundness of the sentences; containing contemplations
of those human passions, which either dissembled or not commonly discoursed of, do yet carry the greatest sway with men
in their public conversation.'[3] Knowledge of the passions, more
generally expressed, knowledge of the motives, is of peculiar
difficulty. The second reason why Hobbes characterizes Thucydides as 'the most politic historiographer that ever writ' is,
therefore, that Thucydides is fully aware of the limits set to
the knowledge of motives. '. . . (he never enters) into men's
hearts further than the acts themselves evidently guide him.'
For 'the inward motive . . . is but conjectural'.[4] Thus it is
from Thucydides that one can best learn the nature both of

---

[1] *English Works*, vol. viii, pp. viii and xxi f. Cf. p. 80, note 1, above.
[2] Compare with this and the preceding passage these sentences from
Hegel's *Vorlesungen über die Philosophie der Geschichte* (quoted from the
translation by J. Sibree, London, 1905): 'The question of the *means* by
which Freedom develops itself to a World, conducts us to the phenomenon
of History itself.' 'The first glance at History convinces us that the actions
of men proceed from their needs, their passions, their characters and
talents. . . . Passions, private aims, and the satisfaction of selfish desires,
are . . . the most effective springs of action' (p. 21).
[3] *English Works*, vol. viii, p. xxix.
[4] Loc. cit., pp. viii and xxvii f.

the passions and of knowledge of them. Hobbes, taught by
Thucydides about those passions which 'carry the greatest sway
with men in their public conversation', reveals his characteristic
moral attitude for the first time in the terse statements of the
introduction to his translation of Thucydides, which treat of
those passions.

A thorough knowledge of the passions is the indispensable
condition for the answering of the question as to the right
ordering of social life, and particularly as to the best form of
State. From the beginning Hobbes gave his preference to
monarchy. One would expect that originally the traditional
arguments of natural theology had convinced him of the pre-
eminence of monarchy.[1] This expectation is proved wrong by
the introduction to his translation of Thucydides. In this
earliest statement the traditional arguments are not even mentioned. We do not believe that Hobbes had already rejected
them, but it is certain that even then they no longer interested
him. From the outset he sought to answer the question of the
best form of State with regard not to man's essential being and
the place occupied by him in the universe, but to experience
of human life, to application, and therefore with particular
reference to the passions. The philosophers, supported by
arguments from natural theology and kindred sources, might
assert the pre-eminence of monarchy—this superiority would
be much more obvious, if monarchy proved itself the best
form of State on the basis of experience, on the basis of a
study of the passions.

In the introduction to his translation of Thucydides, Hobbes
proves the superiority of monarchy with reference solely to the
power of the passions. Indeed, he speaks less of the superiority
of monarchy than of the disadvantages of the other forms of
State: recognition of what is defective leads to recognition of
what is right.[2] As far as democracy is concerned, he states that
in it 'the emulation and contention of the demagogues for
reputation and glory of wit', the desire for 'authority and sway
amongst the common people' play a part which is disastrous
to the common weal. In an aristocracy it is still worse. Each
aristocrat 'desireth to be the chief; and they that are under-

[1] See above, p. 60.   [2] Cf. above, p. 105.

valued, bear it with less patience than in a democracy'.[1] The
passions which determine human society are a striving after
rank and precedence or modifications of that striving, and
because that is the case, monarchy is the best form of State.
For—one must complete the argument thus—in a monarchy
that striving cannot have so disastrous an effect as in the other
forms of State.

The first presupposition for the preference for monarchy is
thus the conviction that the striving after rank and precedence,
or, as we should say according to our earlier exposition,[2] that
vanity is the most dangerous passion. That Hobbes held that
view at the time of writing the introduction to the translation
of Thucydides is proved also by the fact that in the dedication
to that work, when praising the virtues of the second Earl of
Devonshire, he emphasizes no less than three times that his
patron was completely free of this passion.[3] From the outset
vanity was for Hobbes the root of all evil. For in vanity he
recognized the power which dazzles and blinds men. Because
man desires to think well of himself, he refuses to recognize
such facts as reveal the limits of his power and intelligence.
Vanity hinders man from perceiving his true situation. Vanity
is nourished by success. Thus man profits more from ill
fortune than from good fortune. Ill fortune prevents him from
over-estimating his power and intelligence, awakens fear in
him, and fear is a good counsellor. As vanity is the power
which dazzles, the diametrically opposed passion, fear, is the
power which enlightens man. Now vanity is co-ordinated with
publicity as fear is with solitude. Man can assure himself of
the justice of the good opinion which he has, or would like to
have, of himself, only by the recognition which comes to him
from others; he must, therefore, hide from others his weakness,
his consciousness of weakness, that is to say, his fear. On the
other hand, he can admit his fear to himself. Therefore, he
prefers the strictest reprimand, the advice most injurious to

[1] *English Works*, vol. viii, p. xvi f.   [2] See above, p. 11 f.
[3] ' . . . there was not any, who more really, and less for glory's sake
favoured those that studied the liberal arts liberally, than my Lord your
father did.' *English Works*, vol. viii, p. iii f. ' . . . his study . . . directed
not to the ostentation of his reading.' ' . . . (he) took no fire either from
faction or ambition.' Loc. cit., p. iv.

his self-love, if they are but privately administered, to any public
disapproval.[1] Consequently, because vanity, which makes men
blind, dominates public life, and thus fear, which advises man
well, dares to show itself only in solitude or among intimates,
because, therefore, generally speaking, any individual is more
reasonable than any assembly, monarchy is the best form of State.

The chain of reasoning which has just been put forward
forms the basis of Hobbes's political philosophy at all stages
of its evolution from the introduction to his translation of
Thucydides onwards. We discussed the fundamental significance of the antithesis of vanity and fear in Chapter II. Here
it need only be recalled that in all the presentations of his
political philosophy Hobbes kept to the connexion of this antithesis with the antithesis of monarchy and democracy (or
aristocracy).[2] Because vanity by nature determines man, not
only is the State necessary, but particularly monarchy is the
best form of State, since in it publicity—vanity's element—is
least powerful.

We draw the conclusion that there was no change in the
essential content of the argument and aim of Hobbes's political
philosophy from the introduction to his translation of Thucydides up to the latest works. What changed was especially the
method. Originally Hobbes supports his argument particularly
by (induction from) history, later by direct study of the passions.
Only the method of the reasoning and therewith also of the
presentation can have been decisively influenced by the 'discovery' of Euclid's *Elements*.

[1] ' . . . there is something, I know not what, in the censure of a multitude,
more terrible than any single judgment, how severe or exact soever . . .'
Loc. cit., p. vii. ' . . . much prosperity . . . maketh men in love with
themselves; and it is hard for any man to love that counsel which maketh
him love himself the less. And it holdeth much more in a multitude than
in one man. For a man that reasoneth with himself, will not be ashamed
to admit of timorous suggestions in his business, that he may the stronglier
provide; but in public deliberations before a multitude, fear (which for the
most part adviseth well, though it execute not so) seldom or never sheweth
itself or is admitted.' Loc. cit., p. xvi. ' . . . men profit more by looking on
adverse events, than on prosperity . . . men's miseries do better instruct,
than their good success . . .' Loc. cit., p. xxiv.

[2] *Elements*, Pt. I, ch. 13, § 3; Pt. II, ch. 5, §§ 4, 7, 8, and also ch. 8, § 3;
De cive, cap. 10, art. 7, 9, 11, 12, and 15; *Leviathan*, ch. 19 (p. 98) and
ch. 25 (p. 138 f.). Cf. above, p. 64 f.

That is not to say that Hobbes was from the beginning completely aware of all the implications of his characteristic moral attitude which is expressed in the antithesis vanity-fear. Originally he considered fear as the main, but not as the sufficient, motive of right behaviour: 'fear . . . adviseth well, though it execute not so.'[1] The sentence recalls the conclusion to Bacon's *Essay on Boldness*: ' . . . boldness is ever blind; for it seeth not dangers and inconveniences. Therefore it is ill in counsel, good in execution. . . . For in counsel it is good to see dangers; and in execution not to see them, except they be very great.' The distinction between planning and execution can be extended to the distinction between two kinds of virtue, virtue in planning and virtue in execution. In this sense we understand the distinction which Hobbes makes in the earliest exposition of his political philosophy, between the virtues of peace (justice and equity) and the virtue of war (honour). Honour is aristocratic virtue.[2] It is due to Hobbes's original conception of fear that he could at first approve aristocratic virtue. Later he understands by fear not only the motive for right planning but also the motive of right execution:

'Per *metum* est quod homines sibi cavent: fuga quidem et latebris, si caveri aliter posse non putant: *saepissime* vero armis atque instrumentis defensionis, quo fit, ut *prodire audentes*, alter alterius cognoscere ingenium possit. Tunc autem, sive *pugnant*, ex victoria; sive consentiunt, ex consensione civitas nasci solet.'[3]

As fear is thus considered the sufficient motive for all right behaviour, and in particular the sufficient motive for the founding of the State, it is impossible to approve any virtues which do not arise from fear, fear of violent death, and whose essence consists in the conquest or denial of fear. Once Hobbes has fully elucidated his conception of fear, he cannot but reject aristocratic virtue. For 'fear' and 'honour' are irreconcilable: 'fear can hardly be made manifest, but by some action dishonourable, that betrayeth the conscience of one's own weakness.'[4] Honour, which was originally recognized by Hobbes as the virtue of war alongside the virtues of peace, is finally directly opposed to justice and therefore to virtue in general.

[1] See above, p. 112, note 1.   [2] See above, p. 47 f.
[3] *De cive*, cap. 1, art. 2, annot. 2.   [4] *Elements*, Pt. I, ch. 19, § 2.

While Hobbes could still say in the *Elements* 'the only law of actions in war is *honour*', in the *Leviathan* he says: '*Force and Fraud*, are in warre the two Cardinall vertues.'[1] When Hobbes replaces 'honour' by 'force and fraud', he gives us to understand that what he formerly esteemed as 'honour' he has now detected as fundamentally unjust and a pretext for injustice. He goes further than that implicit criticism; he says:

' . . . Nor does it alter the cause of Honour, whether an action (so it be great and difficult, and consequently a signe of much power,) be just or unjust: for Honour consisteth onely in the opinion of Power. Therefore the ancient Heathen did not thinke they Dishonoured, but greatly Honoured the Gods, when they introduced them in their Poems, committing Rapes, Thefts, and other great, but unjust, or unclean acts: In so much as nothing is so much celebrated in Jupiter, as his Adulteries; nor in Mercury, as his Frauds, and Thefts . . .'[2]

And since honour as virtue of war is identical with valour, the negation of honour as a virtue means the negation of valour as a virtue.[3] Because Hobbes finally recognizes fear of violent death as the basis of all virtue, he must finally question every obligation which causes a man to risk his life, and with that the reason for all obligatory esteem of valour: 'When Armies fight, there is on one side, or both, a running away; yet when they do it not out of treachery, but fear, they are not esteemed to do it unjustly, but dishonourably.'[4] Valour may be the virtue of a particular profession, of the soldier's profession—it ceases to count as virtue of man.

Hobbes's moral ideas thus went through a clearly recognizable transformation; from appreciation of aristocratic virtue in the beginning, Hobbes went on to a progressively more and more decided criticism of aristocratic virtue. Aristocratic virtue, which originally embraced all virtue, is later recognized as virtue only in war. Afterwards it becomes the virtue of the barbaric epoch, in which 'rapine was a trade of life'; it is thus

---

[1] Ch. 13 (p. 66). Compare also the following passage from the dedication to *De cive*: ' . . . recurrendum etiam bonis est, si se tueri volunt, ad virtutes Bellicas vim et dolum, id est, ad ferinam rapacitatem.'

[2] *Leviathan*, ch. 10 (p. 47). Cf. also ch. 12 (p. 58).

[3] See above, p. 18, and also p. 50.   [4] *Leviathan*, ch. 21 (p. 115).

reduced to a virtue of the state of nature.[1] Finally all moral virtue is denied it; it is taken from the theory of virtues and assigned to the analysis of passions.[2] After it had thus lost all binding force and is seen as a mere pretext and ornament of affective life, it finds for the time being a last refuge in poetry. Hobbes speaks most fully of 'honour' as virtue in his characterizations of 'heroic virtue', which, as we have seen,[3] is for him identical with honour. Now, the characterizations of 'heroic virtue' occur only in definitions of the heroic poem. But even as the virtue of primitive ages or of poetry, heroic virtue holds its own only so long as the new values, which Hobbes was the first to develop in full consciousness of their range and bearing, did not dominate public opinion. After that heroes were no longer tolerated even in history or poetry. There came a time when it was demanded that history and poetry should concern themselves not 'with the affairs only of Kings', but particularly with 'the affairs of the common people', and that they should be 'rather familiar than heroic'.[4]

It may be assumed that criticism of aristocratic virtue means, in the first instance, substituting prudence for honour. This

---

[1] *Elements*, Pt. I, ch. 19, § 2. With this is connected the fact that the virtues of the heroes are characterized as 'virtues of nature', which amounts to denying that they are genuine virtues. See above, p. 48, note 1.

[2] That the analysis of honour in the *Leviathan* (ch. 10) really belongs to the analysis of passions is shown by the connexion between the parallel passage in the *Elements* (Pt. I, ch. 8) and the theory of the passions which follows immediately in this earliest presentation. This connexion, which was done away with by Hobbes in the *Leviathan*, in order to comply with mechanistic psychology, is restored by Hume in the 2nd Book of the *Treatise of Human Nature*. Hume treats what Hobbes discussed under the headings 'Power' and 'Honourable', in the framework of the analysis of 'Pride and Humility' as 'causes' of these passions.

[3] See above, p. 47 f.

[4] Compare the beginning of Thackeray's *Esmond*. Thackeray's *Vanity Fair* may also be indicated, whose sub-title 'A novel without a hero' expresses that the central personages of the novel are not heroes, *because* they keep clear of Vanity Fair (see particularly ch. 31). According to Hobbes, on the other hand, '(one of the indecencies of an heroic poem) is the dialect of the inferior sort of people, which is always different from the language of the court. Another is, to derive the illustrations of anything from such metaphors or comparisons as cannot come into men's thoughts, but by mean conversation, and experience of humble or evil arts, which the person of an epic poem cannot be thought acquainted with.' *English Works*, vol. iv, p. 455.

substitution seems to have taken place in the course of the sixteenth century and seems in particular to be the basis of philosophy's turn to history.[1] Indeed, in the earliest presentation of his political philosophy, in which he shows much keener interest in history than in later writings,[2] Hobbes says of prudence that it is 'the same with virtue in general'. Yet in the parallel passages in *De cive* and the *Leviathan*, prudence is not even mentioned, and in *De homine* its moral value is expressly denied.[3] Hobbes's criticism of aristocratic virtue thus does not mean the replacement of honour by prudence. It is rather justice and charity which take the place occupied before by honour. These virtues, which in Hobbes's view, are the only moral virtues, have, however, their ultimate foundation in fear of violent death. The criticism of aristocratic virtue thus, in the last analysis, means the replacement of honour by the fear of violent death. And even though one may characterize Hobbes's morals as utilitarian morals, it is only with the important limitation that these morals are based on the fear of violent death, on a passion which is not in itself prudent, but which *makes* man prudent. Precisely, this attempt to give a foundation to utilitarian morals by having recourse to a force which imperatively *compels* prudence, is the peculiarity of Hobbes's political philosophy. Only by this foundation does Hobbes ensure the distinction between moral and immoral motives.

The concrete significance of Hobbes's morals comes out most clearly in one of his latest works, in *Behemoth*. This critical presentation of the causes and course of the Civil War is directed primarily against the Presbyterian clergy and the

---

[1] See above, p. 93 f.   [2] See above, p. 96 f.

[3] Cf. *Elements*, Pt. I, ch. 17, § 14; *De cive*, cap. 3, art. 32; *Leviathan*, ch. 15 (p. 81); *De homine*, cap. 13, art. 9 (see p. 18 above). Compare with the passage quoted in the text, the following passage from the digest of the *Nicomachean Ethics* (mentioned on p. 42 above): 'Virtus proprie dicta, vel communior est, seu dirigens, ut Prudentia, Justitia Universalis, vel directa et specialis est, ut Fortitudo, Temperantia etc. Orditur Aristoteles revera doctrinam virtutum a Fortitudine, respexit enim ad objectum, quod cum in Fortitudine sit maxime arduum, idcirco illam ordine proposuit: Verum methodus pro arbitrio non nunquam variari potest, et melius nunc visum est, methodum illam sequi, quae ducitur ex ordine universalium ad particularia' (p. 12). In accordance with this, *prudentia* is treated first.

middle class. These two groups are, according to Hobbes's assertion, primarily responsible for the outbreak of the Civil War. The Presbyterian clergy accommodated their preaching to the interests of the middle class:

'they did never in their sermons, or but lightly, inveigh against the lucrative vices of men of trade or handicraft; such as are feigning, lying, cozening, hypocrisy, or other uncharitableness, except want of charity to their pastors and to the faithful: which was a great ease to the generality of citizens and the inhabitants of market-towns, and no little profit to themselves . . . they did, indeed, with great earnestness and severity, inveigh often against two sins, carnal lusts and vain swearing; which, without question, was very well done. But the common people were thereby inclined to believe, that nothing else was sin, but that which was forbidden in the third and seventh commandments . . . and therefore never made much scruple of the acts of fraud and malice, but endeavoured to keep themselves from uncleanness only, or at least from the scandal of it. . . . Yet divers of them did preach frequently against oppression . . . but it was before such as were free from it; I mean the common people, who would easily believe themselves oppressed, but never oppressors.'[1]

The middle class, thus supported by the Presbyterian clergy, was the natural vehicle of the Revolution:

' . . . the city of London and other great towns of trade, having in admiration the great prosperity of the Low Countries after they had revolted from their monarch, the King of Spain, were inclined to think that the like change of government here, would to them produce the like prosperity.'[2]

' . . . those great capital cities, when rebellion is upon pretence of grievances, must needs be of the rebel party: because the grievances are but taxes, to which citizens, that is, merchants, whose profession is their private gain, are naturally mortal enemies; their only glory being to grow excessively rich by the wisdom of buying and selling.'

And as though to deny all value to the middle class Hobbes replies to the objection 'But they are said to be of all callings the most beneficial to the commonwealth, by setting the poorer sort of people on work' as follows:

'That is to say, by making poor people sell their labour to them

---

[1] *Behemoth*, p. 25 f.   [2] Ibid., p. 3 f.

at their own prices, so that poor people, for the most part, might get a better living by working in Bridewell, than by spinning, weaving, and other such labour as they can do . . .'[1]

Hobbes thus seems to be a determined opponent of the middle class. If one looks more closely, one notices, however, that his attack is really directed against the policy of the English middle class, and by no means against the middle class itself, its being and its ideal. His final word is not that the middle class is the natural vehicle of any and every revolution, but that, in so far as it is so, it is acting against its own real interest, and that, if it rightly understood its own desire for private gain, it would unconditionally obey the secular power:

'I consider the most part of rich subjects, that have made themselves so by craft and trade, as men that never look upon anything but their present profit; and who, to everything not lying in that way, are in a manner blind, being amazed at the very thought of plundering. If they had understood what virtue there is to preserve their wealth in obedience to their lawful sovereign, they would never have sided with the Parliament. . . .'[2]

Not only does Hobbes not attack the middle class which is sensibly aware of its own interests, he even provides it with a philosophical justification, as the ideals set up in his political philosophy are precisely the ideals of the bourgeoisie. It is true that he condemns the desire 'to grow excessively rich', but 'justly and moderately to enrich themselves' is 'prudence . . . in private men'.[3] It is true that he condemns the exploiting of the poor, but he takes it for granted that 'a man's Labour also is a commodity exchangeable for benefit, as well as any other thing'.[4] For 'the value of all things contracted for, is measured by the Appetite of the Contractors: and therefore the just value, is that which they be contented to give'.[5] Private property and private profit are so little objectionable in themselves that they are rather the inevitable condition for all peaceful life:

'For maintaining of peace at home, there be so many things necessarily to be considered, and taken order in, as there be several causes

[1] *Behemoth*, p. 126.   [2] Ibid., p. 142.
[3] Ibid., p. 44.   [4] *Leviathan*, ch. 24 (p. 130).
[5] Ibid., ch. 15 (p. 78); cf. alao *Elements*, Pt. I, ch. 16, § 5, and *De cive*, cap. 3, art. 6.

concurring to sedition. And first, it is necessary to set out to every subject his propriety, and distinct lands and goods, upon which he may exercise and have the benefit of his own industry, and without which men would fall out amongst themselves, as did the herdsmen of Abraham and Lot, every man encroaching and usurping as much of the common benefit as he can, which tendeth to quarrel and sedition.'[1]

Along with peace at home and abroad, freedom for individual enrichment is the most important aim of corporate life. The sovereign power has, apart from assuring peace, no further duty than seeing to it that the citizens 'quantum cum securitate publica consistere potest, locupletentur (et) ut libertate innoxia perfruantur'.[2] For there is no real good outside sensual goods and the means to acquire them.[3] Even science—however great the pleasure it may afford the individual—has no other publicly defensible aim than the increase of human power and human well-being.[4] Well-being is achieved mainly by labour and thrift. The gifts of nature are less important for its acquisition than trade and industry:

'Ad locupletandos cives necessaria duo sunt, labor et parsimonia; conducit etiam tertium, nempe terrae aquaeque proventus naturalis . . . priora duo sola necessaria sunt. Potest enim civitas in insula maris constituta, non majore, quam ut habitationi locum praestet, sine semente, sine piscatura, solâ Mercaturâ et opificiis ditescere.'[5]

Thus neither income or fortune, but only consumption, should be taxed; taxation of consumption puts a premium on thrift and a penalty on extravagance.[6] It is the duty of the government to compel the able-bodied poor, who cannot support themselves, to work, and also to provide work for them, and

---

[1] *Elements*, Pt. II, ch. 9, § 5; cf. *De cive*, Ep. ded., and *Leviathan*, ch. 24 (p. 131 f.).

[2] *De cive*, cap. 13, art. 6. Compare also the explanation of 'liberty of subjects' in *Leviathan*, ch. 21 (p. 112).

[3] *De cive*, cap. 1, art. 2.   [4] *De corpore*, cap. 1, art. 6.

[5] *De cive*, cap. 13, art. 14. ' . . . Plenty dependeth (next to God's favour) meerly on the labour and industry of men. . . . there have been Commonwealths that having no more Territory, than hath served them for habitation, have neverthelesse, not only maintained, but also encreased their Power, partly by the labour of trading from one place to another, and partly by selling the Manifactures, whereof the Materials were brought in from other places.' *Leviathan*, ch. 24 (p. 130). Cf. also *De cive*, cap. 12, art. 9.

[6] *Elements*, Pt. II, ch. 9, § 5; *De cive*, cap. 13, art. 11; *Leviathan*, ch. 30 (p. 184).

on the other hand to forbid excessive display, for the purpose of encouraging thrift.¹ Along with 'justice and charity', Hobbes obviously recognizes only industry and thrift as virtues. In contrast to industry and thrift, war is no certain means of securing well-being; only 'when all the world is overcharged with Inhabitants, then the last remedy of all is Warre';² but as long as this extreme case has not come about, war should be waged only for defence,³ and to this end it is best to maintain a mercenary army. Thus the relationship between 'Leviathan' and subject is changed to its opposite; the sovereign power is the hireling of the individuals, who apply themselves to just and modest self-enrichment, who buy and sell labour like any other commodity, and who also can pay for the work of their defence: 'the Impositions, that are layd on the People by the Soveraign Power, are nothing else but the Wages, due to them that hold the Publique Sword, to defend private men in the exercise of severall Trades, and Callings.'⁴ The king and his professional army, whose duty it is to protect the private people, must, therefore, *nolens volens* be courageous: 'Fortitude is a royal virtue; and though it be necessary in such private men as shall be soldiers, yet, for other men, the less they dare, the better it is both for the Commonwealth and for themselves.' Far from allowing the citizen to be led astray from his own virtue by royal virtue, Hobbes holds up the middle-class virtues to the king as model: 'Frugality (though perhaps you will think it strange) is also a royal virtue; for it increases the public stock, which cannot be too great for the public use. . . .'⁵ The king exercises his sovereign right in the spirit and in the interest of the bourgeoisie; he provides for equality before the law and for legal security; he chooses his counsellors in consideration not of hereditary privileges but of personal capacity; he opposes the pride and presumption of the aristocracy.⁶ However much Hobbes personally esteemed the aristocracy, and esteemed the

---

¹ *De cive*, cap. 13, art. 14; *Leviathan*, ch. 30 (p. 184 f.).
² Cf. *Leviathan*, ch. 30 (p. 185) and also *De cive*, Ep. ded., with *Elements*, Pt. II, ch. 9, § 9, and *De cive*, cap. 13, art. 14.
³ The motive of the war of conquest is vanity; cf. *English Works*, vol. vi, p. 12, and *Leviathan*, ch. 13 (p. 64); see above, p. 11.
⁴ *Leviathan*, ch. 30 (p. 184).   ⁵ *Behemoth*, p. 45.
⁶ *Leviathan*, ch. 30 (p. 187 f.).

specific qualities of the aristocracy,[1] his political philosophy is directed against the aristocratic rules of life[2] in the name of bourgeois rules of life. His morality is the morality of the bourgeois world. Even his sharp criticism of the bourgeoisie has, at bottom, no other aim than to remind the bourgeoisie of the elementary condition for its existence. This condition is not industry and thrift, not the specific exertions of the bourgeoisie, but the security of body and soul, which the bourgeoisie cannot of itself guarantee. For this reason the sovereign power must be permitted unrestricted power of disposal even over property, because it is only on that condition that the sovereign power can really protect the lives of the subjects. For neither poverty nor oppression nor insult is the greatest and supreme evil, but violent death or the danger of violent

---

[1] See above, p. 45. All the same it is said incidentally in *Behemoth* (p. 69): 'I believe that the Lords, most of them, following the principles of warlike and savage natures, envied his (Strafford's) greatness, but yet were not of themselves willing to condemn him of treason.' The words 'following the principles of warlike and savage natures, envied his greatness, but yet' do not occur in the older editions and were first published by Tönnies from the manuscript.

[2] That this is the case was clearly seen by Clarendon; he says in *A brief view and survey of the dangerous and pernicious errors to Church and State, in Mr. Hobbes's book, entitled Leviathan* (1676): Hobbes 'must not take it ill, that I observe his extreme malignity to the Nobility, by whose bread he hath bin alwaies sustain'd, who must not expect any part, at least any precedence in his Institution; that in this his deep meditation upon the ten Commandments, and in a conjuncture when the Levellers were at highest, and the reduction of all degrees to one and the same was resolv'd upon, and begun, and exercis'd towards the whole Nobility with all the instances of contemt and scorn, he chose to publish his judgments; as if the safety of the People requir'd an equality of Persons and that "the honor of great Persons is to be valued for their beneficence, and the aids they give to men of inferior rank, or not at all; and that the consequence of partiality towards the great, raised hatred, and an endeavor in the people to pull down all oppressing and contumelious greatness"; language lent to, or borrowed from the Agitators of that time' (p. 181). The phrases quoted by Clarendon occur in *Leviathan*, ch. 30 (p. 184). ' "Good counsell", he saies, "comes not by lot or inheritance, and therefore there is no more reason to expect good advice from the rich, or the noble, in the matter of State, then in delineating the dimensions of a Fortress"; and is very solicitous, like a faithful Leveller, that no man may have priviledges of that kind by his birth or descent, or have farther honor then adhereth naturally to his abilities . . .' (p. 182). The phrases quoted occur in *Leviathan*, ch. 30 (p. 187). In the Latin version of the *Leviathan*, which was published after the Restoration, Hobbes left out the phrases which were hostile to the aristocracy. Compare in this connexion the previous note.

death. It is true Hobbes prefers country people to the inhabitants of the great cities;[1] but in the last analysis this has no other meaning than the related fact that he prefers the horrors of the state of nature to the spurious joys of society.[2] Hobbes 'prefers' these terrors of the state of nature because only on awareness of these terrors can a true and permanent society rest. The bourgeois existence which no longer experiences these terrors will endure only as long as it remembers them. By this finding Hobbes differs from those of his opponents who in principle share his bourgeois ideal, but reject his conception of the state of nature.[3]

That Hobbes penetrated more deeply into the matter than the later writers was recognized by no one more clearly than by Hegel. Hegel's analysis of the bourgeois corroborates the identity of Hobbes's morality and bourgeois morality which we have attempted to show. For Hegel is not content to characterize the bourgeois by just and modest self-enrichment and similar features. Obviously following Hobbes, he emphasizes that protection against the danger of violent death, the denial of fortitude as a virtue and thus the fear of violent death, are the primary conditions of bourgeois existence.[4] And as Hegel recognizes the fear of violent death as the basis of the bourgeois existence, he prefers Hobbes's conception of the state of nature to later conceptions: 'Hobbes looks at this condition in its true light, and we find in him no idle talk about a state of natural goodness; the natural condition is really far more like that of the animals—a condition in which there is an unsubdued individual will.' Even though Hegel rejects Hobbes's 'views' as 'shallow and empirical', he nevertheless admits that 'the reasons he gives for them, and the propositions he makes concerning

---

[1] '. . . there is . . . an insincereness, inconstancy, and troublesome humour in those that dwell in populous cities, like the mobility, blustering, and impurety of the air; and a plainness, and, though dull, yet a nutritive faculty in rural people, that endures a comparison with the earth they labour.' *English Works*, vol. iv, p. 444.

[2] Compare the description of these joys in *De cive*, cap. 1, art. 2.

[3] I have treated this rather more fully in my 'Anmerkungen zu Carl Schmitt, Der Begriff des Politischen', *Archiv für Sozialwissenschaft und Sozialpolitik*, vol. lxvii, p. 738 f.

[4] Cf. Hegel's *Schriften zur Politik und Rechtsphilosophie*, ed. G. Lasson, Leipzig, 1913, pp. 379 ff., 472 f., and 477 ff.

them, are original in character'.[1] Hegel's criticism of the
bourgeoisie was made possible not only by the new understanding of Platonic political philosophy, but also by the new understanding of the justification of the bourgeois ideal which must
be traced back to Hobbes.

By characterizing the state of nature as a condition of mutual
fear, Hobbes makes this assumption: the essential relationship
between men is by nature this, that each human individual is at
the mercy of other human individuals. But this would not be
possible if man were not altogether exposed; if '*Nature* (should
not) . . . dissociate, and render men apt to invade, and destroy
one another'.[2] The belief that man is exposed by a Nature which
is not ordered and ordering, but the principle of disorder, to
all hazards; in other words, the denial of creation and providence, is the presupposition for Hobbes's conception of the
state of nature. Only if man is not subject to a higher power
with binding force over his conscience can the relation of men
among themselves be determined, as it is according to Hobbes,
not by mutual obligations, but by (justified or unjustified)
claims of each on each. While Hobbes in the *Elements* had
still said: 'Considering men therefore again in the state of
nature, *without covenants* or subjection one to another, as if
they were but even now all at once *created* male and female,'
he says in *De cive*: 'Ut redeamus iterum in statum naturalem,
consideremusque homines tanquam si essent jamjam subito
e terra (*fungorum more*) *exorti* et adulti, *sine omni* unius ad
alterum *obligatione* . . .'[3] If man is thus completely at the mercy

[1] 'Vorlesungen über die Geschichte der Philosophie', *Werke*, vol. xv,
p. 396, quoted from the translation by Elizabeth S. Haldane and Frances H.
Simson (London, 1895), vol. iii, p. 317. ' . . . the state of nature (is) that of
injustice and violence, of untamed natural impulses, of inhuman deeds, and
feelings.' 'Vorlesungen über die Philosophie der Geschichte', p. 51 (quoted
from the translation by J. Sibree, London, 1905).

[2] *Leviathan*, ch. 13 (p. 65).

[3] *Elements*, Pt. II, ch. 3, § 2, and *De cive*, cap. 8, art. 1. Compare in this
connexion the comparison of the atheist and the theist theories of the
origin of the world in *De homine*, cap. 1, art. 1, where Hobbes obviously
prefers the former. Recognition of teleology here and there (*De homine*,
cap. 1, art. 4, and cap. 12, art. 5; *Leviathan*, ch. 11, p. 53; *English Works*,
vol. vii, p. 176) is, if it is sincere, to be explained only as a residue of tradition, which contradicts the whole of Hobbes's philosophy. Cf. Tönnies,
loc. cit., pp. 182–4.

of the universe which with the harshness of indifference now injures and now profits him, he has no reason to be grateful to the 'First Cause' of that universe. Hobbes says explicitly: 'The Right of Nature, whereby God reigneth over men; and punishes those that break his Lawes, is to be derived not from his creating them, as if he required obedience, as of Gratitude for his benefits; but from his Irresistible Power.'[1] If man's natural condition is such that he has no grounds for gratitude, he will consider chance good fortune as a danger rather than a gift. For as the idea of thanking God for it cannot occur to him, he will consider himself the cause of his good fortune: 'much prosperity . . . maketh men in love with themselves.'[2] That good fortune blinds man is certainly a commonplace; that it cannot but blind him, that it cannot enlighten him, is a characteristic view by which Hobbes makes a stand against tradition. The more sober Aristotle had said: 'Men that prosper have this ill; to be more proud and inconsiderate than others. And this good, that they worship God, trusting in him, for that they find themselves to receive more good than proceeds from their industry.'[3] In the section of his anthropology, which is based on the passage quoted from Aristotle's *Rhetoric*, Hobbes mentions only the evil consequences of good fortune —pride and presumption. That good fortune calls forth gratitude, he either does not or will not recognize.[4] Only ill fortune, especially unforeseen ill fortune, teaches men.[5] For man must be brought to recognize his position by the violent resistance of the real world, and against his natural inclination, which is to deceive himself as to the horror of his natural situation by weaving a cocoon of vain dreams about himself. For the man who has once come into contact with this world, joy and laughter are over.[6] Man must be serious and that exclusively. It is the fearfulness of death rather than the sweetness of life

[1] *Leviathan*, ch. 31 (p. 191 f.). Compare also Hobbes's mocking reply to Bishop Bramhall's criticism of this proposition in *English Works*, vol. iv, p. 288 f.   [2] See above, p. 112, note 1.
[3] *Rhetoric*, ii. 17, quoted from Hobbes's digest, *English Works*, vol. vi, p. 471 f.   [4] Cf. *De homine*, cap. 13, art. 5. (See p. 40 f.)
[5] See above, p. 19, and p. 112, note 1.
[6] Compare Hobbes's explanation of laughter as an expression of vanity in *Elements*, Pt. I, ch. 9, § 13.

which makes man cling to existence.[1] Since man is at the mercy of a fate utterly unconcerned as to his weal or woe, a fate which one may call God's irresistible power, because man experiences only force, and not kindness from the overwhelming power of the universe, he has no choice but to help himself.[2] He has to live, not in gratitude, but in the serious and oppressive consciousness of his freedom, of himself as a free being, of his capacity to free himself. Constantly aware of the desperate seriousness of his situation, it will not occur to him to be proud of his freedom, and, therefore, he will, above all, be on his guard against taking that freedom as the object of his speculations, against contemplating himself in his freedom and taking pleasure in it. It is better and more becoming to the situation of man to deny that freedom theoretically by mechanistic physical science, and to assert it practically by the conquest of nature, and particularly of human nature, with the help of that science. Not grateful contemplation of nature, and still less vain contemplation of man, is fitting to man's situation, but the utilization and cultivation of nature. For man can assert himself only by increasing and improving nature's deceptive and niggardly gifts by his labour and exertions; and the more he makes himself independent of nature by his labour, the further he draws away from nature, and makes the gifts of nature disappear behind his own free activity, the more highly is his labour to be valued;[3] trade and industry are more to be prized than agriculture and fishing. Because Hobbes's point of departure is that man is at the mercy of nature, he distrusts good fortune and the fortunate, distrusts their gratitude and their gaiety, distrusts, in particular, in spite of all personal affection, the aristocracy, whose virtues are only 'virtues of nature'. Thus he is on the side of those who are

---

[1] Compare the founding of the State in Hobbes's political philosophy on the basis of the fear of death, with Aristotle's quite different statement in the *Politics* ($1278^{b}24-30$).

[2] Hobbes sees man, as it were, as the proletarian of creation. Man, as understood by Hobbes, stands in the same relation to the universe as Marx's proletarian to the bourgeois world: he has nothing to lose by his rebellion, except his chains, and everything to gain.

[3] Connected with this is the exclusion of all receptive perception from science (*De corpore*, cap. 1, art. 2). Compare also Hobbes's conception of political philosophy as *a priori* science. See above, p. 106.

prepared to owe their good fortune exclusively to their own achievement and their own serious labour.

It would seem to us that Hobbes's political philosophy is the most important testimony to the struggle which has been fought against the aristocracy in the name of bourgeois virtue. It bears witness to the struggle particularly in that this struggle is fought out within that political philosophy itself; the genesis of Hobbes's political philosophy is nothing other than the progressive supplanting of aristocratic virtue by bourgeois virtue. For Hobbes came only gradually to a clear realization that the moral attitude he adopted as a standard demanded the unconditional rejection of aristocratic virtue. The antithesis could, for a time, remain hidden from him, because in spite of their antithesis,[1] aristocratic virtue and bourgeois virtue have something fundamental in common.

Aristocratic virtue as Castiglione sees it and bourgeois virtue as Hobbes sees it, are in accord in that they are, and are understood as, the virtues of civilized men. In the name of 'letters' Castiglione fought against the older view, which was defended particularly by the French aristocracy of his time, and which admits only 'noblenes of armes'. The courtier is certainly to pass soldiering off as his main profession, 'and all the other good qualities for an ornament thereof'. But he is to know that apart from moral virtue, to which valour essentially belongs, 'the true and principall ornament of the minde in every man . . . are letters'.[2] He is to know that the object of war is peace, defence and not conquest, the civilization of subject peoples and not barbaric tyranny over them.[3] He is to have left the coarseness of country life behind him, like all martial, 'Scythian' coarseness.[4] It is an urban ideal that Castiglione has before him, as had Hobbes.[5] So it is not surprising that Castiglione also considered it a prince's duty 'to shew favour to marchant men, and to helpe them also with stockes' and 'set a stint to

---

[1] Compare especially the passages on laughter in Castiglione's *Courtier* (pp. 137 ff.) and in Hobbes's writings (e.g. in *Elements*, Pt. I, ch. 9, § 13).
[2] Castiglione, loc. cit., pp. 68, 35 f., and 72.
[3] Loc. cit., pp. 280, 288 ff., and 300.   [4] Loc. cit., p. 129.
[5] Compare Hobbes's observation as to the connexion between philosophy and urban life in the *Leviathan*, ch. 46 (p. 364): 'Where first were great and flourishing Cities, there was first the study of Philosophy.'

the over sumptuous buildings of private men, banquetings
. . .'[1] Hobbes and Castiglione, one may sum up, are at one,
because they are both heirs of the tradition of classical antiquity. They had not to choose between Caesar's ideals and
those of Ariovistus. Both feel the deepest repugnance for the
baseness of provocative arrogance and cruelty which characterize the barbarians in Caesar's descriptions. A knowledge of
one's own limitations and of human limitations, modesty in the
full sense, is thus for Castiglione as for Hobbes[2] the necessary
condition of virtue: 'How much doe we take pleasure in a
Gentleman that is a man at armes, and how much more worthy
praise is he if he bee modest, of few wordes, and no bragger,
than an other that alwaies craketh of himselfe, and blaspheming
with a braverie seemeth to threaten the world.'[3]

Aristocratic and bourgeois virtue are at one not only in that
both presuppose the idea of civilization in the sense given to
it by the tradition of classical antiquity; the loss of classical
naïveté is also the common basis of both ideals. It is from this
that we understand how Castiglione came to speak his 'new
word'[4] about grace. Grace arises from a noble negligence,
which is the virtue of self-display, the art of concealing one's
own art.[5] It is true that in Castiglione's case this art is only a
highly refined art of self-display and ostentation, but that this
refinement was necessary proves that self-display had lost its
naïveté. Carried to its extreme, the criticism not only of boasting
but above all of affectation, which is contained in Castiglione's
discussions of grace, leads to the replacement of self-confidence
by fear.[6] In principle aristocratic virtue and bourgeois virtue
are virtues of self-consciousness. That virtue understood as

---

[1] Loc. cit., p. 293.

[2] To what extent Hobbes's political philosophy leads once more to the
undermining of knowledge of human limitations, was indicated on p. 107
above. Cf. Plato's *Protagoras*, 327 c ff.

[3] Castiglione, loc. cit., p. 48. Compare also the following caricature of a
boaster: 'And an other saide that hee occupied no looking glasse in his
chamber, because in his rage hee was so terrible to behold, that in looking
upon his own countenance he should put himselfe into much feare.' Ibid.,
p. 38.   [4] Loc. cit., p. 46.   [5] See above, p. 52 f.

[6] Castiglione says in passing: 'I will have our courtier to keepe fast in his
minde one lesson, and that is this, to bee alwaies warie . . . and rather
fearefull than bolde (diffident rather than forward) . . .' Loc. cit., p. 71.

honour, as magnanimity, has this character, needs no further explanation; but the fear of violent death also, the principle of Hobbes's morals, is a form of self-consciousness. The fear, as Hobbes understands it, includes man's attitude to that fear,[1] and therewith the consciousness that there is reason for fear; it is consciousness of one's own weakness.[2] According to aristocratic and to bourgeois virtue, the right life of man is understood exclusively as an emanation of his right self-consciousness. Right self-consciousness is, however, not right 'self-knowledge' as knowledge of man's essential being, of the nobility and baseness which make up that being; it is, in other words, not knowledge of the place which is essentially due to man in the cosmos, but is a right consciousness in the human individual of himself in relation to other human individuals, and of the situation in which he finds himself face to face with other human individuals. Thus[3] the two ideals are in contrast to all those conceptions which recognize obedience either as the essence of, or as an essential moment in, right living. Hobbes expresses this state of things when he introduces both 'glory or pride' and fear of violent death as substitute for justice.[4]

In the movement from the principle of honour to the principle of fear, Hobbes's political philosophy comes into being.

---

[1] 'Ego ea voce (sc. metuere) futuri mali prospectum quemlibet comprehendo. Neque solam fugam, sed etiam diffidere, suspicari, cavere, ne metuant providere, metuentium esse judico.' De cive, cap. 1, art. 2, annot. 2.

[2] Elements, Pt. I, ch. 19, § 2; De cive, cap. 15, art. 7. Cf. also Elements, Pt. I, ch. 10, where 'vain fear' and 'vain dejection' are used as synonyms.

[3] See above, p. 93 f. and 106 f.　　　　[4] See above, p. 99, note 1.

VIII

THE NEW POLITICAL SCIENCE

THE genesis of Hobbes's political philosophy is characterized by the following processes: (1) the movement away from the idea of monarchy as the most natural form of State to the idea of monarchy as the most perfect artificial State; (2) the movement away from the recognition of natural obligation as the basis of morality, law, and the State to the deduction of morality, law, and the State from a natural claim[1] (and thus to the denial of every natural obligation); (3) the movement away from the recognition of a superhuman authority—whether of revelation based on Divine will or a natural order based on Divine reason—to a recognition of the exclusively human authority of the State; (4) the movement away from the study of past (and present) States to the free construction of the future State; (5) the movement away from honour as principle, to fear of violent death as principle. The explanation of the inner connexion between these movements must be reserved for an analysis of Hobbes's political philosophy. For this philosophy is nothing other than the homogeneous connexion between the final stages of the movements mentioned. The unity of this connexion, in its turn, proceeds from the unity of Hobbes's moral attitude.

This moral attitude does not by any means appear only at the end of a long process, but directs this process from the beginning. Not the moral attitude itself, but the unfolding of its universal significance, of the whole nexus of its presuppositions and consequences, is the result of the genesis of Hobbes's political philosophy. This moral attitude is thus not only objectively 'prior' to the argument and presentation of his political philosophy (both of which were influenced by mathematics and exact science), but also in Hobbes's development it precedes his preoccupation with the exact sciences. There remains the question how Hobbes's mathematical and scientific studies furthered or hindered his political philosophy; in other

[1] See below, pp. 155 ff.

words, what had to be added to his fundamental moral attitude, in order that his political philosophy should take on its final form.

Before the 'discovery' of Euclid, Hobbes still believed in the authority of traditional (Aristotelian) moral and political philosophy. But although, or rather because, he took the validity and applicability of the traditional norms as a matter of course, his interest centres not so much on those norms as on the method of their application. He investigates not so much the essence of virtue and vice as 'the method of obtaining virtue and of avoiding vice'. The problem of application, in itself secondary, actually becomes the central problem, as the presupposition is made that reason is, in principle, impotent. Thus Hobbes's turning to history has philosophic significance. Taught by tradition what man should be, he seeks to discover, by the study of the historians and by induction from history, what man is, what forces really determine him, in order to gain from this knowledge rules for the application of the traditional norms. He discovers especially the passions as forces of this type. Among the passions he pays particular attention to vanity and fear. The view which guides this selection is the relationship of the passions to reason, or more accurately, the fitness or unfitness of the various passions, to function as substitutes for impotent reason. For vanity is the force which makes men blind, fear is the force which makes men see. With this the reciprocal and unequivocal co-ordination of the two passions with the basic forms of human corporate life (publicity and solitude) is given, and with it the answer to the question of the best form of State (the unconditional preference for monarchy). It is true, the traditional norms limited the horizon within which Hobbes at first took his bearings; what really interested him was, however, not those norms, but phenomena, which cannot be understood within the traditional horizon— at all events if they are to be conceived in such a way as Hobbes from the outset conceived them. By emphasizing the antithesis of vanity and fear of violent death, Hobbes was already going beyond the traditional horizon.

As early as his humanist period Hobbes had not only the historians (and poets) at his disposal for the study of the passions.

He doubtless, at this time, already knew the scientific analysis of the passions in Aristotle's *Rhetoric*, to which, as we have seen,[1] his political philosophy owes so much. Hobbes's earliest scientific ambition was perhaps to write an analysis of the passions, in the style, i.e. according to the method of the *Rhetoric*, in order thus to further the theory of application of the moral precepts. Had such a plan been carried out, a very free, a very independent adaptation of the *Rhetoric* would have come into being. For Hobbes's approach to the passions and kindred phenomena was from the outset an interest peculiar to himself and diverging from Aristotle's. Whereas Aristotle discusses honourable and estimable passions with the same emphasis as base and blameworthy ones, the emphasis for Hobbes is from the beginning laid on the 'dissembled passions', which are *eo ipso* to be condemned. It is true that Aristotle, no less than Hobbes is concerned with those passions which 'carry the greatest sway with men in their public conversation';[2] but for him the positive connexion of a passion with public life does not mean a criticism of that passion, since among the passions which appear in public life there are estimable as well as despicable ones. Hobbes, on the other hand, finds from the beginning that the passion which counsels men well is hardly or not at all displayed in public.[3] With this is connected the fact that for Hobbes the delusion brought about by good fortune is in the foreground, whereas Aristotle discusses the good and evil consequences of good fortune in the same equable tone.[4] Such characteristic deviations from the *Rhetoric* are found in the few sentences of the introduction to the translation of Thucydides which touch upon themes of the *Rhetoric*. We may therefore take it as certain that if at this time Hobbes had made a coherent exposition of the passions and the like, he would even then have presented them in a way fundamentally different from Aristotle's. What this exposition would have been like may be seen if one compares the central chapters of Hobbes's anthropology, which arose out of the study of the *Rhetoric*, with their model. For since some of the changes which Hobbes makes in Aristotle's assertions cannot possibly

---

[1] See above, p. 35 ff.   [2] *English Works*, vol. viii, p. xxix.
[3] See above, p. 112, note 1.   [4] See above, p. 124.

be explained by the influence of mathematics and natural science, and since, on the other hand, they completely correspond to the difference between the introduction to the translation of Thucydides and the *Rhetoric*, precisely these divergences may be taken as original reservations on Hobbes's part against Aristotle. However it may be with this well-founded supposition, the comparison which we attempt in the following pages is necessary for a reason more cogent than interest in Hobbes's development. Its main object is to give a more accurate conception of how far Hobbes could depart from Aristotle in substance, without making a break with the method of the *Rhetoric*, i.e. without following Euclid's method. For only when this has been established can there be an answer to the question of how much Hobbes's political philosophy owes to mathematics.

A large part of the changes which Hobbes makes in his model is to be explained by his fundamental opinion that fear, or more accurately fear of death, is the force which makes men clear-sighted, and vanity the force which makes men blind. The change in the estimate of fear is shown by the fact that Hobbes in his enumeration of good things[1] mentions life as the first good in the first place, whereas Aristotle mentions happiness in the first place and life only in the penultimate place.[2] Besides, Hobbes speaks in the same connexion with particular emphasis of good things which are good precisely because they serve the protection of life, whereas Aristotle stresses good things which produce good, rather than good things which preserve good.[3] Moreover, in his comparison of good things,[4] Hobbes, deviating from Aristotle, declares the regaining of a lost good to be better than the undisturbed possession of that good; the memory that that good was once imperilled is the condition of a sound estimate of it, just as the frightfulness of death rather than the sweetness of life reveals the value of

---

[1] See above, p. 40.
[2] As early as the longer English *Rhetoric*-digest, in his reproduction of *Rhetoric*, i. 6, Hobbes had 'forgotten' happiness. See *English Works*, vol. vi, p. 431.
[3] Cf. *De homine*, cap. 11, art. 6–8, with *Rhetoric*, i, 6, §§ 6–7 and 10–15. For the same reason Hobbes, here also deviating from Aristotle, counts poverty without penury among the goods.   [4] See above, p. 40.

living.[1] Finally, in his discussion of anger Hobbes names only fear as an antidote against anger, whereas Aristotle among many other things mentions respect as well as fear.[2] The change in the estimate of vanity is shown by the fact that Hobbes in his discussion of emulation and envy makes no mention of the difference in value of these two passions, according to which emulation is nobler than envy.[3] Besides, he traces the pleasure of victory to vanity, whereas Aristotle characterizes the reason for this pleasure as a conception of superiority.[4] Moreover, in Hobbes's enumeration of the causes of crime, he names vanity in the first place, diverging from Aristotle.[5] Finally, Hobbes's analysis of shame shows no trace of what is the background of the Aristotelian analysis of this passion; according to Aristotle shame is no virtue, but a passion, but, nevertheless, it is that passion which holds noble youths in check, whereas the base can be held in check only by fear— according to Hobbes, shame, as confusion arising from disgrace endured, is only the opposite of satisfied vanity.[6] The original difference between Hobbes and Aristotle becomes completely clear when one compares the two philosophers' enumeration

[1] *De homine*, cap. 11, art. 14. Cf. above, p. 125, note 1.

[2] See above, p. 37. Cf. *English Works*, vol. vi, p. 453 f. and *De homine*, cap. 12, art. 4. Cf. also above, p. 20 f.

[3] See above, p. 39.

[4] . . . τὸ νικᾶν ἡδύ . . . φαντασία γὰρ ὑπεροχῆς γίγνεται. *Rhetoric*, i, 11, § 14. '. . . victoria, jucunda: facit enim bene de se sentire . . .' *De homine*, cap. 11, art. 12. Connected with this is the fact that in the passage quoted Hobbes says, deviating from Aristotle (*Rhetoric*, i, 11, § 15), 'Placent autem *maxime* certamina ingeniorum . . .' For interpretation of this passage see above, p. 19.

[5] *Leviathan*, ch. 27 (p. 157). The sections which follow were obviously influenced by *Rhetoric*, i, 12, §§ 1–4. Compare also the treatment of degrees of crime in *Leviathan*, ch. 27 (p. 161 f.) with *Rhetoric*, i, 14.

[6] See particularly the juxtaposition of *gloriatio* and *pudor* in *De homine*, cap. 12, art. 6. Cf. also *Elements*, Pt. I, ch. 9, § 3. In Aristotle cf. (apart from *Rhetoric*, ii, 6) *Eth. Nicom.* 1108^{a}32, 1116^{a}28 ff., 1128^{b}1 ff., and 1179^{b}12 ff. Cf. also Plato, *Legg.*, 646 E ff. The difference in the estimate of shame, which is still more clearly seen if one considers the treatment of shame in Mandeville's 'Fable of the Bees', which was influenced by Hobbes, is of particular interest, because in it the vanity-fear antithesis, which characterizes Hobbes's view of human nature, finds its most vivid expression. The disparagement of shame, the replacement of shame by fear is the necessary consequence of preferring the shameless 'honest' admission of fear, which renounces all claim to honour, to 'vain' hiding of fear, which is solicitous of honour. Cf. above, p. 21 f.

of pleasant things.[1] In Aristotle's view the typical or normal example of what is pleasant is the ease which constitutes or accompanies the achievement of or return to a natural and, therefore, also a customary state, and he therefore begins his enumeration with this; thus everything which one can do without compulsion and exertion, with ease and convenience, counts as pleasant, among other things, freedom from care, idleness, sleep, play, jesting, laughter. Such things are not even mentioned in Hobbes's list. They are disregarded as are the sensual enjoyments which Aristotle discusses immediately after. In his enumeration of pleasant things, Hobbes names in the first place *progress*; ease of any kind, 'the repose of a mind satisfied', is in his opinion a state neither desirable nor attainable: 'continual delight consisteth not in having prospered, but in prospering,' not in possession and enjoyment, but in successful striving and desiring.[2] Leisure cannot be a good to aspire to in such a life of tension which, far from moving between many and varied states of repose, is complete restlessness. Thus, diverging from Aristotle, Hobbes names in his enumeration of pleasant things, work or occupation.[3] As Hobbes teaches that the most pleasant thing of all is the progress to ever-farther goals, that even enjoyment has in it an essential dissatisfaction, that there is nothing pleasant without the keen pang of dissatisfaction, he stands in sharp contrast to Aristippus, according to whose theory pleasure is identical with gentle movement, and also to Aristotle and Plato and Epicurus, who say that the greatest pleasure is pleasure free from any alloy of pain, the purest pleasure. Thus, diverging from Aristotle, Hobbes characterizes that which is 'more vehement' as better.[4] According to Hobbes the pleasant is not so much what is naturally

[1] See above, p. 40.

[2] *Elements*, Pt. I, ch. 7, § 7; *Leviathan*, ch. 11 (p. 49); *De homine*, cap. 11, art. 12 and 15.

[3] *De homine*, cap. 11, art. 11. Cf. also above, p. 34, note 1.

[4] *De homine*, cap. 11, art. 14. Cf. V. Brochard, 'La théorie du plaisir d'après Épicure' (*Études de philosophie ancienne et de philosophie moderne*, Paris, Vrin, 1926, pp. 262 f., 273 f., and 288), on the fundamental difference between English utilitarianism on the one hand, and Epicurus and classical philosophy altogether on the other. For the development after Hobbes, I would refer the reader particularly to Locke's *Essay on Human Understanding* (Book II, ch. 20, § 6) and Nietzsche's *Wille zur Macht* (Aphorisms 693 ff.).

pleasant, as the 'pleasant' movement from one pleasant thing
to another pleasant thing, to a pleasanter thing, the consciousness which accompanies this movement, more accurately, self-
consciousness. Self-consciousness is, however, constituted only
by a comparison of the individual with other individuals: man
does not merely strive after ever-farther goals, but after goals
more remote than any other man has as yet attained to.[1] If
the pleasant which is worth mentioning exists only in comparison with others, in trying conclusions with others, in
matching oneself *against* others, it is not surprising that in his
enumeration of pleasant things, Hobbes, differing from Aristotle, mentions neither friends nor the doing or receiving of
good, but immediately after progress itself, as it were interpreting progress, *malum videre alienum*.[2] The difference between Hobbes's and Aristotle's enumeration of pleasant things
—this difference, which is perhaps the best key to an understanding of all the latent presuppositions of Hobbes's morals—
is to a considerable extent identical with the difference between
Bacon and the philosophic tradition.[3] With this we gain further
corroboration for our contention that the difference between
Hobbes and tradition is in decisive points independent of the
turn to mathematics and modern science. Indeed, if one takes

[1] ' . . . as men attain to more riches, honours, or other power; so their
appetite groweth more and more; and when they are come to the utmost
degree of one kind of power, they pursue some other, *as long as in any kind
they think themselves behind any other.*' *Elements*, Pt. I, ch. 7, § 7.

[2] That Hobbes here thinks particularly of the misfortunes of friends is
shown by the parallel to *De homine*, cap. 11, art. 11 ('Malum videre alienum,
jucundum: placet enim non ut malum, sed ut alienum. Inde est, quod
soleant homines ad mortis et periculi aliorum spectaculum concurrere'), in
Elements, Pt. I, ch. 9, § 19, which concludes with the words 'men usually
are content . . . to be spectators of the misery of their *friends*'. Aristotle had
merely said: καὶ αἱ περιπέτειαι καὶ τὸ περὶ μικρὸν σώζεσθαι ἐκ τῶν κινδύνων·
πάντα γὰρ θαυμαστὰ ταῦτα (*Rhetoric*, i, 11, § 24). As early as his *Rhetoric*-
digest Hobbes gives these paragraphs a harsher turn: 'And *other men's*
dangers, so they be near. And to have escaped hardly' (*English Works*,
vol. vi, p. 442).

[3] Cf. *Elements*, Pt. I, ch. 7, § 7 with Bacon, Essay xix, and *De homine*,
cap. 11, art. 15, *in fine*, with Bacon, *Works*, ed. Spedding and Ellis, vol. iii,
p. 426 f. We have already indicated the fundamental harmony between
Bacon and Hobbes in another connexion (pp. 89 ff. and 98). Modern
investigators usually under-estimate Bacon's influence on Hobbes, simply
because they over-estimate the significance of Galileo's method for Hobbes's
political philosophy.

into consideration the personal and literary relationship between Bacon and the young Hobbes,[1] it corroborates the more
far-reaching contention that this difference precedes the 'discovery' of Euclid in Hobbes's life also.

But the new moral attitude is one thing, and the consciousness of its novelty and the rebellion against tradition, which is
the concomitant of that consciousness, is another. Hobbes's
break with tradition was doubtless the result of his turning to
mathematics and natural science. Precisely for this reason he
became conscious of the antagonism of the new moral attitude
to the whole tradition, only in the form of antagonism between
the new and the traditional *science*. That the main point was
not the proclamation, but the grounding of the new ideals,
that such grounding, that political science in general, was possible and necessary—this fundamental assumption of the philosophic tradition was not doubted for a moment by Hobbes,
who has otherwise cast the tradition, as a whole, aside. Before
he became acquainted with Galileo and Euclid he in principle kept—in spite of the doubts and dissatisfaction to which
his turning to history bears witness—to traditional political
philosophy. After his 'discovery' of Euclid, he became clearly
aware of the need for a new political philosophy. The possibility and necessity of political philosophy as a science is always
taken as a matter of course. Not the idea of political science
but its method became a problem through the study of Euclid.
That, however, means that the might of the scientific tradition,
which did not permit the more fundamental question of the
purport of science as such to come up, is the reason why the
need for a reform of political philosophy comes into being
primarily as the need of a new method in political philosophy,
and why it is felt only in the moment when Hobbes becomes
acquainted with the new method.

The explicit break with the whole tradition of political
philosophy, which Hobbes claims—and rightly—to be the first
to make, thus becomes possible only after 'Euclid'. This fact
is incontestable, but what 'Euclid' signifies in this connexion
is more important and more obscure. According to Hobbes's
own view, the application of mathematical method to political

[1] Aubrey, *Brief Lives*, ed. Clark, Oxford, 1898, i, 331.

philosophy means that politics is now for the first time raised
to the rank of a science, a branch of rational knowledge. That
politics hitherto was not a science is shown clearly enough by
the fact 'that they that have written of justice and policy in
general, do all invade each other, and themselves, with contradiction'. The reason for this is that in politics up to that time,
not reason, but passion had found expression. The only completely passionless, purely rational science, and therefore the
only science, which is already in existence, is mathematics;
thus only by orientating oneself by mathematics, i.e. by progressing as mathematicians do from self-evident principles by
means of evident conclusions,[1] can politics be reduced 'to the
rules and infallibility of reason'. Political philosophy must be
just as exact and accurate as the science of lines and figures.
But exactitude in political philosophy has a scope and significance quite different from that of mathematics; exact passionless mathematics is indifferent to passions; exact passionless
political philosophy is in conflict with the passions.[2] And exact
political philosophy attacks not only the passions themselves
but also and especially the opinions which are born of the
passions and nourished by them, those opinions which are in
their turn the strongest weapon of the passions; and therefore,
as all opinions of the good and the fitting, considered as
opinions, and as distinct from true knowledge, are the product
and the weapon of passion, exact political philosophy attacks
all opinions of the good and fitting.[3] The need for exact
political philosophy is thus justified by no means only in reference to the failure of traditional political philosophy, but also
and especially in reference to the wrongness of opinions as
such,[4] which is betrayed first by the fact that most opinions

[1] ' . . . si . . . doctrinae moralis et civilis fuissent demonstratae, cur non
credam et illas pro mathematicis haberi debuisse? Non enim subiectum,
sed demonstrationes faciunt mathematicam.' *Opera latina*, vol. iv, p. 23.
Cf. also loc. cit., p. 390.

[2] *Elements*, Ep. ded. and Pt. I, ch. 13, §§ 3–4; *De cive*, Ep. ded. and
praefatio; *Leviathan*, ch. 4 (p. 15) and 11 (pp. 52 ff.); *De corpore*, cap. 1,
art. 1 and 7.

[3] *De cive*, Ep. ded. and cap. 3, art. 31–2.

[4] For in spite of its wrongness traditional political philosophy already
shows an attempt to find a remedy for the unreliability of opinion. Cf. *De
cive*, cap. 3, art. 32.

are wrong.[1] Because all opinion as such is wrong, the true knowledge of the good and fitting must be opposed to all opinion, must be exact knowledge, completely free of the character of opinion. Thus Hobbes's political philosophy is directed not only against the political science of tradition, but against all norms and values which are based on opinion, against any and every system of morals which is popular and pre-scientific. The ideal of exact scientific political philosophy means, therefore, that only science discloses to man the obligatory aims of his volition and action.[2] Thus, with this ideal there is already the anticipation of the systematic overstepping of ordinary values, a morality opposed to pre-scientific morality, a truly paradoxical morality and a form of politics which is Utopian and outstrips all experience. Whereas scientific mathematics does not stand in opposition to pre-scientific mathematics, to everyday counting and reckoning, scientific moral and political philosophy as Hobbes understands it is opposed to pre-scientific morals and politics, i.e. to everyday praise and blame. Confronted with this significance of 'mathematical' exactness in political philosophy, a significance which could not be foreseen from the mathematical standpoint, one cannot hold that it is a sufficient explanation of Hobbes's reform of political philosophy to recall Hobbes's opinion that mathematics is the model for all the sciences and for political philosophy in particular, and therefore to emphasize the importance of the 'discovery' of Euclid in Hobbes's life. One must try rather to define the philosophical meaning of the turning to 'Euclid' on the basis of what that turning means for political philosophy.

During his humanist period Hobbes had tried to remedy the (alleged or real) defects of Aristotle's moral philosophy by studying history in order to discover the forces which in reality determine men. Precisely by this he had endangered the possibility of taking up a free position towards men's actions and conduct. As though he had become aware of this danger, as though his eyes had been opened to the precariousness of any and every subjection to 'reality', he turned away from history,

---

[1] *Elements*, Pt. I, ch. 13, § 3 and ch. 17, § 14.

[2] Therefore Hobbes can say: 'regula aliqua et mensura certa . . . quam hactenus nemo constituit . . .' *De corpore*, cap. 1, art. 7.

not towards the Aristotelian moral and political philosophy, but to an exact moral and political philosophy. By this very fact he stands for the first time in explicit opposition to Aristotle's political philosophy. For just this was Aristotle's contention that the subjects of political philosophy, the beautiful and the just, do not permit of as exact a treatment as the subjects of mathematics; in accordance with this, Aristotle wished to treat those subjects not with an exactness ill adapted to them, but roughly and in outline; he sought to fix their meaning in accordance with the definiteness peculiar to them, but for that very reason not accurately.[1] With this Aristotle had in his part turned against Plato, who had demanded that the most important subjects—the just, the beautiful and, above all, the good—should be treated not in outline but with the greatest accuracy.[2] The confusion with regard to the good, the just, and the beautiful, which caused Aristotle to acknowledge and maintain the peculiar lack of definiteness of these subjects which explains that confusion, was for Plato a reason for transcending the whole field in which such confusion was possible. Whereas Aristotle's political philosophy is and means to be in harmony with opinion as to the just, the beautiful, and the good, and with political experience, Plato's political philosophy is in principle paradoxical and ready to make demands which cannot be fully justified by political experience.[3] Thus, when Hobbes, stimulated by mathematics, demands an exact and paradoxical political philosophy, he is departing from Aristotle and going back to Plato. The turning to Euclid is to be characterized at first as a return to Plato.

We have already pointed out[4] that Hobbes, who at the end of his humanist period still had no objection to raise against the traditional view that Aristotle is the philosopher *par excellence*, later designates Plato as 'the best of the ancient philosophers'. If we inquire further why Hobbes preferred Plato to Aristotle, Hobbes answers that Plato's philosophy 'was much in credit . . . with the better sort, that founded their doctrine

---

[1] *Eth. Nicom.* 1094^{b}12 ff. and 1098^{b}5 ff. Cf. *Rhetoric*, i. 10, *in fine*.

[2] *Republic*, 484 C and 504 D–E; *Legg*, 964 D–965 C.

[3] *Republic*, 473 C, 452 A–D, 506 C; *Eth. Nicom.* 1127^{b}25 ff., 1145^{b}3 ff. and 22 ff. Cf. *Republic*, 505 A, with *Eth. Nicom.* 1096^{b}36 ff.; cf. further Aristotle's *Politics*, 1264^{a}1 ff.   [4] See above, p. 32 f.

upon the conceptions and ideas of things, and Aristotle's with those that reasoned only from the names of things, according to the scale of the categories'.[1] In other words, whereas Plato frees himself from the spell of words, Aristotle remains under that spell. Thus Aristotle's ethic is guided in the definition of virtue and vice by what is praised or blamed, i.e. what is called good or bad.[2] But men in each case call that good or bad which seems to them good or bad, because they desire it or abhor it. If, therefore, one makes praise or blame the token of virtue or vice, one makes one's judgement dependent on the passions or on the passionate likes and dislikes of oneself or of others. Aristotle's ethic remains enmeshed in this dependence.[3] As that ethic took its bearing by words, it is nothing but a description of passions.[4] The completely adequate proof of this at first sight astounding statement must have been in Hobbes's eyes the fact that Aristotle in his analysis of the virtues discusses magnanimity and liberality and so forth—i.e passions.[5] Plato, on the other hand, who does not follow words, arrives at the four cardinal virtues, to which Hobbes can take much more kindly,[6] instead of the long list of Aristotelian virtues, into which so many passions have insinuated themselves. And whereas in his *Politics* Aristotle merely reduces the practice of the Greek republics to rules, Plato has the possibility of elaborating a political philosophy which systematically and from the

[1] *English Works*, vol. vi, p. 100. 'Aristoteles . . . non tam ad res respexit, quam ad voces . . .' *Opera latina*, vol. iii, p. 498. 'Cepit opinor Aristotelem libido quaedam pro authoritate sua, cum rerum non posset, verborum tamen censum peragendi . . .' *De corpore*, cap. 2, art. 16.

[2] 'They estimate virtue, partly by a mediocrity of the passions of men, and partly by that that they are praised. Whereas, it is not the much or little praise that makes an action virtuous, but the cause . . .' *English Works*, vol. vi, p. 218. Cf. also *Opera latina*, vol. iii, p. 502, and *De cive*, cap. 3, art. 31.

[3] 'Aristotle, Cicero, Seneca, and others of like authority . . . have given the names of right and wrong, as their passions have dictated; or have followed the authority of other men . . .' *Elements*, Pt. II, ch. 8, § 13.

[4] 'Their Morall Philosophy is but a description of their own Passions . . . they make the Rules of Good, and Bad, by their own Liking, and Disliking . . .' *Leviathan*, ch. 46 (p. 366; cf. also p. 372).

[5] In all presentations of his political philosophy Hobbes discusses magnanimity only as a passion among other passions. Compare also the mention of liberality, &c., among the passions in *Leviathan*, ch. 6 (p. 26).

[6] Cf. *De cive*, cap. 3, art. 32, and *De homine*, cap. 13, art. 9.

outset avoids the fallacy of concluding from what is or was, what ought to be.[1] Aristotle's orientation by words has as a necessary result incapacity to formulate an uncompromising criticism of opinion, passions—and in view of the connexion between opinion, passions, and sensuality—sensuality. Plato, on the other hand, is the classical critic of sensuality.[2] Liberation from the spell of words is necessary because speech, above all, speech about good and evil, is indefinite and ambiguous, the origin of all strife and all contradiction. Strife and contradiction cease, when it comes to counting, reckoning, and weighing.[3] Thus Plato's insight into the problematic nature of speech is inseparable from his esteem for mathematics.[4] Plato is thus, not only in fact but also according to Hobbes's opinion, the originator of at least the demand for an exact and paradoxical political science. Therefore, for a thorough understanding of the new political science, the examination of Hobbes's conception of Plato is indispensable.

The most profound expression which Hobbes finds for the difference between Plato and Aristotle is that Plato's philosophy starts from ideas, and Aristotle's from words; that Plato frees himself from the spell of words, whereas Aristotle remains under that spell. This judgement appears at first sight to be a caricature of the actual position, a caricature which was almost inevitable, for Hobbes, as a result of his disdain for classical philosophy, did not consider an unbiased study of the sources necessary. For, in truth, it is precisely Plato who originally 'takes refuge' in speech, and Aristotle was in so far only his disciple and successor. And as for the difference between Plato and Aristotle, which develops in the course of an approach which was common to them both, it consists rather in this, that Plato, much more than Aristotle, orientates himself by speech. Thus the basis for Plato's theory of the strict unity of virtue is that since, whenever we speak of virtue

---

[1] Cf. *Elements*, Pt. II, ch. 9, § 8 and *Leviathan*, ch. 21 (p. 113) with *Leviathan*, ch. 31 (p. 197) and ch. 20, *in fine*.

[2] *Opera latina*, vol. v, p. 251.

[3] Cf. *Elements*, Ep. ded. with Plato, *Euthyphro*, 7 B–C.

[4] ' . . . in the school of Plato (the best of the ancient philosophers) none were received that were not already in some measure mathematicians.' *English Works*, vol. vii, p. 346. Cf. also *Leviathan*, ch. 46 (p. 365).

—whether we attribute virtue to a man, a woman, a child, or a slave—whether we characterize temperance, courage, or justice as virtue—we, in all these cases, use the same word virtue, we always mean the same thing. Thus Plato's theory that the causes of things, the ideas, have a transcendent independent existence, rests on the fact that the ideas show this independence in speech. It is against this very orientation that Aristotle's criticism is directed. His 'recensio verborum', which Hobbes censured, had as its task precisely the liberation from the delusion born of language, by showing that the same word can be used with various meanings—that, for instance, 'virtue' said of a man means something other than 'virtue' said of a woman[1]—and that that which in speech is 'prior'—as, for instance, 'good' in speech, is 'prior' to 'man'—is therefore by no means 'prior' in being.[2] However considerable and however portentous Hobbes's misunderstanding may be, it is by no means complete; it is based not only on a mere misinterpretation of Aristotle's efforts to reveal the various meanings of words, as involving indifference to things. That this is the case may be seen by considering why and in which sense Plato is more bound by speech than is Aristotle, or, what amounts to the same thing, why Plato asserts the transcendence of ideas.

Plato 'takes refuge' from things in human speech about things as the only entrance into the true reasons of things which is open to man. Anaxagoras and others had tried to understand the things and processes in the world by their causes, by tracing them back to other things and processes in the world. However, this procedure affords no possibility of true understanding.[3] Against this explanation of nature by the physiologists there is not only the objection that it is an insufficient explanation or no explanation at all; physics of the type of the Anaxagorean, 'Epimethean'[4] physics, which as such takes—

---

[1] Compare the polemic against *Meno*, 72–4, in Aristotle's *Politics* $1260^a 21$ ff.; cf. further *Eth. Nicom.* $1096^b 24$–6.

[2] Aristotle's *Metaphysics*, $1077^b 1$ ff. Cf. J. Klein, Die griechische Logistik und die Entstehung der Algebra, apud: *Quellen und Studien zur Geschichte der Mathematik usw.*, Abteilung B, iii, 72 and 95 f.

[3] *Phaedo*, 97 B ff.

[4] That is to say a physics where mind, thinking, comes 'after' the work, as distinguished from a 'Promethean' physics, where mind, thinking, precedes the work.

whether expressly and intentionally or implicitly and unin-
tentionally is of no importance—not the ordering power of
reason, but disorder and irrationality as the principle of nature,
necessarily leads to the destruction of all certain and independent standards, to finding everything in man's world very
well as it is, and to subjection to 'what the Athenians *believe*'.[1]
Confronted with this absurd conclusion, Plato does not without
further ado oppose to materialist-mechanistic physics a spiri-
tualist-teleological physics,[2] but keeps to what can be understood without any far-fetched 'tragic' apparatus, to what the
'Athenians' *say*.[3] What men, in particular the Athenians, and
in particular their spokesmen the Sophists, say, is contradictory.
The contradictions make necessary an investigation into which
of the conflicting assertions is true. Whatever the result of the
investigation, one of the conflicting ἔνδοξα must be given up,
the opposed ἔνδοξον must be maintained. Thus the latter
ἔνδοξον becomes truly paradoxical; but by making unanimity
and understanding of each with himself and with others possible, it proves itself true.[4] The fact that what men say is
contradictory proves that there is truth hidden in what they
say, and the art of the truth-revealing discussion, of dialectic,
is nothing else but directing the discussion in the right way
and at the right time to the true ἔνδοξον which is to be maintained. The most obvious contradictions which underlie every
contention and every enmity, concern the just, the beautiful,
and the good.[5] And yet men are in greater concord as regards
the good than as regards any other subject, and in such a
fashion that this real concord is the ultimate ground of all

---

[1] *Protagoras*, 320 C–328 D. Protagoras begins his long speech by stating
that it was Epimetheus, and not Prometheus, who was responsible for the
distribution of powers to mortals, and he continues it and ends by justifying
what the Athenians believe (see particularly 324 C and 328 C). What Plato
means by Protagoras' speech is that Protagoras does not understand the
necessary connexion between a justification of the existing state of things
and an 'Epimethean' doctrine of the formation of the world or of human
civilization, and thus that he does not in the least understand what he is
saying. Cf. also 361 C–D. [2] *Phaedo*, 99 C–E.
[3] Cf. *Meno*, 75 B–D with 76 D–E; cf. further, *Phaedo* 100 C–E. It must
be pointed out that Protagoras, in the above-mentioned passage, speaks
almost exclusively of what people believe (and not of what they say).
[4] Cf. *Republic*, 457 B and *Crito*, 46 D–E.
[5] *Euthyphro*, 7 B–D, and *Phaedrus*, 263 A; cf. *Republic*, 523 A–524 C.

possible concord. All say of the good that they really wish it. That means that they want the truly good and not merely the appearance of good,[1] and further they wish to have it, to possess it; they pursue it, they desire it, they know, therefore, that they lack it,[2] and that it is external to them. This true, external good makes things go well with men, when they attain it, when it falls to their lot. It is the reason for the well-being of men who 'partake' of the good. Now a moment's reflection shows that what men usually conceive of as good—wealth, honours, and so forth—is not the same good as they mean; for they mean by 'good' what is in every respect the contrary of evil, that which is completely free from evil. The result of this reflection is confirmed by what men also say: that the good is virtue and wisdom. Thus it is precisely of this better understood good that what men say of misunderstood good holds: that only by partaking of the true external transcendent good as such, which is the reason of their virtue and wisdom, are men virtuous and wise.[3] For what men mean when they say 'virtue', virtue as unequivocally different from vice, the idea of virtue, is never found in all its purity in the works of men. This is admitted at least by virtuous youths, when they seek teachers of virtue, seek to become virtuous, and thus express that they have not virtue. What the youths confess of themselves is true of all men,[4] if one is only exact enough, if one only considers accurately what speech means by virtue—virtue as absolutely unalloyed with vice. The virtue which is not found in the works of men is found in speech alone,[5] in the divinatory,

---

[1] *Republic*, 505 D–E, and *Theaetetus*, 177 D; cf. Aristotle's *Rhetoric*, i, 7, §§ 36–7. Even the sophist, who contents himself with appearances with regard to being and to the true, cannot but maintain the intrinsic value of the good. Cf. *Theaetetus*, 167; *Euthydemus*, 286 B ff., and *Cratylus*, 385 E ff.

[2] *Symposium*, 204 A and 204 E–205 D; cf. *Meno*, 77 C–D, *Gorgias*, 468 D, *Euthydemus*, 278 E–280 B, *Hipp. Mai.* 291 D–C and 294 A.

[3] It is true that knowledge is 'in' the soul (*Republic*, 518 B–C), but it has reached it 'from above', from the gods (*Republic*, 416 E), and higher than knowledge is 'being' (Ep. vii, 342 A ff.), is measure (*Philebus*, 66 A–B). Cf. also *Phaedo*, 79 D.   [4] See especially *Laches*, 188 B.

[5] *Republic*, 473 A. (It is from this passage that *Phaedo*, 99 E–100 A, is fundamentally to be understood). Cf. also *Republic*, 479 A ff. and 592 A. It is explained by the reason given that Socrates is called merely the justest man among his contemporaries, and by no means 'just'. (*Phaedo, in fine*, and Ep. vii, 324 E). Cf. *Republic*, 472 B–C.

'supposing' and 'founding' knowledge incorporated in speech.[1] Speech alone, and not the always equivocal deeds, originally reveals to man the standard by which he can order his actions and test himself, take his bearings in life and nature, in a way completely undistorted and, in principle, independent of the possibility of realization.[2] This is the reason for Plato's 'escape' into speech, and for the theory thereby given of the transcendence of ideas; only by means of speech does man know of the transcendence of virtue.[3]

When Hobbes says that Plato philosophizes *not* from 'words' but from 'ideas', he therefore fundamentally misunderstands him, and how disastrous the effect of this misunderstanding was we shall immediately have to consider. However, as Plato turns away from things, not to speech in itself, but to speech in its contradictoriness, as he opposes to 'physiology' not an 'ontology' but dialectic,[4] it is certain that it is just the apparently pedantic allegiance to speech which he observes, that brings him into opposition to what men usually say and believe. And thus Hobbes's conception of Plato is, to a certain extent, justified. At all events there arises from Plato's specific approach—from the turning to speech in its contradictoriness— the demand for an exact and, therefore, paradoxical philosophy which Hobbes recognizes, and a series of further consequences with reference to which Hobbes again takes up the cudgels against Aristotle in favour of Plato.

Let us first recall the significance which is attributed in Plato's moral philosophy to the antithesis between true and pseudo-virtue.[5] Pseudo-virtue differs from true virtue in this, that true virtue has as its basis a complete change of objective, whereas pseudo-virtue is based entirely on ordinary human aims and interests. True virtue as opposed to pseudo-virtue

---

[1] Cf. *Republic*, 505 E with *Protagoras*, 330 C, *in princ.* and *Phaedo*, 100 B.

[2] *Republic*, 472 C ff. and 592; *Legg.*, 746 B–C.

[3] For this reason also, virtue is knowledge. Cf. with *Republic*, 473 A, *Apology*, 23 A–B.

[4] For this reason the Platonic question as to the essence of virtue cannot be answered by the Aristotelian definition of virtue. In other words, for this reason the perception that virtue is always the virtue of a specific being (*Republic*, 353 B–E) does not for Plato take on the fundamental importance which it has for Aristotle.

[5] *Symposium*, 212 A; *Theaetetus*, 176 C; *Republic*, 536 A.

is the result of 'divinely inspired madness', a 'purification' of the soul, a conversion of the whole soul. It is essentially wisdom.[1] True virtue differs, therefore, from pseudo-virtue, by nothing else than its reason.[2] Pseudo-virtue is pseudo-virtue because its aim is not virtue itself, but the appearance of virtue, reputation for virtue, and the honour which results from that reputation.[3] Pseudo-virtue seeks what is imposing and great, true virtue what is fitting and right.[4] One gains the clearest conception of the antithesis between true and pseudo-virtue, if one compares the life and fate of a truly just man, who has no appearance of justice, whose justice is hidden,[5] with the life and fate of a truly unjust man, who enjoys a reputation for justice and whose injustice is hidden.[6] It is not a mere matter of chance that Plato thus compares the just and the unjust, and not the courageous man and his opposite. Courage, the virtue of the warrior, is inseparable from military glory. No virtue seems more brilliant,[7] more worthy even of reverence than courage; for courage is the standard ideal of the Lacedaemonian and Cretan laws. And yet it is the lowest virtue.[8] Its problematic nature shows itself in full clearness only when one considers it not in its archaic form, in which its sense is, as it were, narrowed and limited by obedience to law, and in which, for that very reason, it is hidden wisdom,[9] but when one considers it apart from this limitation, in itself. This consideration of courage in isolation is all the more fitting, since courage seems more sharply delimited from other virtues

---

[1] *Phaedo*, 68 c–69 c; *Phaedrus*, 244 D and 256 E; *Symposium*, 203 A; cf. *Republic*, 518 c and 521 c.

[2] The question of the reason as the one reason especially characterizes Plato's theory of the change of constitutions, as Aristotle stresses in controversy. (See *Politics*, 1316.)

[3] *Theaetetus*, 176 B; *Republic*, 363 A and 367 B.

[4] Cf. *Republic*, 423 c and E.

[5] Compare the completely different treatment of the problem of 'hidden' virtue in Aristotle's *Eth. Nicom.* (1178^{a}28 ff.) and *Politics* (1263^{b}8 ff.).

[6] *Republic*, 365 A ff.

[7] *Eth. Nicom.* 1177^{b}16 f.

[8] *Legg.*, 630 c–631 c (cf. 963 E ff.). The scale of virtues set up in the passage mentioned also influences the structure of the *Nicomachean Ethics*, in so far as there a beginning is made with courage, and we then rise to justice and finally to science (respectively wisdom).

[9] Cf. *Protagoras*, 342 B, with *Republic*, 429 c–430 c.

than are the other virtues one from another.[1] Courage, as it
is usually understood, is the virtue of the man, his capacity,
without fear or effeminacy, to help himself, to protect himself
from injustice or injury, to assert and save himself. According
to this ideal, the perfect man is the tyrant, who disposes of the
greatest possible power to do what he will.[2] The tyrant as an
ideal is the perfect expression, the most seductive and therefore
the most revealing form of the popular ideal of courage, and
thus challenges to searching criticism of that ideal. In limitless
self-love, in frenzied arrogance, the tyrant seeks to rule not
merely over men but even over gods.[3] From this a light falls
on the more 'innocent' ideal of courage. This ideal is nothing
more noble, and nothing else, than a disguise of man's natural
self-love, of man's natural hedonism.[4] If the unequivocal co-
ordination of virtue with manliness is thus called into question,
the equality of the sexes in the ideal State becomes inevitable
in principle. It is not courage which is the highest virtue—
self-mastery stands higher,[5] and higher still than self-mastery
stand wisdom and justice. In itself wisdom stands supreme,
but justice stands supreme from an exoteric point of view.
This explains why Plato does not assert, as does Aristotle, the
superiority of the theoretical life to ethical virtue. Aristotle
teaches that the ethical virtues, headed by justice, are available
to men, as men, whereas his true happiness, which to a certain
extent transcends human limitations, consists in philosophy.[6]
That the philosophers are the only men who live on the 'island
of the blessed' is an opinion which Plato and Aristotle share.
Plato only denies that the philosopher has a right to seek his
own happiness, without a thought for the unphilosophic many.
However much the philosophers, assimilating themselves to
God, transcend human limitations, they are, and remain, men,

---

[1] *Protagoras*, 349 D; cf. *Gorgias*, 495 C.

[2] *Meno*, 71 E; *Gorgias*, 469 C, 483 A–B, 491 B, 512 D; *Republic*, 549 D–
550 A.   [3] *Republic*, 573 C; *Legg.*, 716 A and 731 D–732 B.

[4] Cf. *Protagoras*, 349 D, with 351 B ff. as well as *Gorgias*, 492 C ff.

[5] *Legg.*, 631 C. The decadent form of σωφροσύνη is εὐήθεια (*Politicus*,
309 E); εὐήθεια is the virtue peculiar to primitive ages (*Legg.*, 679 C). For
both these reasons it is adapted to ironical representation of Socrates'
σωφροσύνη (*Phaedo*, 100 D, and *Meno*, 75 C) which is in contrast to the ἀνδρεία
of the sophists (*Euthydem.*, 275 B, e.g.).

[6] *Eth. Nicom.* 1177ᵇ27 ff.

and thus form only one species of men among others, and are thus under allegiance to the laws of the State, which has as its aim the maintenance of the whole and not the happiness of the parts. The law of the ideal State compels the philosophers to take thought for other men and to watch over them and not 'to turn whither each will'.[1] Because the pursuit of philosophy as a human undertaking is under a higher order, justice, with regard to men, stands higher than wisdom. Whereas Aristotle, by unreservedly setting theoretic life higher than ethical virtue, unconditionally oversteps the limits of the State and thus indirectly attains the possibility of recognizing virtues which are not really political virtues but virtues of private life,[2] for Plato there are only political virtues.[3]

When Hobbes, following Plato, recognizes the ideal of an exact paradoxical moral philosophy, the chain of reasoning which we have just indicated and which is implied in this ideal, becomes the backbone of his political philosophy. In his moral philosophy also, the antithesis between pseudo-virtue, which aims at reputation and honour, and true virtue is a constituent part. He also teaches that true virtue on the one hand, and pseudo-virtue and vice on the other, differ only in their reason.[4] He also finds himself forced into searching criticism of the natural ideal of courage. He also recognizes only political virtues. For him also the antithesis between the fitting and the great is of supreme importance, and as a result he also distrusts rhetoric, in a way which recalls Plato.[5] Con-

---

[1] *Republic*, 519 D–520 C. Another expression for this is that philosophizing means striving to die, but the philosopher may not end his life at his own will. Cf. *Phaedo*, 61 D ff. and *Crito*, 48 B–E.

[2] It is connected with this that Aristotle, differing from Plato, distinguishes between σοφία and φρόνησις. Cf. particularly *Eth. Nicom.* 1140ᵇ7 f. (the recognition of the 'popular' characterization of Pericles as φρόνιμος) with *Gorgias*, 515 C ff.

[3] That the expression 'political virtue' is used by Plato (as also by Aristotle and Plotinus) not in this sense, but in order to characterize popular virtue, important as it otherwise is, need not be taken into consideration here.

[4] Compare the polemic, which is based on this theory, against the Aristotelian conception of virtue in *De cive*, cap. 3, art. 32. The next source of this polemic is probably Grotius, *De iure belli ac pacis, Prolegomena*, §§ 43–5. Grotius takes as his authority for his criticism of Aristotelian moral philosophy the Platonists *inter alios*.

[5] 'A pleader commonly thinks he ought to say all he can for the benefit

nected with this is a series of further changes which he made in his model, Aristotle's *Rhetoric*. By reason of his Platonic approach, he thought the difference between the analysis of ordinary values and of passions given in the *Rhetoric* on the one hand, and the theory of the *Ethics* on the other, not nearly great enough. While in Aristotle's view the common passionate valuations have a peculiar consistency and universality, Hobbes, by reason of his radical criticism of opinion as such, cannot but deny them this dignity.[1]

What Hobbes's political philosophy owes to Platonism is, therefore, its antithetic character, the constituent conception of the antithesis between truth and appearance, the fitting and the great, in the most extreme formulation, between reason and passion. That one antithesis—the antithesis between vanity and fear—is of fundamental importance for morals, was Hobbes's conviction from the outset. But at the beginning he understood the antithesis as an antithesis within the domain

of his client, and therefore has need of a faculty to wrest the sense of words from their true meaning, and the faculty of rhetoric to seduce the jury, and sometimes the judge also, and many other arts which I neither have, nor intend to study.' *English Works*, vol. vi, pp. 6–7. Compare the passages mentioned above, p. 41, note 1. The significance of Hobbes's criticism of rhetoric and its connexion with his Platonism is most clearly seen if one compares his observations on rhetoric with those of Bacon. It is from this point that Hobbes's final criticism of history is also to be fully understood. The most precise expression of this criticism is that the historian takes the great as his standard, while the philosopher is concerned with the right and the true. (*De cive*, Ep. ded.; compare the beginning of Thucydides' history.) Greatness is the standard also in the rhetoric of the sophists (*Gorgias*, 518 E; cf. also p. 82 above for the connexion between rhetoric and history in tradition). History thus finally has for Hobbes the same significance as sophistry had for Plato. According to Plato's view also, there was a connexion between sophistry and what modern usage would call 'historical interest'. Cf. *Protagoras*, 347 C–348 A with 338 E ff.

[1] Aristotle defined pity and indignation thus: 'Pity is a perturbation of the mind, arising from the apprehension of hurt or trouble to another that doth not deserve it. . . . Indignation . . . is grief for the prosperity of a man unworthy.' Hobbes takes over this definition only with a limitation which indicates the problematic nature of these valuations: ' . . . when (calamity) lighteth on such as *we think* have not deserved the same, the compassion is the greater. . . . Indignation is the grief which consisteth in the conception of good success happening to them whom *they think* unworthy thereof.' (See above, p. 38 f.). The same tendency is shown by the fact that in his enumeration of goods, Hobbes, differing from Aristotle, does not mention the virtues, and, in his analysis of the passions, omits the moral judgements on the passions.

of the passions. As a result of his turning to Plato and then to the Stoa, he came to conceive this antithesis between vanity and fear as the antithesis between passion and reason. He interprets all passions as modifications of vanity, and he identifies reason with fear.[1]

Hobbes's agreement with Plato, his option for Plato against Aristotle, must be recognized in its full bearing—and the previous pages are only a first attempt in this direction, and need elaboration in every respect—if his opposition to Plato is to be properly understood. If one may say that the turning to Euclid is to be characterized first as a return to Plato, one must immediately add that, on the other hand, this turning hides the deepest antithesis to Plato which can be imagined. However resolutely Hobbes demands a completely passionless, purely rational political philosophy, he desires, as it were, in the same breath, that the norm to be set up by reason should be in accord with the passions.[2] For the norm which Hobbes seeks is to be applicable under all circumstances, under the most unfavourable circumstances, in the extreme case. Respect for applicability determines the seeking after the norm from the outset. With this Hobbes does not merely tacitly adopt Aristotle's criticism of Plato's political philosophy[3] but goes much beyond Aristotle.[4] The predominating interest in application, which is thus the primary reason for Hobbes's oppo-

---

[1] Cf. p. 11 f. above, and F. Tönnies's Introduction to *Thomas Hobbes, Naturrecht*, Berlin, 1926, p. 9. The identification of reason with fear finds its most pregnant expression in the comparison of life with a race, with which Hobbes concludes his earliest and most perfect exposition of the passions, and in which 'almost all the passions before mentioned' occur, but fear finds no place (*Elements*, Pt. I, ch. 9, § 21): fear, which moderates the unchecked race of the state of nature, in which force and fraud are the two cardinal virtues, to reasonable competition, to the regulated 'play' of the civil state, is for that very reason exalted above the passions, and, therefore, replaces reason.   [2] See above, p. 101.

[3] See particularly *Eth. Nicom.* 1096ᵇ30 ff. The observation that 'Soveraigns, and their principall Ministers . . . need not be charged with the Sciences Mathematicall, (as by Plato they are)' (*Leviathan*, ch. 31, *in fine*) is also in harmony with Aristotle's criticism of Plato, as a comparison of the educational precepts of Aristotle's *Politics* with the 7th Book of Plato's *Laws* shows.

[4] Aristotle's argument against community of goods (that it must necessarily lead to strife) becomes for Hobbes the very foundation of his political reflections. See *De cive*, Ep. ded.

sition to Plato, now is the motive for turning to Euclid as to the 'resolutive-compositive' method.

In accordance with this method, the given object of investigation is first analysed, traced back to its reasons, and then by completely lucid deduction the object is again reconstituted.[1] The reasons which are brought to light in this process are, in principle, to be defined as the matter of the object: 'Quod attinet ad methodum . . . *a civitatis materia incipiendum, deinde ad* generationem et *formam* eius, et iustitiae originem primam, progrediendum esse existimavi. Nam ex quibus rebus quaeque res constituitur, ex iisdem optime cognoscitur.'[2] If the form of the State is deduced from its matter, there is a guarantee that no elements enter into the State which are not contained in its matter, man, and finally in the 'nature', understood as matter, of man, i.e. in what falls to man's share before all education.[3] The execution corresponds to this programme; the axioms which Hobbes gains by going back from the existing State to its reasons, and from which he deduces the form of the right State, are man's natural selfishness and fear of death, i.e. motives on whose force one can depend in the case of all men under all circumstances. Thus all chance, all arbitrariness is excluded and the unconditional applicability of the ideal of the State, thus arrived at, vouched for. Hobbes's political philosophy is, therefore, different from Plato's, that in the latter, exactness means the undistorted reliability of the standards, while in the former, exactness means unconditional applicability, applicability under all circumstances, applicability in the extreme case. Thus the 'resolutive-compositive' method corresponds perfectly to Hobbes's original intention, the interest in application.

Hobbes took this method over from Galileo. He believes that he can by this means achieve for political philosophy what Galileo achieved for physics. But obviously the adequacy of this method for physics does not guarantee its fitness for political philosophy. For while the subject of physics is the natural body, the subject of political philosophy is an artificial body; i.e. a whole which has to be made by man from natural wholes. Thus the concern of political philosophy is not so

---

[1] See above, p. 2.   [2] *De cive*, praefatio.
[3] Ibid., cap. 1, art. 2, annot. 1.

much knowledge of the artificial body as the production of that body. Political philosophy analyses the existing State into its elements only in order that by a better synthesis of those elements the right State may be produced. The procedure of political philosophy is, therefore, much less like the procedure of physics than that of the technician, who takes to pieces a machine that has broken down, removes the foreign body which prevents the functioning of the machine, puts the machine together again; and who does all this in order that the machine may function. Thus political philosophy becomes a technique for the regulation of the State. Its task is to alter the unstable balance of the existing State to the stable balance of the right State.[1] Only in so far as political philosophy becomes a technique of this kind can it make use of the 'resolutive-compositive' method. That means that the introduction of this method into political philosophy presupposes the previous narrowing-down of the political problem, i.e. the elimination of the fundamental question as to the aim of the State. The introduction of Galileo's method into political science is thus bought at the price that the new political science from the outset renounces all discussion of the fundamental, the most urgent question.

This neglect of the truly primary question is the result of Hobbes's conviction that the idea of political philosophy is a matter of course. Hobbes does not question the possibility and necessity of political philosophy; in other words, he does not ask first 'what is virtue?' and 'can it be taught?' and 'what is the aim of the State?', because these questions are answered for him by tradition, or by common opinion. The aim of the State is for him as a matter of course peace, i.e. peace at any price. The underlying presupposition is that (violent) death is the first and greatest and supreme evil.[2] This presupposition does not seem to him to require criticism, debate, or discussion.[3] After finding this presupposition as a principle when he analysed the existing State, he proceeds to deduce from it the right State; diametrically opposed to Plato, whose con-

---

[1] Cf. E. Cassirer, *Die Philosophie der Aufklärung*, pp. 25 ff.

[2] Not that peace is the condition of all civilization. See particularly *De cive*, cap. 1, art. 2, *in fine*.   [3] Cf. Plato, *Apology*, 29 A–B.

sideration of the genesis of the State seems superficially akin, but has the character of reflection, of deliberate questioning of what is good and fitting.[1] The 'resolutive-compositive' method thus presupposes nothing less than a systematic renunciation of the question of what is good and fitting. Convinced of the absolutely typical character of mathematical method, according to which one proceeds from self-evident axioms to evident conclusions, 'to the end', Hobbes fails to realize that in the 'beginning', in the 'evident' presuppositions whether of mathematics or of politics, the real problem, the task of 'dialectic', is hidden.[2] 'Dialectic' is the discussion and testing of what men *say* of the just and the unjust, of virtue and vice. Hobbes considers it superfluous, even dangerous, to take as one's point of departure what men say about justice and so forth: 'the names of Vertues, and Vices . . . can never be true grounds of any ratiocination.'[3] That one can base no reflection on how men usually apply the terms of virtues and vices, is not a datum which Hobbes would be justified in pitting against the tradition founded by Socrates-Plato, for the Socratic-Platonic reform of philosophy rests precisely on the perception of the unreliability and contradictoriness of ordinary speech. But it does not follow from this perception that one is to consider 'not the words but the things'. For to give up orientation by speech means giving up the only possible orientation, which is originally at the disposal of men, and therewith giving up the discovery of the standard which is presupposed in any orientation, and even giving up the search for the standard.[4]

The application of the 'resolutive-compositive' method to political philosophy is of doubtful value, not merely in principle, but also from the point of view of Hobbes's presuppositions. We have said that by the adoption of this method Hobbes was prevented from asking the question as to the standard. That does not mean that he simply forgets this question, but that he only asks it, and answers it inadequately, i.e. at a later stage. He begins his political philosophy not with the question as to the essence of virtue, or with the question (which to a certain extent is equivalent) as to the

---

[1] *Republic*, 370 B.
[2] Ibid., 510 B ff.
[3] *Leviathan*, ch. 4, *in fine*.
[4] Cf. *Republic*, 472 C–E.

'nature' of man in the sense of the idea of man, but with the question as to the 'nature' of man in the sense of that which falls to all men before education. From the analysis of man's 'nature', thus understood, by 'standardless testing'[1] emerges a standard, which is, according to Hobbes's view, the only significant standard, i.e. the only one which warrants unconditional application. But even this way of answering the question as to the standard is made impossible by the 'resolutive-compositive' method. In accordance with this method Hobbes traces the existing State back to its principles in human nature —limitless self-love on the one hand, and the fear of violent death on the other. From these principles the right State is afterwards to be deduced. If this procedure is to be significant, the principles themselves must contain the answer to the question as to the right State, as to the standard. This is, indeed, the case. Hobbes characterizes the two principles which he has gained from his analysis as the principle of natural appetite and the principle of natural reason, i.e. as the principle of the wrong and the principle of the right. But this characterization does not arise from the analysis, for the analysis can only show the principles of the existing State, and cannot, therefore, teach anything about the rightness and wrongness of those principles; and, on the other hand, this characterization is the presupposition of the synthesis, which—as a synthesis of the right State—cannot arise until it has been established what is the right. The qualification—a qualification which follows the analysis and precedes the synthesis—of the two principles of human nature as right and wrong, i.e. the answer to the question of standard, is thus certainly inserted into the frame of the 'resolutive-comparative' method; but it is not to be understood from this method, either in general or even less in particular. The justification of the standard, which is the fundamental part of the political philosophy, is hidden by the 'resolutive-compositive' method and even made unrecognizable. For how otherwise is it to be explained that all interpreters of Hobbes who have followed his method have not noticed that the principle of natural reason (fear of violent death as the greatest and supreme evil) or, what comes to the same thing,

[1] Cf. above, p. 105.

the principle of the 'right of nature' which he seems only to presuppose, is in reality justified by him?[1]

What is justified in this way is indeed not strictly a standard, a norm, a law, an obligation; but a right, a claim. According to Hobbes, the basis of morals and politics is not the 'law of nature', i.e. natural obligation, but the 'right of nature'.[2] The 'law of nature' owes all its dignity simply to the circumstance that it is the necessary consequence of the 'right of nature'. It is from this standpoint that we can best recognize the anti-thesis between Hobbes on the one hand, and the whole tradition founded by Plato and Aristotle on the other, and therewith at the same time the epoch-making significance of Hobbes's political philosophy. For what is the peculiarity of modern political philosophy in relation to classical political philosophy? 'While modern thought starts from the rights of the individual, and conceives the State as existing to secure the conditions of his development, Greek thought starts from the right of the State.'[3] The 'right of the State' is, however, the law: 'Freely as the spirit of Socrates ranged, he acknowledged himself the slave of the law. And what is true of Socrates is true of the Athenian people. They might appear, as they stood assembled

---

[1] This justification occurs in De cive, cap. 1, art. 7.

[2] This right is the minimum claim which as such is fundamentally just and the origin of any other just claim; more exactly, it is unconditionally just because it can be answered for in face of all men in all circumstances. A claim of this kind is only the claim to defend life and limb. Its opposite is the maximum claim, which is fundamentally unjust, for it cannot be answered for in the face of any other man. The maximum claim, the claim man makes by nature, i.e. as long as he is not educated by 'unforeseen mischances', by damnorum experientia, is the claim to triumph over all other men. This 'natural' claim is checked by fear of violent death and becomes man's rational minimum claim, and thus 'right of nature' comes into being, or at least comes to light. That is to say, the 'right of nature' is the first juridical or moral fact which arises if one starts from man's nature, i.e. from man's natural appetite. The 'law of nature' belongs to a much later stage of the progress from human nature to the State: natural 'right' is dealt with in the first chapter of De cive, natural 'law' in the second and third chapters. (The same order is to be found in the Elements, and though less clearly there, in the Leviathan.) How a right which does not presuppose a law, but precedes all law, is to be understood, is indicated by the following sentence of Fichte: 'Das Urrecht läuft in sich selbst zurück, wird ein sich selbst berechtigendes, sich selbst als Recht constituirendes, d.i. ein abso-lutes Recht . . .' (Sämtliche Werke, vol. iii, p. 119.)

[3] E. Barker, Plato and his Predecessors, p. 27.

in their Pnyx, sovereign under heaven. But they too recognized the sovereignty of the laws.'[1] Modern and classical political philosophy are fundamentally distinguished in that modern political philosophy takes 'right' as its starting-point, whereas classical political philosophy has 'law'.[2] What has been said is valid in particular with regard to the relationship of modern socialism to Plato's 'socialism': ' . . . if, like Plato, (the modern socialist) appeals to the conception of "justice", "justice" does not mean to him, as it means to Plato, the duty of discharging an appointed function, but the right of receiving an adequate reward for the function discharged.'[3] If modern and classical political philosophy stand in this relation to one another, there is no possible doubt that Hobbes, and no other, is the father of modern political philosophy. For it is he who, with a clarity never previously and never subsequently attained, made the 'right of nature', i.e. the justified claims (of the individual) the basis of political philosophy, without any inconsistent borrowing from natural or divine law. He himself was aware that the precise subordination of Law to Right, that even a clear and consistent distinction between them, was an innovation. He says: 'though they that speak of this subject, use to confound Jus, and Lex, Right and Law; yet they ought to be distinguished; because Right, consisteth in liberty to do, or to forbeare; Whereas Law, determineth, and bindeth to one of them: so that Law, and Right, differ as much, as Obligation, and Liberty . . .'; and in another passage: 'I find the words Lex Civilis, and Jus Civile, that is to say, Law and Right Civil, promiscuously used for the same thing, even in the most learned authors; which neverthelesse ought not to be so.'[4] How justified Hobbes's verdict is may be seen if one compares that passage in earlier literature which corresponds perhaps

[1] Loc. cit., p. 38.

[2] One may even say ' . . . in the political thought of Greece . . . the conception of rights seems hardly to have been attained. . . . They had little if any conception of the sanctity of rights'. Loc. cit., p. 7. Cf. also Fustel de Coulanges, *La Cité antique* (iii, 11 and iv, 11), and Gierke, *Das deutsche Genossenschaftsrecht*, iii, § 3 (particularly n. 41).

[3] E. Barker, loc. cit., p. 212. 'Plato, we may perceive, is a teacher not so much of woman's rights as of woman's duties.' Loc. cit., p. 221.

[4] *Leviathan*, ch. 14 (p. 66) and ch. 26 (p. 153). Cf. *Elements*, Pt. II, ch. 10, § 5.

most closely to his demands, the following interpretation in Grotius:

'Ab hac iuris significatione (*sc.* ius est, quod iustum est) diversa est altera, sed ab hac ipsa veniens, quae ad personam refertur: quo sensu ius est, Qualitas moralis personae competens ad aliquid iuste habendum vel agendum. . . . Qualitas autem moralis perfecta, facultas nobis dicitur . . . Facultatem Iurisconsulti nomine sui appellant, nos posthac ius proprie aut stricte dictum appellabimus: sub quo continentur potestas, tum in se, quae libertas dicitur, tum in alios; ut patria, dominica . . .'[1]

Grotius, as a successor of the Roman jurists,[2] is, indeed, on the way to Hobbes concept of 'right', but that he does not reach it (and does not seek to) is shown by the fact that *ius proprie aut stricte dictum*, as he understands it, presupposes *lex*.[3] Because Hobbes was the first to distinguish with incomparable clarity between 'right' and 'law', in such a way that he sought to prove the State as primarily founded on 'right', of which 'law' is a mere consequence—in other words, because Hobbes's political philosophy, as the harshest critic which that philosophy has recently found, remarks with obvious surprise 'is itself based . . . on assumptions representing an extreme form of individualism: an individualism more uncompromising than that of Locke himself'[4]—Hobbes is for that very reason the founder of modern political philosophy.

Hobbes marked an epoch not only by subordinating law to right. He was at the same time 'the first writer to grasp the full importance of the idea of Sovereignty . . . he must take

[1] *De iure belli ac pacis*, lib. i, cap. 1, §§ 3–5. Cf. also Suarez, *Tr. de legibus ac de Deo legislatore*, i, cap. 2, §§ 4–5. Fortescue devotes a chapter of his *De natura legis naturae* (1, cap. 30) to the difference of Law and Right. What regards the development after Hobbes, see Gierke, *Althusius*[3], pp. 113, 301, n. 94, and 305.

[2] For the significance of Roman jurisprudence in the genesis of the modern conception of 'right', compare the following statement by Maine: ' . . . it is evident, I think, that the Law of Contract, based as it is on the complete reciprocity and indissoluble connection of rights and duties, has acted as a wholesome corrective to the predispositions of writers, who, if left to themselves, might have exclusively viewed a moral obligation as the public duty of a citizen in the Civitas Dei.' *Ancient Law*, p. 290.

[3] Cf. loc. cit., §§ 3 and 9, and also *Prolegomena*, §§ 8–11.

[4] C. E. Vaughan, *Studies in the History of Political Philosophy before and after Rousseau*, Manchester, 1925, vol. i, p. 23.

the credit of being the first to see that the idea of Sovereignty
lies at the very root of the whole theory of the State; and the
first to realize the necessity of fixing precisely where it lies,
and what are its functions and its limits.' By this also Hobbes
stands in contrast to classical political philosophy: 'Amongst
the most notable omissions of Greek philosophy is the absence
of any clear attempt to define the nature of Sovereignty, to
determine its seat, or settle the ultimate sanction on which it
rests.'[1] The two fundamental innovations which are to be
attributed to Hobbes, the subordination of law to right and
the recognition of the full significance of the idea of sovereignty,
are closely connected. One sees their common origin when one
retraces the condition which made possible the problem of
sovereignty. In classical times the analogy to that modern
problem is the question 'Who or what shall rule?' The answer
of antiquity runs 'The law.' Philosophers who could not
acquiesce in the divine origin of law justify this answer in the
following way: the rational should rule over the irrational (the
old over the young, the man over the woman, the master over
the slave) and therefore law over men.[2] A problem of sovereignty arises only when the right to rule on the part of reason
and reasonable people is called into question. The doubt falls
at first only on the applicability[3] of the principle, that he or
what is rational is justified in ruling. Granting that there are
men who by force of reason are undoubtedly superior to others,
would those others submit to them merely on this ground,
and obey them? would they recognize their superiority?[4] But

[1] Loc. cit., p. 55.

[2] ' . . . lex est ratio summa insita in natura, quae iubet ea, quae facienda
sunt, prohibetque contraria. Eadem ratio cum est in hominis mente
confirmata et confecta, lex est.' It is true 'populariter interdum loqui necesse
erit et appellare eam legem, quae scripta sancit quod vult aut iubendo aut
vetando, ut vulgus appellat. Constituendi vero iuris ab illa summa lege
capiamus exordium, quaeque saeculis omnibus ante nata est quam scripta
lex ulla aut quam omnino civitas constituta.' Cicero, *Legg.*, 1. 6. 18-19.

[3] Interest in application at the same time causes the turning to history.
There is thus a direct connexion between Bodin's interest in history (see
above, p. 83 f. and 94) and his theory of sovereignty. Compare his *République*,
ii, ch. 6, *in princ.*

[4] Compare especially the polemic against Aristotle's *Politics* in *De cive*, cap.
3, art. 13 and in *Leviathan*, ch. 15 (pp. 79-80). 'Would you have every man
to every other man allege for law his own particular reason? There is not

doubt does not stop at that. It is denied that any considerable difference in reasonableness exists between men. In all practical affairs, one man is, in principle, as wise as any other, bent on the perception of his interest and as capable of perceiving that interest as any other. By nature all men are equally reasonable; and as far as the superiority gained by study, experience, and reflection is concerned, it is insignificant because 'it is possible long study may increase, and confirm erroneous sentences . . . and of those that study, and observe with equal time, and diligence, the reasons and resolutions are, and *must* remain discordant'.[1] Because reason is essentially impotent, it is not enough to reply that reason is the origin and seat of sovereignty. Thus it becomes fundamentally questionable which of the men who are equal and alike is to rule over the others, and under which conditions and within which limits they have a claim to rule. Thus the *problem* of sovereignty arises. Because all men are equally 'reasonable', the reason of one or more individuals must arbitrarily be made the standard reason as artificial substitute for the lacking natural superiority of reason in one or more: '(The) common measure of all things that might fall in controversy . . . some say, is right reason: with whom I should consent, if there were any such thing to be found or known *in rerum natura* . . . But . . ., seeing *right reason is not existent*, the reason of some man, or men, must supply the place thereof; and that man, or men, is he, or they, that have the sovereign power.'[2] For the same cause which made the substitution of sovereign power for reason necessary, i.e. because reason is impotent, the rational 'law of nature' also loses its dignity.[3] In its place we have the 'right of nature' which is, indeed, according to reason but dictated not by reason but by the fear of death. The break with rationalism is thus the decisive presupposition for the concept

amongst men a universal reason agreed upon in any nation, besides the reason of him that hath the sovereign power.' *English Works*, vol. vi, p. 22.

[1] *Leviathan*, ch. 26 (p. 143); cf. ch. 13 (p. 63).

[2] *Elements*, Pt. II, ch. 10, § 8. Cf. *Leviathan*, ch. 5 (p. 19). 'Yet though (the reason of him that hath the sovereign power) be but the reason of one man, yet it is set up to supply the place of that universal reason, which is expounded to us by our Saviour in the Gospel . . .' *English Works*, vol. vi, p. 22.   [3] Cf. above, p. 24.

of sovereignty as well as for the supplanting of 'law' by 'right', that is, the supplanting of the primacy of obligation by the primacy of claim. This break with rationalism is, therefore, the fundamental presupposition of modern political philosophy in general. The acutest expression of this break which can be found in Hobbes's writings is that he conceives sovereign power not as reason but as will. The role of right reason, which is not existent *in rerum natura*, is filled not so much by the reason of him or those holding the sovereign power, as by his or their will.[1] Hobbes expressly turns against the view still predominant in his age that the holder of the sovereign power is in the same relation to the State as the head to the whole man. The holder of the sovereign power is not the 'head', that is, the capacity to deliberate and plan, but the 'soul', that is, the capacity to command, in the State.[2] There is only a step from this to Rousseau's theory that the origin and seat of sovereignty is *la volonté générale*. Rousseau made completely clear the break with rationalism which Hobbes had instituted.[3] For Rousseau explicitly replaced the classical definition of man as 'animal rationale' by a new one: 'Ce n'est pas tant l'entendement qui fait parmi les animaux la distinction spécifique de l'homme que sa qualité d'agent libre.'[4] The explicit break with rationalism is thus the reason for the antithesis of modern political thought to classical, an antithesis which is thus characterized: 'The Greeks believed in the need of education to tune and harmonise social opinions to the spirit and tone of a fixed and fundamental law. The modern belief is the need

[1] Cf. Montesquieu's saying: 'La volonté du souverain est le souverain lui-même.' *L'Esprit des lois*, ii. 2.

[2] *De cive*, cap. 6, art. 19. Compare also the mention of will in the definition of the State in *De cive* (quoted above, p. 33, note 1). Compare in this connexion Gierke, *Althusius*[3], pp. 74 (n. 44) and 280. See above, p. 150, note 1.

[3] This is not to deny what A. Cobban is doubtless justified in stressing (*Rousseau and the Modern State*, London, 1934, p. 144): Rousseau's 'theory is altogether on the side of reason if we compare it with that which came after and in the name of emotion, sentiment, tradition, upheld the aristocratic and monarchical system of the past against the new, Rousseauist democratic ideas.' But in judging the historical significance of Rousseau we are primarily concerned with the relation of his theory to earlier theories, and compared with these, Rousseau's theory is certainly not on the side of reason.

[4] *Discours sur l'origine de l'inégalité*, première partie.

of a representation to adjust and harmonise a fluid and changing and subordinate law to the movement of a sovereign public opinion or "general will".[1] For the development after Rousseau altered nothing in this relationship, which is seen first and most precisely in Hobbes. By closer definition of *la volonté générale* as 'folk-mind' or 'class-consciousness' the turning—the turning away from rationalism—which Hobbes had inaugurated was not doubted at all. Its consequences were thus corrected indeed; but precisely therewith the presupposition of that turning was from that time onwards petrified into dogma. This presupposition, as we have already said, is the belief in the impotence of reason, or to put it perhaps more plainly in other words, the emancipation of passion and imagination.[2]

The view of classical rationalism, that only reason justifies dominion, found its most radical expression in Plato's saying that the only necessary and adequate condition for the weal of a State is that the philosophers should be kings and the kings philosophers. That amounts to stating that the setting up of a perfect commonwealth depends exclusively on 'internal policy' and not at all on any conditions of foreign policy. Indeed, no other philosopher asserted the primacy of internal policy as did Plato. The unconditional primacy of internal policy—thus may one sum up Plato's theory of justice. For this theory says: there is no happiness for men without justice; justice means attending to one's own business, bringing oneself into the right disposition with regard to the transcendent unchanging norm, to which the soul is akin, and not meddling into other people's affairs; and justice in the State is not different from justice in the individual, except that the State is self-sufficient and can thus practise justice—attending to its own business—incomparably more perfectly than can the individual who is not self-sufficient. Accordingly for the properly constituted State its self-assertion against other States is an accidental result of its proper constitution and not its main object. The citizens of the perfect State, who for their own

---

[1] E. Barker, loc. cit., pp. 38–9.

[2] It is thus not a matter of chance, that *la volonté générale* and aesthetics were launched at approximately the same time.

sake are 'hard-boned lean dogs', for that very reason to foreigners
happen to be either allies to be esteemed or foes to be feared.[1]
Aristotle criticizes Plato's radicalism in this matter also as
usual. The legislator, he objects, must pay heed not only to
the land and its inhabitants, but also to neighbouring States.[2]
But in the systematic recognition of the primacy of internal
policy, Aristotle undoubtedly agrees with Plato.[3] The reason
for this agreement is the view which the two philosophers hold
in common, that what lends to a thing its being, its peculiar
essence, what limits it—that essence is what we mean when
we speak, e.g., of a horse as a horse—takes precedence over all
other reasons for the thing in question, and particularly over
all external conditions. If the essence of the thing is to be
preferred to its external conditions, to the self-realization and
self-assertion of that thing against its external conditions, then,
for instance, the right constitution of the body, its health, is
to be preferred to its return to health, to its recovery after loss
of health. In this example Plato makes clear that the good
statesman carries out his legislation with an eye to peace, that
is to the good internal constitution of the State, and not with
an eye to war, that is, to the assertion of the State against
external conditions.[4] Precisely by this example one penetrates
to the ultimate reason which caused Hobbes to presuppose the
primacy of foreign policy, in contrast to the primacy of internal
policy in classical political philosophy. Hobbes, differing from
Plato and Aristotle, asserts that the recovery of health is to be
preferred to the undisturbed possession of health.[5] He would
not be the consistent thinker which he is admired for being
if he did not also assert that 'as for very little commonwealths'
—and the perfect States for Plato and Aristotle are 'very little
commonwealths'—'there is no human wisdom'—therefore, in
particular not the wisdom of the philosopher-kings—'can uphold them, longer then the Jealousy lasteth of their potent
neighbours'.[6] While for Plato and Aristotle, in accordance
with the primary interest they attach to home policy, the ques-

---

[1] *Republic*, 422.   [2] *Politics*, 1265ª.
[3] Cf. particularly *Politics*, 1324ᵇ–1325ᵇ.
[4] *Legg.*, 628.   [5] See above, p. 132 f.
[6] *Leviathan*, ch. 25, *in fine*.

tion of the number of inhabitants of the perfect State, that is, the limits set to the State by its inner necessity, is of decisive importance, Hobbes brushes this question aside in the following words: 'The Multitude sufficient to confide in for our Security, is not determined by any certain number, but by comparison with the Enemy we feare. . . .'[1] The primacy of foreign policy is taught not only by Hobbes but in all specifically modern political philosophy, whether implicitly or explicitly. This assertion needs no proof in view of the theories of 'power politics'. As for pacifist theories, we can save ourselves a detailed analysis, for which this is not the place, by quoting the 'seventh proposition' from Kant's *Idee zu einer allgemeinen Geschichte in weltbürgerlicher Absicht*. It runs: 'The problem of establishing a perfect civil constitution is dependent on the problem of a lawful external relation between the States and cannot be solved independently of the solution of the latter problem.'

The antithesis between classical and modern political philosophy, more accurately between Platonic political philosophy and that of Hobbes, reduced to principle, is that the former orientates itself by speech and the latter from the outset refuses to do so. This refusal arises originally from insight into the problematic nature of ordinary speech, that is, of popular valuations, which one may with a certain justification call natural valuations.[2] This insight leads Hobbes, just as it did Plato, first to the ideal of an exact political science. But while Plato goes back to the truth hidden in the natural valuations and therefore seeks to teach nothing new and unheard-of, but to recall what is known to all but not understood, Hobbes, rejecting the natural valuations in principle, goes beyond them, goes forward to a new *a priori* political philosophy, which is of the future and freely projected. Measured by Aristotle's classical explanation of natural morals, Platonic moral philosophy is paradoxical, as is Hobbes's. But whereas the paradoxical nature of Platonic moral philosophy is as irreversible as the 'cave' existence of men bound to the body, Hobbes's

---

[1] *Leviathan*, ch. 17 (p. 88). Compare in this connexion *Leviathan*, ch. 8, *in princ.*: 'Vertue generally . . . consisteth in comparison.'

[2] For this use of the word 'natural', cf. Klein, loc. cit., p. 66.

moral philosophy is destined sooner or later to change from paradox to an accepted part of public opinion.[1] In other words, the paradoxical nature of Platonic moral philosophy is the paradox of the unpretentious old and eternal, the paradoxical nature of Hobbes's moral philosophy is the paradox of the surprising new, unheard-of venture. Whereas in Plato the true virtues have the same names as the (popular) pseudo-virtues, in Hobbes's work they are different even in name. As a result Hobbes must raise an incomparably greater claim for his political science than Plato had done. Whereas Plato retraces natural morals and the orientation provided by them to their origin, Hobbes must attempt in sovereignty, and without this orientation, to discover the principle of morals. While thus for Plato the 'concreteness', the 'materiality' of morals was and could be no problem, Hobbes travels the path which leads to formal ethics and finally to relativist scepticism. The enormous extension of the claims made on political science leads at last to a denial of the very idea of political science and to the replacement of political science by sociology.[2] A further stage, the final stage of modern political philosophy is also to be understood from this point. Plato does not question the virtue-character of courage, to which speech bears witness, but simply opposes the over-estimation of courage which underlies the popular opinion about courage. Hobbes, because he renounced all orientation by speech, goes so far as systematically to deny the virtue-character of courage. And just as disdain of speech

[1] 'Tua illa, quamquam paradoxa, vera tamen sunt, ut mihi videntur, et *futura aliquando endoxa*. Interea tu, qui defendis omnem doctrinam Hobbianam, quid dicturus es ad ea quae habet in Physica sua et Politica?' *Opera latina*, vol. iv, p. 226.

[2] Burke's struggle against 'abstract principles' must especially be recalled in this connexion. In his polemic against Rousseau and those of a similar mind, Burke appeals to the importance of 'circumstances', *ad homines* with the greatest justification, because modern political philosophy in contrast to classical political philosophy had claimed unconditional applicability (applicability under any circumstances) for its theories. What Burke does not see is that precisely this interest in the systematic conquest of 'circumstances', in the exclusion of all 'arbitrariness' (even and precisely the arbitrariness with which the sensible man at times does the sensible thing), that, in other words, the predominance of the interest in application was the real reason why 'general theories' and 'abstract principles' were ever produced.

finally leads to relativist scepticism, the negation of courage leads to the controversial position of courage which becomes more and more acute on the way from Rousseau by Hegel to Nietzsche and is completed by the reabsorption of wisdom by courage, in the view that the ideal is not the object of wisdom, but the hazardous venture of the will.[1]

Relinquishing orientation by speech does not mean that Hobbes 'forgets' the question of standards, but that he poses this question only as an afterthought, and, therefore, inadequately. Whereas Plato distinguishes between two kinds of reasons, the good and the necessary,[2] Hobbes recognizes only one kind, the necessary. Since as a result of this he is obliged to take into account the inevitable difference between the good and the necessary within the necessary itself, the question of the standard, of the good, becomes for him the question of what is *par excellence* necessary, and he discovers the retreat from death as the necessary *par excellence*.[3] The reason underlying this procedure is the denial of the existence of a natural law, that is, of a natural standard. That this denial is only the result of relinquishing orientation by speech can here only be asserted. For Hobbes the denial of natural standards was irrefutably evident on the basis of his materialistic metaphysics. Thus this metaphysics is the implicit presupposition even of his turning to Euclid, provided that the acceptance of the 'mathematical' method presupposes the negation of absolute standards.[4] But one cannot acquiesce in this finding and its consequence that Hobbes's political science is only the result of his natural science. For the question arises: why did Hobbes decide in favour of materialism? on the ground of what primary conviction was materialism so vividly evident for him?[5]

[1] 'Les mythes révolutionnaires . . . ne sont pas des descriptions de choses, mais des expressions de volontés. L'utopie est, au contraire, le produit d'un travail intellectuel . . .' G. Sorel, *Réflexions sur la violence*, Paris (Rivière), 1930, p. 46. Cf. p. 160 above.

[2] Cf. *inter alia*, *Timaeus*, 68 E, and *Republic*, 493 C.

[3] Cf. p. 17, note 3, and p. 25 above.

[4] Cf. also p. 151 above, on the philosophical meaning of Hobbes's 'materialism'.

[5] That this primary conviction can be discovered from an analysis of Hobbes's style has been shown very finely by Basil Willey, *The Seventeenth Century Background* (London, 1934), pp. 98-9.

The question may be more sharply put. Are the latent presuppositions of Hobbes's materialism not most easily to be explained by the analysis of his political philosophy? We limit ourselves here to rough indications. Hobbes's turn to natural science is to be explained by his interest not so much in nature as in man, in self-knowledge of man as he really is, i.e. by the interest which characterized him even in his humanist period.[1] The humanist or moral origin of his scientific question is revealed even in his answer to that question. The fundamental concept of his theory of motion, the concept of conatus, appears first in his analysis of appetite.[2] Nor is that all. His scientific explanation of sense-perception is characterized by the fact that it interprets perception of the higher senses by the sense of touch; and the preference for the sense of touch which this presupposes is already implied in Hobbes's original view of the fundamental significance of the antithesis between vanity and fear.[3] Finally, in his physics Hobbes never attained to an adequate understanding of the principle of inertia. The least one must say is that he treated straight and circular motion as equivalent and that he did not consider it necessary to understand circular motion as a modification of straight motion.[4] In his theory of human nature, on the other hand,

[1] He himself recounts: 'Natura sua, et primis annis, ferebatur ad lectionem historiarum et poetarum . . . Postea autem cum in congressu quodam virorum doctorum, mentione facta de causa sensionis, quaerentem unum, quasi per contemptum, Quid esset sensus, nec quemquam audisset respondentem, mirabatur, qui fieri potuerit, ut qui sapientiae titulo homines caeteros tanto fastu despicerent, *suos ipsorum sensus*, quid essent, ignorarent.' Starting from the question of man's senses, he discovers that the origin of all things is to be sought in the nature and variety of movements. And after this discovery 'Quaesivit *inprimis*, qualis motus is esse posset, qui efficit sensionem, intellectum, phantasmata, aliasque proprietates animalium'. *Opera latina*, vol. i, pp. xx, xxi, and xiv.

[2] Cf. F. Brandt, *Thomas Hobbes' Mechanical Conception of Nature*, Copenhagen/London, 1928, p. 300 f.

[3] See above, p. 27. Among the Hobbes papers at Chatsworth there is an excerpt from Scaliger's *De subtilitate*, in which among other items Exercitatio 286 has been summarized. This treats, in express controversy with Aristotle, of the pre-eminence of the human sense of touch over that of animals.

[4] Brandt, op. cit., p. 333. Compare especially the following observation by Hobbes: 'Maximam partem effectuum naturalium deducit ille (*sc.* Hobbius) a motu quodam, quem vocat circularem simplicem . . .' *Opera latina*, vol. iv, p. 226.

he expresses with all definiteness that 'vita motus est perpetuus, qui, cum rectâ progredi non potest, convertitur in motum circularem'.[1] If Hobbes's natural science in its questions and answers is thus dependent on his 'humanist', that is moral, interests and convictions, on the other hand a particular conception of nature is the implicit basis of his views in moral and political philosophy. But it is necessary to raise the question whether the conception of nature which is the presupposition of his political philosophy is identical with the conception of nature which he explains in his scientific writings. It is certain that there is a kinship between these two conceptions of nature, conceptions which in principle are to be kept separate. It is for this reason and only for this reason that his scientific investigations could exert a positive influence on the evolution of his political philosophy. He could not have maintained his thesis that death is the greatest and supreme evil but for the conviction vouched for by his natural science that the soul is not immortal. His criticism of aristocratic virtue and his denial of any gradation in mankind gains certainty only through his conception of nature, according to which there is no order, that is, no gradation in nature.[2] The idea

[1] *De homine*, cap. 11, art. 15. That the pre-eminence of straight motion over circular can be asserted on non-mechanistic, even anti-mechanistic presuppositions, is shown by the following passage from Bergson, which should be compared with *De homine*, cap. 11, art. 15. 'La vie en général est la mobilité même; les manifestations particulières de la vie n'acceptent cette mobilité qu'à regret et retardent constamment sur elle. Celle-là va toujours de l'avant; celles-ci voudraient piétiner sur place. L'évolution en général se ferait, autant que possible, en ligne droite; chaque évolution spéciale est un processus circulaire.' *L'Evolution créatrice*, Paris (Alcan), 1907, p. 139. Hobbes's theory, no less than that of Bergson, is based primarily on self-knowledge, and not on reflections of a scientific nature.

[2] From this standpoint we can understand the difference between Hobbes's conception of pride (which we interpreted by speaking of 'vanity') and the traditional conception. 'Pride' in the traditional sense means rebellion against the gradation of beings; it presupposes, therefore, the existence and obligatory character of that gradation. Hobbes's conception of 'pride', on the other hand, presupposes the denial of natural gradation; this conception is, indeed, nothing other than a means of 'explaining', i.e. of denying that gradation: the allegedly natural gradation concerning the faculties of the mind proceeds from 'a vain conceipt of ones own wisdom, which almost all men think they have in a greater degree, than the Vulgar'. (*Leviathan*, ch. 13, p. 63; compare also the harsh criticism of Aristotle's contrary opinion in ch. 15, p. 79 f. and in *De cive*, cap. 3, art. 13). The revolutionary

of civilization achieves its telling effect solely by reason of the presupposition that the civilization of human nature can go on progressing boundlessly, because what tradition in agreement with common sense had understood as given and immutable human nature is for the main part a mere 'natural limit' which may be overpassed. Very little is innate in man; most of what is alleged to come to him from nature is acquired, and therefore mutable, as conditions change; the most important peculiarities of man—speech, reason, sociality—are not gifts of nature, but the work of his will.[1] But precisely by the last-mentioned example it becomes clear that the conception of nature which Hobbes's political philosophy *presupposes* is dualistic: the idea of civilization presupposes that man, by virtue of his intelligence, can place himself outside nature, can rebel against nature. This dualism is transparent all the way through Hobbes's philosophy,[2] not least in the antithesis of *status naturalis* and *status civilis*. The antithesis of nature and human will is hidden by the monist (materialist-deterministic) metaphysic, which Hobbes *teaches*, which he found himself forced to adopt simply because he saw no other possibility of escaping the 'substantialist' conception of mind, and therefore 'the kingdom of darkness'. This dilemma, which was not swept aside until Kant and his successors, is the decisive reason for Hobbes's materialist-deterministic theory, which is not only not needed for his political philosophy, but actually imperils the very root of that philosophy. It is a sign of this: that the moral basis of his political philosophy becomes more and more disguised, the farther the evolution of his natural science progresses. That this is the case is seen if one compares his theory of the passions in the *Elements of Law* with the theory in the *Leviathan*. To the same connexion belongs the fact that in the *Elements of*

character of this conception of pride—it is this conception which underlies modern criticism of 'illusions' and 'ideologies'—is obvious. How far the Puritans, who, in their criticism of ecclesiastical and secular hierarchy, also understood that hierarchy as proceeding from pride, anticipated this conception, must here remain an open question.

[1] *Elements*, Pt. I, ch. 5, §§ 1–2; *Leviathan*, ch. 5 (p. 21); *De cive*, cap. 1, art. 2; *De corpore*, cap. 1, art. 2; *De homine*, cap. 10, art. 1.

[2] Cf. above, p. 7 f. The antithesis nature–human will is equivalent to the antithesis body–speech. The latter occurs, e.g. in *De homine*, cap. 10, art. 2, *in fine*.

Law Hobbes treats exclusively within the analysis of honour the themes which in the *Leviathan* he treats also and previously within the analysis of power.[1] In other words, with the progressive elaboration of his natural science, vanity, which must of necessity be treated from the moral standpoint, is more and more replaced by the striving for power, which is neutral and therefore more amenable to scientific interpretation.[2] Hobbes certainly took great care not to follow this path to its logical conclusion. Consistent naturalism would have been the ruin of his political philosophy. That is shown in the case of Spinoza. Spinoza, more consistently naturalistic than Hobbes, relinquishes the distinction between might and right and teaches the natural right of all passions. Hobbes, on the other hand, by virtue of the basis of his political philosophy, a basis which was not naturalistic but moral, asserts the natural right only of the fear of death. It is shown in another way in the case of Montesquieu. Montesquieu, carrying the naturalistic analysis of the passions to its logical conclusion, comes to the result that the state of nature cannot be the war of all against all.[3] If, then,

---

[1] Cf. *Elements*, Pt. I, ch. 8, §§ 5-6, with *Leviathan*, ch. 10 (pp. 43-4). Cf. also p. 115, note 2, above.

[2] Cf. pp. 13-14 above. In this connexion some changes which Hobbes made in the text of the *Leviathan* in the later Latin version are very instructive, especially in the important comparison of man with the other 'political creatures'. We quote the English version and give the variations in the Latin version in brackets: 'men are continually in competition for Honour and Dignity, which these creatures are not; and consequently amongst men there ariseth on that ground (propter eam, *inter alias*, causam), Envy and Hatred, and finally Warre; but amongst these not so (inter illa rarissime) . . . man, whose Joy consisteth in comparing himselfe with other men, can relish nothing but what is eminent (Homini autem in bonis propriis nihil tam iucundum est, quam quod alicuius sunt maiora).' Ch. 17 (p. 88) and *Opera latina*, vol. iii, p. 129. The analysis of the passions which lead to crime begins in the English version with the proposition: 'Of the Passions that most frequently are the Causes of Crime, one, in Vain-glory, or a foolish over-rating of their own worth . . .'; in the Latin version, on the other hand: 'Passionum, quae crimina potentissime suadent, sunt ira, avaritia, caeteraeque cupiditates vehementiores, sed non sine spe.' Ch. 27 (p. 157), and *Opera latina*, vol. iii, p. 214. To the same connexion belongs the fact that in the English version it is said: in the state of nature 'no action can be unjust' while the Latin version has: 'Nihil . . . est injustum.' Ch. 15 (p. 74), and *Opera latina*, vol. iii, p. 111 f. Cf. p. 24, note 1, above.

[3] 'Le désir que Hobbes donne d'abord aux hommes de se subjuguer les uns les autres n'est pas raisonnable. L'idée de l'empire et de la domination

only inconsistent naturalism is compatible with Hobbes's political philosophy, the consistent naturalism which Hobbes displays in his scientific writings cannot be the foundation of his political philosophy. The foundation must be another conception of nature. The elaboration of this conception of nature, which is related to naturalism but by no means identical with it, is the most urgent task for an exact analysis of Hobbes's political philosophy.

To sum up: The foundation of Hobbes's political philosophy, that is the moral attitude to which it owes its existence and its unity, are objectively as well as biographically 'prior' to the mathematical scientific founding and presentation of that philosophy. The turning to Euclid as well as to naturalism is certainly motivated in Hobbes's original moral-political view, and thus these two intellectual forces were able to exert a positive influence, which is not to be underestimated, on the evolution of his political philosophy, on the elucidation of the whole nexus of presuppositions and conclusions of the original moral attitude. On the other hand, the mathematical method and materialistic metaphysics each in its own way contributed to disguise the original motivation-nexus and thus to undermine Hobbes's political philosophy. From these findings is drawn the methodic conclusion for the study of Hobbes's political philosophy that the most mature presentation of that philosophy, that is the *Leviathan*, is by no means an adequate source for an understanding of Hobbes's moral and political ideas. It is true that the presuppositions and conclusions of the fundamental moral attitude are more clearly manifest in the *Leviathan* than in the earlier presentations, but, on the other hand, in the earlier presentations the original motives of Hobbes's political philosophy are generally more clearly shown.

est si *composée* et dépend de tant d'autres idées, que ce ne serait pas celle qu'il aurait d'abord.' *L'esprit des lois*, i. 2.

INDEX